THE END OF SUPPLICATION

AF075015

THE END OF SUPPLICATION

The Invention of Prostrate Blackness as a Replacement for the Maroon

Yannick Giovanni Marshall

LONDON • NEW YORK • OXFORD • NEW DELHI • SYDNEY

Zed Books
50 Bedford Square, London, WC1B 3DP, UK
1359 Broadway, 12th Floor, New York, NY, 10018, USA
29 Earlsfort Terrace, Dublin 2, Ireland

BLOOMSBURY and Zed Books are trademarks of Bloomsbury Publishing Plc

First published in Great Britain 2025

Copyright © Yannick Giovanni Marshall, 2025

Yannick Giovanni Marshall has asserted his right under the Copyright, Designs and Patents Act, 1988, to be identified as Author of this work.

Cover design by Paul Smith

All rights reserved. No part of this publication may be reproduced or transmitted in any form or by any means, electronic or mechanical, including photocopying, recording, or any information storage or retrieval system, without prior permission in writing from the publishers.

Bloomsbury Publishing Plc does not have any control over, or responsibility for, any third-party websites referred to or in this book. All internet addresses given in this book were correct at the time of going to press. The author and publisher regret any inconvenience caused if addresses have changed or sites have ceased to exist, but can accept no responsibility for any such changes.

A catalogue record for this book is available from the British Library.

Library of Congress Control Number: 2025937423

ISBN: HB: 978-1-3503-7510-9
PB: 978-1-3503-7509-3
ePDF: 978-1-3503-7512-3
eBook: 978-1-3503-7511-6

Typeset by Deanta Global Publishing Services, Chennai, India
Printed and bound in Great Britain

To find out more about our authors and books visit www.bloomsbury.com and sign up for our newsletters.

For Dad,
and the Native Quarters

Contents

INTRODUCTION: FELLING THE LINCOLN MEMORIAL	1
Chapter 1 "A CERTAIN NEGRO MAN NAMED ADAM": A BLACK ANTI-COLONIAL LIFE IN A WHITE SUPREMACIST TOTALITARIAN COLONY	13
Chapter 2 KILLING THE MAROON, BIRTHING THE SUPPLICANT NEGRO	43
Chapter 3 THE MUZZLE OF CIVIL RIGHTS	85
Chapter 4 SUPPLICATION IN THE SPECTACLE	123
CONCLUSION: THE BRAVE RUN	153
Notes	159
Selected Bibliography	192
Index	199
About the Author	208

INTRODUCTION
FELLING THE LINCOLN MEMORIAL

On Capitol Hill, in the capital of the colony called by the colonists the United States, there stands the "Emancipation Memorial" monument. The sculpture, built in 1875 in the closing days of *Reconstruction* and at the dawn of *Redemption* depicts President Abraham Lincoln standing with his hand either raised in a gesture of emancipation or petting an unnamed Black man—depending on where the viewer is positioned.

The man representing the slave with shackles broken and kneeling over the words "Emancipation" was modeled after Archer Alexander, "the last Missouri enslaved man captured under the Fugitive Slave Law" of 1850. It was funded solely by formerly enslaved people—beginning, the story goes, with a donation from a formerly enslaved person from Virginia, Charlotte Scott, who gave her employer $5 for a monument for Lincoln.[1]

An alien visiting this statue might be forgiven if they read into it evidence that, as the colonists preach, America is the last bastion of freedom in the world. The monument represents a story of Black freedom in the settler-colony as won by the benevolence of the state and the generosity of its spirit personified in Honest Abe. Nowhere can a tinge of regret be discerned in Lincoln's manly face as his "United States" was collapsing around him and he stood in the charred remains of one of the last holdouts in the Western Hemisphere in the battle to keep Africans in chains—a place where a quarter million white men bled and died for the right to peddle and strip off Black flesh. Nowhere in the statue's inscription, nor in Lincoln's Emancipation Proclamation, is it revealed that Lincoln himself was for the forcible deportation of Africans and was championed by writers such as Thomas Dixon Jr., who might be called the poet laureate of the Ku Klux Klan. Or that shortly after his proclamation he was murdered by a white supremacist who deemed Lincoln not racist enough and who assisted in the capturing of another calculatingly less celebrated white "great emancipator" John Brown, and shouted "Sic semper tyrannis! The South is avenged"[2] after assassinating the president, delivering a blow against the "government overreach" and woke ideology, which forced the horsewhip out of the fists of noble gentlemen. Instead, that foreigner, arrived from a country not deemed a shithole, wearing an Alexis de Tocqueville cravat, is through the old Lincoln Memorial presented with a story of white state benevolence and African passivity, and reception of said benevolence. He might even be tempted upon seeing the contemporary conditions of the Black lumpen in the native quarters of Washington DC to agree with the old slave master tenet that the blacks are ungrateful.

The present work is not concerned with what this alien thinks but with what Charlotte Scott got for her hard-earned money. The figure of the Black, often naked, and kneeling man is ubiquitous in colonist anti-racist discourse. It appears everywhere from Josiah Wedgwood's anti-slavery medallion depicting the kneeling slave asking of white society, "Am I not a Man and a Brother," to Mark Twain's "Nigger Jim" faithfully assisting Huckleberry Finn on his adventures. The Supplicant Negro is a sort of gender counterpart to the Mammy figure,[3] who was a de-sexualized and over-maternalized,[4] subservient domestic Black woman, as seen, for example, in the character "Mammy" in *Gone with the Wind* and "Old Aunt Jemima" from minstrel shows and then the pancake syrup brand. This figure also replaces the threat of the negro fiend,[5] the war and fire organizing negress, the "negro wench" figure and is put to the same use, flattering white power with depictions of Black impotence. But in white supremacist patriarchy, where Blackness is gendered male[6] supplication becomes a descriptor of the "race" and essence of Africanity. From Colin Kaepernick's gesture of taking a knee to representations of an angelic, begging George Floyd—a man murdered with the knee of a police officer. The figure attempts to win pity from white society, countering the bestializing imagery of slave masters, colonists, and police apologists who depict the Africans they sought to retain in their shackles as devils, savages, and violent criminals. It also, and this is the subject of the present work, replaces the history of global Black revolts in pursuit of radical autonomy from plantation power with a story of the peaceful pursuit of integration into an always-to-be-adequately reformed colony. The figure of the supplicating negro has been used to associate the pursuit of Black freedom with pleading, requests and "demands," dramatized vulnerability, and submission. It draws in the horizons of the Black freedom dreams until they match the border of the settler-colony, so that the absolute community autonomy won by escaping the reach of master and police power, that is, marronage, disappears and these dreams are replaced with the requirement to peacefully march to an always oncoming day of equality and Civil Rights. The labor of Ms. Scott and other emancipated slaves who gave of their wages to build a monument to freedom was used to keep them depicted as forever on their knees. But Black freedom, where it is won, however transitory in white supremacist hegemony, has been won in anti-colonial war, plantation arson, escapes, spontaneous lumpenproletariat prison riots and uprisings against police, maroon wars, and national revolutions. The specter of the Black fugitive everywhere haunts white power. For this reason, it must be beaten back and melded into images of Black supplication, by colonists, be they styled liberal or conservative so that the Black girl with "behavioral issues" cussing out a police officer can be given a sticker of Martin Luther King Jr. and told the way to win her cause is through ensuring authority is not in danger. Through a visit to scenes in the history of this sleight of hand, this book is an attempt at a step toward self-emancipation from white abolition, Civil Rights, and other colonist anti-racisms. It is also, partly, if not a late participant in the expanding, international Black anti-colonial revolt (not the 2020 summer protests as containment efforts have described them) of felling statues and monuments[7] to white power; it is an attempt to repay Charlotte Scott and Archer Alexander with a smaller monument to escape.

The first chapter, "'A Certain Negro Man Named Adam': A Black Anti-Colonial Life in a White Supremacist Totalitarian Colony," tells the story of Adam, "a negro slave," and his late seventeenth-century conflict with the man who considered himself to be his master, John Saffin. Adam's treatment and the conflict over a promise of his manumission inspired celebrated white abolitionist and magistrate Sam Sewall to pen *The Selling of Joseph: A Memorial* which the *Colonial Society of Massachusetts* two hundred years later praised as "the first public plea for the emancipation of the negro."[8] Adam's story, papered over by Sewall's tract, is read to reveal his insolent revolt, as well as sketch out settler-colonial racial totalitarianism via one man's experience of forced servitude. Adam's survival, despite every colonial institution militating against his freedom, the victory in his partial freedoms despite all attempts to capture him, and the autonomy and threat inherent in his walking saucily about town is presented as a model of the urban maroon, that is, the fugitive African often only nominally captured, but walking with swagger in radical autonomy despite being surrounded by colonial power.

Chapter 2, "Killing the Maroon, Birthing the Supplicant Negro," presents an impression of marronage in the eighteenth century of the borderless Western Hemisphere, and the violent murder and then the disappearance of the artists of Black liberty, the runaways, and their replacement with the figure of the Supplicant Negro. Special attention is paid to moments of a trial, as recorded by court recorder Daniel Horsmanden, of enslaved Africans for the conspiracy to burn New York in 1741. Far from the dotish, submissive Black figures said to be worthy of freedom in abolitionist novels and campaigns, the trial documents reveal an African hatred of masters and masters' society and a will to burn it to the ground. The chapter includes scattered scenes of Black revolt, beyond New York to present a political tradition of revolt and marronage, far more threatening, effective, and frequent than the peaceful protest or agitation for "change" which both colonial abolitionist and pro-slavery advocates have worked in tandem to bury. The second half of the chapter focuses on this burial and the replacement of the maroon with the "half child." It opens with a return to the scene of conflict between Adam and John beginning with a reading of Sam Sewall's first abolitionist tract as an attempt to paper over Adam's shovel-wielding violence and John's conservative reply. Finally, Josiah Wedgwood's anti-slavery medallion and the caricature of Jim in Mark Twain's *Adventures of Huckleberry Finn*, two discourse-shifting instruments, are examined as moments in the white abolitionist effort to seal the coffin on the violent revolt of the enslaved African.

Chapter 3, "The Muzzle of Civil Rights: Lift Thine Eyes to the State," shows how the ossification of supplicant Blackness set the stage for the narrative of Black appeal to masters, the master race, and the masters' society to be recast in the twentieth century into an appeal to the state for justice. In Chapter 3, we record the narrative of "Civil Rights" being presented as a campaign of love and "brotherhood" and as the demand for America to "live up to its ideals." It regurgitates the Supplicant Negro theme and displaces Black radical thinkers and the histories of Black radical traditions of action against US anti-Black pogroms and apartheid. A Civil Rights narrative supplanted Black radicalism just as the Wedgwood anti-slavery medallions stamped out the shadow of slave revolts. As a direct appeal to the colony, "Civil Rights" was also the vehicle for the domestication of Black liberatory politics. The ending of all coloniality—the aim of marronage and rebellion—was redirected into a campaign for reformed governance and improved colonialism. The savior of Black people became a white supremacist society eventually enlightened and more sympathetic—not one in ruins. The chapter demonstrates how Civil Rights—as its name testifies—sought to contain the struggle for Black life within the confines of the colonial state and colonial justice. It aimed to lead Black politics by the bit away from traditional Black radical thought (such as David Walker's *Appeal*) that looked beyond colonialism and its expression in nation-form, that is, America. Thus, in addition to reproducing Black supplication in the face of white supremacist violence, contemporary liberal discourse on race pushes for a framing that presents white supremacist violence as a problem unique to America and one which that colony has within its power to rectify. Moments from Dr. King's "I have a dream" and Barack Obama's "A More Perfect Union" speeches are examined in detail as speeches that orient Black freedom toward a call for Black supplication to the state. The influence of the Civil Rights tradition, the chapter argues, functions as a muzzle on what can be said about Black freedom and blinders on what can be imagined for Black life outside of the colonial state.

Chapter 4, "Supplication in the Spectacle," presents the contemporary society of white supremacist spectacle.[9] There, before the public destruction even of prostrate Black people, radical uprisings are beaten back into submission not only by riot police but also by the disciplining force of the enduring Civil Rights ideology, which is revealed as a new Black code of peaceful protest. The chapter examines the liberal media and its interest in giving white supremacists the benefit of the doubt to any point of absurdity. It also examines its leveling of the disciplinary power of Civil Rights discourse to help police the Black lumpenproletariat-led uprising. The Black Codes of peaceful protest are a natural outgrowth of the representation of Black campaigns for justice as supplication from the downtrodden slave—a being never to be armed, and always to have their body and language regulated and contorted into performances of obsequiousness. Three contemporary expressions of the problem of the Supplicant Negro are analyzed. First, white cable news hosts who have interviewed Black preachers and professors who plead for justice and improved "race relations"—to the exclusion of Black radical youth activists at the heart of the uprising.[10] The Black guests chosen to speak during flare-ups of racial violence fulfill a comforting role as the pleading, native informants. Chris Hayes's stated wish that Kyle Rittenhouse turn his life around and the violence of liberal hope is discussed as well as an example of giving white supremacists the benefit of the doubt. Second, New Jersey senator Cory Booker's speech on the Senate floor during the 2020 Black uprising. The senator, it is argued, channeled the Supplicant Negro figure to help neutralize the uprising and recenter the moribund campaign for equal rights for Black people in colonialism.

Finally, the chapter analyzes Black Lives Matter as a supplicating plea in late fascism. The chapter argues that ours is the age of Trump's discovery, namely, the conservative's discovery that open racism is not taboo and has few political drawbacks. On the contrary, it is cheered on by the "silent majority." That which excited lynch mob society a century ago continues to excite it today. The Civil Rights struggle only wobbled open racism in the public square—it did not knock it out. The masks of fiscal conservatism, tradition, and "values and principles" today are constantly dropped, revealing the same old mob with the same old nooses. While open anti-Blackness was never absent from the public sphere from any majority-white country, as Boris Johnson's editorials[11] and Italian parliaments prove,[12] this discovery set in motion competition among conservative figures and has launched a race for who could push the bar furthest in open racism.[13]

The book concludes by arguing that in such a world where open racism and racist massacres are accelerating, the fetter that is the old hat-in-hand Supplicant Negro figure must be destroyed. If there is to be an end, once and for all, to the subject position of peoples of African descent, a historical narrative and politics of Black marronage and anticolonialism must supplant it. The time of negotiation, protest, and even "radical demands" such as those set out in the Ten-Point Program of the Black Panther Party must be set aside. Talks have failed and the fire is in fact this time. It is unreasonable and unhelpful for Black people to continue to be expected to shuffle between the two poles of white supremacy: liberal abolitionism and Nazism, pleading the case for justice while the meager rights won continue to be stripped from them. It should be given up that any meaningful hope could be drawn from more polite requests, and all further attempts at pleading should be ended. America should be left and divested from before the reintroduction of rule by "planters."

Methodology: Traipsing through What Has Been Said

It must be admitted from the outset that I am untrained. I spent the majority of what was to be my formal academic training in the gutters of the university, in the rooms with the steel chairs of suspect quality and shakily lit backrooms offered to Black Studies and Caribbean Studies or the beautified marginalized studies of the disobedient Area Studies and Ethnic Studies. And even in this I've skirted training, leaving required courses to go to the stacks, electing, against the wisdom of my mentors, to put together a patchwork of different Black Studies without developing expertise in a region or a sensible and recognizable methodology, creolizing and bastardizing my studies. Self-exiled, I am forced to rebrand my inadequacies as strengths, and advocate for there being something in window-shopping through the disciplines and sitting on the stoop of scholarship fearing to enter the halls.

And there is something in it. In staying on the outside, uninvited, but pretending to resist the lasso. There is a lot lost, of course. You are ever unequipped, and worse, a foreigner trampling on the most closely held beliefs of people without any tool to gauge how closely they are held. However, I claim the right to be excused—as long as Alexis de Tocqueville is still the reigning prince explaining what makes America great to the Americans: the foreigner christening the colony, a Black pauper raised not so far away, sojourning for longer stretches of time in the big cities and small towns than he can be allowed to bark against the colonial occupation de Tocqueville garlanded.

There is something one sees more clearly when provincializing academia. To not merely echo the activist students in their recognition that "these schools were not meant for us," but to imagine oneself not as trespassing at all. Not interrupting the stability of traditional white power with one's presence but imagining oneself on its outside, refusing integration. From this vantage point, academic training feels less than a preparation for interpreting the world and entering into a respected career path than it does the undoing of thought and its replacement with citations and talking points. A tannery that represents itself as a dressing room. In the time when Black books are banned[14] and Black Studies and history are increasingly contraband, and lynch mob society has learned to no longer shout "low down abolitionist!" but "woke" in order to slap books unflattering to slavery out of Black children's hands, it may have proved wise not to fully commit to academia in colonialism. Prescient to have trained oneself in the old traditions of slave literacy in secret and the enjoyment of unsanctioned texts as the latest Redeemer administration positions the wrecking ball near the stacks and orders the elimination of all art save line-dancing. In "lynch mob society," I refer to the continuation of what has come to be known as the Jim Crow period (ca.1870–1970). Not merely a "new Jim Crow," that is, not only to the "Age of Mass Incarceration," as Michelle Alexander puts it, but the continuation and expansion of anti-Black colonial culture from the slave codes to the neo-Black codes. The latter including the strictures of the peaceful protest and the police encounter, the public spectacle of Black lynching death, gerrymandering and voter restrictions, normalized white supremacist violence and mainstreaming of white supremacist media and political parties, police impunity, the apartheids of redline legacies, homelessness, and unspoken vagrancy laws, and so on. Informal apartheid, settler pleasure at the sight of the publicly abused "black," which is to say the settler-colonial same that is, rule by supremacist mob.

Even before colonial totalitarianism switched gears from coded and surreptitious to overt in preparation for the settler overtake of the state, scholarship was unenticing. The archives[15] are sticky with anti-Blackness and one has to wade through mounds of crap that are some version of the warning "Black boy do not be a runaway." The traces of the voices of the slave revolt are few and far between and as I learned from Angela Zimmerman when they are found like Martin Delaney's Blake on Black international anti-slavery revolution, they are, too often, in pieces. More often than not the record of our lives does not even make it to threadbare. "What we had to say was not even considered important enough to record. You think you are reading an accurate chronicle written at the time, but if who we are and what we care about are deemed irrelevant it won't be in there," writes Rebecca Hall in a book about women-led slave revolts that was itself temporarily black-labeled as sensitive on "X."

Add to the unfriendly archives hearing of my students' dorms being raided by campus police. And before this, as an undergrad, a secret attempt to build a case against me (revealed by a mistakenly sent email) after challenging the colonist patriotism in my Canadian politics class, being fresh from street postcolonial studies in Gaborone. And being suspended for challenging my Canadian high school teacher's insistence that Africa was "underdeveloped" because of its "tragic" postcolonial mismanagement. I have not come to scholarship with the warmth I've seen projected during campus tours and student orientation.

In these conditions, the methodology I have had to develop, which I have long accepted as inadequate, is a traipsing through what has been said. Temporary sojourning. A rejection of expertise and mastery and of masters. This is perhaps to be understood as the expected defensive maneuver from impostor syndrome's impostor who has never graduated to accepting that things are better now. More, even colonial-critical voices are included. But I prefer to reject even this welcome into the fold and remain speaking at the academy from an unsettled place. I am one impostor happy to be found out, caught by those who are openly unaware of Black lumpen thought. It is not always pathological, impostor's syndrome—some of us are impostors for real.

The stench of anti-blackness in scholarship is so ubiquitous that it isn't much more salvageable than an old kitchen rag. I have no interest in "contributing" to it or to feel included and I feel more comfortable petulant than at anyone's service. I do not believe that my task here is to educate and/or increase "knowledge production." A book can be something other than polished sticky notes. A Black writer is more than a wet nurse to a moribund academic industry. Nor do I have much interest in the production line and criticisms that this argument is old or does not say something new, an industry-based idea where thought is the equivalent to waiting outside the sneaker shop for the latest release, produced and already en route to the landfill, all the time greatly exaggerating its utility. I have no hope in "decolonizing scholarship" and the promises to produce a more equitable and inclusive colonial education. Anti-colonialism can fathom no such thing. Is it possible to decolonize the British military and the Israeli police? Is decolonizing diversifying? This seems the modern sense of decolonization, which is the colonists' sense. It is removed from the angry fists of the colonized and given over to their caretakers. The diversity is not so much of thought but of the bodies tasked with representing standard, licit thought. Of advertisements, tokens with additional lines, and park murals of sunny, smiling, diverse communities which happen to still not represent the inmate and the vagrant (though this is a blessing as it would be worse if they forced their social dead to grin).

I have not learned to quit books and so found it better to saunter aimlessly around campuses for as long as colonialism will entertain them. Black Studies has been a halfway house. There one can remain in the capaciousness of it, the alterity of it, even as it is still stained with the government and university—but housed physically and symbolically in its gutters, always among the first to be displaced, cut, banned by those who see houselessness as unsightly and smell the threat of disorder. Until there is only Black revolt, Black Studies will have to do. Its genre-bending and marginality are enough to cook up ideas in the slave quarters as there is still time before it is dragged fully into respectability. A place before the regimented method, collage and unfixity.[16] Not interdisciplinarity but the potential for antidisciplinarity, its uneasiness in the shackles, derided for moving around even as all other "Disciplines" have followed its lead. Jack of all trades, expert in none, as if Jack the tradesman is so wildly inferior to the experts.

Still, except for some moments, Black Studies can also be devilishly uninspiring. Not because of a lack of brilliance but in the selling that brilliance to the highest state bidder. In the disused rooms given to Black Studies, the Black liberal is still king, peddling Martin Luther King to a student body that has long left him and has enrolled or sneaks into the few Black radical classes out of anger with the traditions of state and Civil Rights genuflecting Black scholarship. A lot can transpire in the smaller offices away from those who still teach that Black people invented peanut butter or American democracy or some other racist shit and brush over the Black invention of the hemispheric slave revolt. Away from the Black academic liberal, now reformist in both their words and their actions[17] who deliver on time their more complicated version of LL Cool J in the Braid Paisley's "Accidental Racist," and on in with the mocked Afrocentrics, the militants, the never-to-be-praised, the unacceptable womanists—a Quilombo where there are less citations and research is compromised by adjunct life, 4:4 teaching loads, side hustles, and fighting university admins.

If there is a method, it is traipsing through what has been said. Not an anthropological look at marronage nor a history of it, not a history of Black supplication nor a close reading of racist texts. A brush of a visit through a number of scenes discovered while finger-walking through the records at the record store. A fealty to Haiti's Shango over Marx or the academic designs of a usable future. A poetics of study allowing itself entry into scholarship rather than apologizing at the door.

> The white fathers told us, I think therefore I am. The Black mothers within each of us—the poet- whispers in our dreams, I feel therefore I can be free. Poetry coins the language to express and charter this revolutionary awareness and demand, the implementation of that freedom . . . there are no new ideas still waiting in the wings to save us as women, as human. There are only old and forgotten ones, new combinations, extrapolations and recognitions from within ourselves, along with the renewed courage to try them out . . . For within structures defined by profit, by linear power, by institutional dehumanization, our feelings were not meant to survive. Kept around as unavoidable adjuncts or pleasant pastimes, feelings were meant to kneel to thought as we were meant to kneel to men. But women have survived. As poets.[18]

Saidiya Hartman noted runaway slave and essayist Frederick Douglass' anger at the amusements the enslaved were forced to participate in, which to him operated as "safety-valves to carry off the explosive elements inseparable from the human mind when reduced to the condition of slavery," and yearned for a dangerous music and dangerous thought.[19] I've often wondered if Black thought, when filtered through the academy and its "scholarship," ends up as jargon playthings, careerist amusements that distract us from the colonial condition, derail dangerous thought, all the while branded as essential by masters who give us our space to fiddle on the slave ship. Of course, there have been exceptions, especially by scholars who were primarily creative writers and revolutionaries, and these I've clung to in order to keep up the fire of the excitement to know despite the barriers constituted by toy readings. But it seems more important than ever, in this yet again period of white supremacist redemption, to be sparing with our writing and attend mainly to dangerous poetry. This work, or this method, is an attempt to pull away from the velcro of colonial scholarship and land into a more poetic mud.

Chapter 1

"A CERTAIN NEGRO MAN NAMED ADAM"
A BLACK ANTI-COLONIAL LIFE IN A WHITE SUPREMACIST TOTALITARIAN COLONY

What acts in a slave towards a white person will amount to insolence it is manifestly impossible to define-it may consist in a look, the pointing of a finger, a refusal or neglect to step out of the way when a white person is seen to approach. But each of such acts violates the rules of propriety, and if tolerated would destroy that subordination upon which our social system rests.[1]

According to Benjamin Rice of the Town of Sudbury in the County of Middlesex in the Province of Massachusetts Bay, Adam, a "negro slave," about five weeks into the year of 1699, ran up to Thomas Shepherd with an ax and tried to hit him with it.[2] Thomas,[3] residing in Bristol County in New England, rented a farm from acclaimed poet, politician, and judge John Saffin—a farm, which contained sheep, cattle, and "a certain Negro man named Adam."

Adam was angry. This was, in part, the natural emotional condition of a life lived self-aware under white supremacist totalitarian control. The affliction of possessing a mind no horsewhip could evangelize into believing that although one's lot was miserably tragic and cursed, with enough good behavior and supplicating prostration in front of the master and master's society, one's suffering might be satisfactorily eased. He was angry because he was subjected to colonialism and was at war against every shackle placed upon him without his consent. More specific to his particular case, Adam was angry because he was under the impression that after he finished a seven-year term of "service" to John's tenant Thomas, he would be set free and was not.

John, in a legal document he signed and entered into the book of *Wills and Inventory* on November 15, 1694, promised Adam his manumission. Adam was to work for Thomas on John's Bristol farm for seven years beginning March 25, 1694, after which he would "enfranchise, clear and make free my said negro man named Adam to be fully at his own dispose and liberty as other free men are or ought to be according to all true intents and purposes whatsoever." He added the condition that Adam was to go about his work cheerfully, quietly, and industriously in lawful business and must carry himself as an honest and true servant ought to, during the seven years.[4] This last condition, the satisfaction of which seemed wholly up to the say of John, was used as the basis for denying Adam his *liberty*.

Adam's telling of the conflict is not recorded. The story of Adam according to John is as follows:

> in the Year 1693 I Let a certain Farm Scituate at the Head of *Mount Hope* Neck, adjoyning to the Town of *Swansey*, called *Boundfield*, together with a Stock of Cattel, and Sheep with this Negro called *Adam*, unto one *Thomas Shepard*, Junior, late of *Charlstown*, for the Terms of Seven years; and knowing the said Negro to be of a proud, insolent and domineering spirit, yet had a cunning serpentine Genious, I thought to work upon his natural Reason; and for his own benefit (if it were possible) to oblige him to obedience, and to go on chearfully, quietly and industriously in his Business, for the mutual benefit of both Landlord and Tenant; and for his encouragement therein, I promised him his Freedom, and to that end, did voluntarily give him it under my Hand and Seal, upon the Conditions therein mentioned.
>
> After which the said Negro about two years carried himself indifferently well, being able (if he list) to do Husbandry work as well as most Negroes, yet he was often very Lazie and Remiss, would favour himself, and (when he could) would sliely make others bear the weight of the work ... Notwithstanding for all this kindness and indulgence [His Master Thomas showed] towards this wretched Negro, he grew so intollerably insolent, quarrelsome and outragious, that the Earth could not bear his rudeness; and this not for a fit of distemper now and then, perhaps that might have been born with; but his general deportment and usual carriage was so vexatious and grievous to the Family, contesting with his Master and his Wife, and beating his Children, with other exorbitant practices, too tedious to be mentioned: So that his Master *Shepard* long before the Expiration of the Term aforesaid, did earnestly intreat me to take the said Negro away, and otherwise to dispose of him, for he was so proud and surlie that he scarce dare speak to him (as he told me) to ask him where he had been, or why he staid so long, *&c*. much more to strike him,

for fear he should do him or his Children some mischief; Though (said he) I could beat him, and lay him at my foot, yet considering that saying, *That he that doth not value his own life, can command anothers* . . . [T]he said *Shepard* told me: . . . he was so quarrelsome and contentious, calling the Maids vile names, and threatning them (as they said) that they were sometimes afraid to be in the Room with him; and both my Wife and my Sister *George*, have often desired me to turn him the said Negro out of the house, for they could not indure his pertinacy. So in the beginning of *March* last, I order'd the said Negro to go up to *Bristol*, (where I was going my self) and had agreed with a man of *Swansey* to set him a work, but he absolutely refused, and would not go; but after I was gone, he took his Cloaths out of the house by stealth, and went about the Town at his pleasure . . . So some time after I came home from *Bristol*, this Villain came to me in a sawcy and surly manner, and told me that I must go to Captain *Sewall*, he would speak with me at his House; I guess'd what the matter was, and soon after I obey'd this Negromantick Summons, and went to know what Captain *Sewall* had to say to me (where was Mr. *Isaac Addington*) who falling into a discourse about the said Negro, he produced a Writing he said I had given the Negro under my Hand for his Freedom . . . he did very gravely admonish me, saying, that since I had given such a thing under my Hand and Seal, I ought to stand to it, and perform it; adding, that Liberty was a thing of great value, even next to life; to which I replied, that if the Negro had in any wise performed the Condition, I should not have made a word about it, to which Mr. *Addington* answered, that there was much to be allowed to the behaviour of Negroes, who are so ignorant, rude and bruitish, and therefore to be considered as Negroes . . . I replied, that the said Negro had not carried in any sort answerable to what might have been justly expected from him, had there been no such encouragement given him; as for small faults I should have winkt at them, but he having behaved himself so diametrically contrary to those Conditions, it was intollerable and not to be born with . . . This is the summe of what then passed, and so we parted without any thing concluded on. Soon after, the next day (as I take it) I requested Lieutenant Colonel *Townsend* to go with me to Captain *Sewall*, deeming it within the Cogniscance of two Justices of the Peace to determine such a matter, *viz.* Whether the said Negro having so egregiously broken the Condition aforesaid should be free, that they might soon put an end to the business, but they were of another opinion, that it was beyond their power; in fine, it was concluded, that Lieutenant Colonel *Townsend* should bind the said Negro over to answer at the next Superiour Court to be held at *Boston* . . . so when the Superiour Court Conven'd, both parties appeared, and the Declaration I had given in by way of complaint, and also the Writing that I had given the Negro, were both Read, and also the Evidences I produced, to prove the Negro had often broken the Conditions were also Read; much discourse there was about it, at last it was concluded, that seeing the Witnesses Sworn, were not there present *Vive voce*, that the matter should be transmitted to the next Superior Court to be held at *Bristol*, which was above nine weeks after; in the mean time this Rascally Negro went about the Town swaggering at his pleasure in defiance of me his Master.

Adam's interest in his freedom and his desire not to work for, or be around, his enemy was interpreted by John as insolence from a violent Black man who could not be brought into humble servitude to John or his tenants.

Furious with Adam's recalcitrance (over and above the loss of his forced labor), John chased Adam, spending time, hassle, and expense, never content to let him go as he promised. After arranging for a police officer to bind Adam over "with another Negro said to be free, named *Dick* to be his Surety"[5] only to see him "swaggering at his pleasure in defiance" of the man who thought of himself as his master, John took matters into his own hands. He somehow managed to get himself promoted from the Inferior Court of Common Pleas to the Superior Court of Judicature in Bristol and had Adam tried there at the suit of the king, apparently conscious of the fact that Black offenses against the slave master and slave masters' class are offenses against the state. Thus, John became a judge in the trial in which he was the plaintiff. According to the magistrate Sam Sewall,[6] not only did Adam have the deck set against him in having the plaintiff in his case also be the judge, but John "tampered with Mr. Kent, the Foreman" of the jury as well as placed another one of his tenants, Mr. Smith, on the jury. Despite some white witnesses testifying to Adam's good character and the preponderance of evidence in Adam's favor, the jury led by the foreman found Adam guilty. The jury apparently agreed with Thomas that he was a "very disobedient Turbulent outragious and *unruly* Servant."[7] The court, however, continued the case, questioning whether it was appropriate for John to be its arbitrator considering his being directly interested in the outcome. Nevertheless, it required Adam be returned to the custody of the man who considered himself to be his master.

1. "A Certain Negro Man Named Adam" 17

As soon as the decision to have Adam remain in John's custody was reached, John declared in open court, "Here I do in the presence of this Honourable Court command you to make hast to *Boston*, and then forthwith to go down to the Castle to work as you did before, till farther order from me." Adam did so, but in his insolence and his freedom, the "vile Negro," according to John's further complaint, "went about the Town ten or twelve days at his pleasure before he went to the Castle."[8]

According to John Griffin, one day while in the castle run by John's new client Timothy Clarke, Adam did not shovel earth to Timothy's liking. Timothy instructed him to do it another way, but Adam refused. Timothy said "you Rascal, why don't you do it as I order you." Adam replied he was no rogue, no rascal, nor a thief. Timothy broke Adam's pipe and said he will do what he says and pushed him. Adam pushed back and told Timothy that if he hit him, he would hit back. Timothy hit him with the stick. Adam took the stick, broke it, and hit the captain with the shovel and, as a witness testified, "might have killed him" but for the other laborers and the garrison soldiers who helped Timothy. According to his deposition, John Griffin said the negro was so furious and outrageous and "putt forth such great strength" that it took six or seven men to restrain him. He managed to bite one of the laborers rescuing the captain before he was sent to the dungeon.

In chains again for his resistance, Adam again frustrated John's attempts to hold him in a new trial, *Dom Rex v. Adam,* in 1702. It was deemed that Adam could not, in fact, be tried at the suit of the king as John was the real plaintiff. Additionally, John was prevented from sending Adam out of the province of Massachusetts Bay as he threatened. John may have preferred to send Adam "down river" to a colony like Virginia, more suitable, he may have thought, for the punishment of Black people than Massachusetts Bay, a relatively liberal white supremacist province. Virginia, famous since the trial of John Punch as the first colony to institute lifelong Black slavery, had by 1691, only a few years before John's hoodwinking of Adam via legal deed, begun discouraging the manumission of slaves. Or John may also have had in mind deporting Adam to South Carolina, free from Massachusetts abolitionist elements and populated by Barbados planters who took the people they enslaved in Barbados to South Carolina[9]—"West Indian Negroes" becoming "African American." Or he might ship Adam to Barbados itself or other Caribbean islands famous for Black torture, where he would become a West Indian. To lose Adam somewhere in the circuitous history of the intra-American slave trade.[10] That is, the sea and land border-crossing hemisphere-wide forced migration of Black peoples fated to frustrate the blood quantum and xenophobic logic of anti-Pan-Africanists. Shy supplicants of the slave state who centuries later would attempt to drown their own Africanness in a bucket and sweep the reality of Black heterogeneity under the rug in order to continue nursing their national identity at the colonial borders.

With John's suit failing, Adam took the opportunity to sue John for his freedom. The courts judged that he should instead take his case to the Common Pleas, but in the meantime, it was decided Adam should be left in peace "until by due process of law he be found a slave." Frustrated again, neither able to force Adam under his hand as property nor send him out of the country, John appealed to the legislative branch after failing to secure a seat on the Council. In his petition to the legislature, he pleaded, with all the white victimhood he could muster, that the defiant insolence of the yet-to-be-captured African was a threat to the safety of all her Majesty's good subjects and a possible contagion in the colony. Again, he identified the slave masters' interests with those of the colonial state and is aware that putting down one insolent slave was in the interests of national security.

> yor Petir is made a meer Yassall to his slave in being at contiuuall cost and charges about him to supply him with all manner of Necessarys, as Cloaths, Bedding food and Phisick, and attendance when lately he had the small pox. Allso to pay the keeper for his keeping in Prison Three Months where he was by the Quarter Sessions committed for his outrages & murtherous attempts at the Castle: generally known, (a Narrative whereof being in Print.) yet for all this the said vile Negro is at this Day set at large to goe at his pleasure, in open Defiance of me his Master in danger of my life, he haveing threatued to be Revenged of me and all them that have cross't his turbulent Humour, to the great scandall and evill example of all Negros both in Town and countrey whose eyes are upon this wretched Negro to see the Issue of these his exorbitant practices . . .
>
> Restoreing Ms said Negro to yo Peti that as an English subject he may Dispose of his said Negro, as he shall see cause for his own safty, and all other of her Majestys good subjects that may be exposed to any Detriment by the sd Negros villainous practices.[11]

The saga ends with Adam being tried again and convicted on August 3, 1703, for not dutifully performing his tasks and therefore required to remain John's slave. Adam appealed on November 2 of the same year, and it was decided, with some finality, that "Adam & his heirs be at peace & quiet & free . . . from the said John Saffin Esq & his heirs for Ever." Thus, John pursued Adam, seemingly into perpetuity, deploying every department of the colonial state and society to maintain Adam's enslavement: the repressive apparatus, the judiciary, the legislature, the white worker citizenry, white innocence, appealing to all who would listen that the free, insolent African was an intestine enemy[12] to the colonial, white nationalist state. Despite every fetter of power thrown at him, Adam managed to escape—constantly. Effectively living out a life free from master and overseers' control, be it expressed through violence or congeniality. A life of marronage within the belly of the white supremacist town. He was known to be a freeman until at least 1711. Free, of course, as far as it is possible to be free while Black within white supremacist totalitarianism. As the 1893 meeting of the colonial society unironically points out, Adam was known to be free as he was on a list of freed Black people forced to work for the state, the 1711 "Act for Regulating of Free Negro" requiring "the Free Negroes of this Town hereafter named each one of them to give their Attendance, faithfully & dilligently to worke on cleansing & Repaireing the High wayes and other Services of this Towne."[13] A foreshadowing of the evolution of slave master society's domination of Black life from the white power of private individuals to the white power of the public sphere.[14]

"The Totalitarian Nature of Colonial Exploitation"

> The colonist is not content with physically limiting the space of the colonized, i.e., with the help of his agents of law and order. As if to illustrate the totalitarian nature of colonial exploitation, the colonist turns the colonized into a kind of quintessence of evil.[15]
>
> —Frantz Fanon

This incomplete life story of Adam, and the insurgency of spirit it reveals, is, of course, in no way exceptional. Innumerable stories of slave revolts of one are to be found throughout the Black-enslaving world. It is revisited here, however, for two reasons. Firstly, because his ill-treatment very likely inspired what the *Colonial Society of Massachusetts* celebrated as the "first public plea for the emancipation of the negro,"[16] one of the first white abolitionist texts. Sam Sewall, one of the magistrates who decided in Adam's favor, would publish a tract in the year 1700 *The Selling of Joseph: A Memorial* that would be regarded as one of the first documents, intended for public consumption, suggesting the abolition of slavery, as well as an admonishment of the master John. In it, some of the first shadings of the drawing of the Supplicant Negro, the candidate for emancipation, begin to emerge. Placed alongside John's countering pamphlet *A Brief and Candid Answer to a late Printed Sheet, Entitled, The Selling of Joseph* vilifying Adam and "the negro" in general as devil and "quintessence of evil," the American white settlers' Manichean representation of Blackness—the liberal's and the conservative's—that is, the full range of settler interpretation of Blackness rallying between Supplicant Negro and brute, half-child and half-devil, comes to light.[17] Consideration of these warring, conjoined depictions is the subject of the following chapters.

Adam's life, a life lived within and against white supremacist totalitarianism, is revisited also because it offers a scale model of Black, non-supplicating life surrounded by colonial power. His insolence, his violence, and his disagreeable nature, the reality of Adam being the inverse of that fabricated figure, the Supplicant Negro. Here, a representative of Black anti-colonial life, Adam is at the center, the target, of a series of concentric and overlapping circles of white supremacist power; the cuffs expanding and contracting in whichever way guarantees the securing of his arrest. These rungs, the limiting space of the slaver's farm, the police, the courts, civil society, or the settler's public, are some elements of the repressive apparatuses[18] of white supremacist totalitarianism which make up colonialism. They are our colonial problem. The problem of those of us who are in the "colonial regions" and native quarters and face the "direct intervention by the police and the military [which ensures] the colonized are kept under close scrutiny, and contained by rifle butts and napalm,"[19] and so they are examined here. The rest of the book examines the problem in the capitalist regions where "the sermonizers, counselors, and confusion-mongers intervene between the exploited and the authorities"[20] keeping the colonized in place through the dissemination of the figure of the Supplicant Negro and their prescribed codes of behavior. Also our colonial problem.

The Farm

Adam enters the frame on the farm. As a means of production. Farm chattel in a series that includes sheep and cattle. He is a defective instrument corrupted by a disagreeable and violent humanity. He is to be smelted into service for the master's use. Trained into obedience for "the mutual benefit of both landlord and tenant." Black life is placed into the vise of the colonists' economy to be severed from its autonomy, its independence, humanity, and interests, and converted into a machine that benefits its purchaser. This chattel-making, the possession, and exploitation of the totality of a human being, crudely shorthanded as enslavement, is the process of making people into things.[21] The process of forcibly ushering African life off the work machine, the making of the "negro slave," the extracting and dispensing with African languages, labor, belief systems, relationships, names, culture, and offspring, and their replacement with education only for servitude and training to help conform to a life under surveillance, sexual humiliation, and public punishment. The enslavement farms of the Western Hemisphere are more complete and perfected than any institution invented by the accused "totalitarian regimes" of the twentieth century. They are older, more enduring, and their afterlives of prison, policing, and negrophobic culture have been more normalized and more championed. The fact that the American slave mill is an afterthought in discussions of totalitarianism and fascism is itself a measure of the extensiveness of the process of African depersonalization.[22] So that even post-Emancipation, Black lives do not appear on the register. The plantation, the slave mill, is nonetheless an incomplete and often unsuccessful attempt at lobotomizing the African. The production of a completely peaceable, patriotic, and supplicating slave is extremely rare if it existed at all. Even genuine Black allies to the plantation cursed overseers when out of earshot. The "contented slave," Saidiya Hartman notes, only appeared after being whipped into subjection, and "happy Sambo" was not enslaved but one of the effects of slavery.[23] The attempt at producing actual supplicant individuals, "house negroes," more often lured slaveholding families into a false sense of security, leading them to believe their field hands to be dimwitted and content, only to find, with their home in flames, a jolly okra-frying mammy with machete raised above them replying, "It [is] me . . . the good slave, the faithful slave, the slave slave, and suddenly my eyes were two cockroaches frightened on a rainy day . . . I struck, the blood spurted: it is the only baptism that today I remember."[24]

The failure of the mill's operation is expressed most clearly in the persistence of the rebellions of the Africans collectively as well as the rebelliousness of the individual African imprinted in Adam as his "proud, insolent and domineering spirit." A sauciness, which at its heart is the declaration of masterlessness and self-ownership, is antithetical to the absolute docility of the man-machine desired in slavery. Insolence simply meant the most secure hold the masters had on those they enslaved was faulty. "The most potent weapon in the hands of the oppressor is the mind of the oppressed"[25] and that mind was spitting in John's face. The sermons attesting the holiness of Black supplication to masters failed, and the repressive apparatus of the police-state jumped in and piled on at every rung of the encircling society. This is why the police must be called to put down the Black girl "with attitude" at the pool party.[26] Why a judge in 1910, Albany, Georgia sentenced three Black teenagers—referred to as "negro women"—each to one year of hard labor in a chain gang for wantonly destroying the flowers and flower pots in their path as they traipsed through a white neighborhood. The judge called it a case of racial antipathy, reading clearly the subtext of revolt in the girls' disrespect.[27] Haughtiness and insolence are performances of superiority or at least equality, declarations with the body that one does not accept oneself as a being subject to another. The managing of Black insolence and disorderliness is always at the same time the quelling of insurgency.

The Baton of Law

> Here you are, on a lone plantation, ten miles from any other, in the swamps; not a white person here, who could testify, if you were burned alive,—if you were scalded, cut into inch-pieces, set up for the dogs to tear, or hung up and whipped to death. There's no law here, of God or man, that can do you, or any one of us, the least good; and, this man! there's no earthly thing that he's too good to do.[28]

Adam, being saucy and surly, did not, according to John, hold up his end of the bargain. Thus, under the law he invented for his slave, he had no obligation to set him free. It was especially insulting to have his slave—the slave who refused his order to go to Bristol and work for his tenant—to present him with a "Negromantick" (a word John apparently coined to associate Black insolence and use of white law against white power with works of the devil) summons to see the magistrate. The magistrates told John that Negroes, who were "ignorant, rude and brutish," could not be expected to perfectly perform according to the agreement he set forth in the document promising Adam his enfranchisement. Because it could be said Adam performed as reasonably as an African could be expected to for the seven years, he should be set free. The court's anti-Black ideas were turned against the slave owner's private interests. John was betrayed.

"The rule of law"[29] is never, as it is presented in their social sciences, a civilizing social contract for the functioning of a democracy. On the contrary, for the masters, it is imagined as a second horsewhip. The law proven defective, as evidenced by the magistrate's siding with Adam, John was free to ignore it. And so he did. The law in the settler-colonial space referred to as New England, as John correctly recognized, is a tool to subject the African to the power of John, the white slave owner. Its pretensions to objectivity, rationality, equality, the "rule of law," are the coats it wears to make the white supremacist instrument more agile. The ruse of law invites liberal white supremacists to its defense with the offer that they can partake in the universalist language of blind justice and thus wash their hands of a device that has proven at all hours, in all settler-colonial spaces, to be an instrument of racial control and racist violence. Again, law in colonialism is a rhetorical instrument dressed up as an objective, wise-if-flawed, estimable code for civilized life but functions simply as an aid in setting in stone the patterns and arrangements of race and class oppression. John expected the law to arrange conditions preferable for his enslaving of Adam and to, like a cudgel, be brought down onto the heads of the negroes that defied the colony's, and his, order of subjugation. He did not acquiesce to the rule of law once it decided against him. He did not worry about the "hypocrisy" in believing in the wisdom of the law yet defying it, or about being seen as a criminal for refusing its wisdom. Hypocrisy has never been a moral barrier to the negrophobe seeking police violence against the African despite the liberals' heroic will to believe in the white supremacist's desire for moral coherence. Wavering in its primary duty, the law was disregarded by John, who went into his second pocket, which held the police lieutenant-colonel. The police officer, always standing at the ready in service of white supremacist power, is prepared to be a more effective and trustworthy binding device when the handcuff of the law is faulty.

Police in the Settlers' Pocket

John went to use the force of the state against Adam, literally walking with it at his side in the person of Lieutenant-Colonel Penn Townsend. Two centuries later in 1892, a white grocer in Memphis, Tennessee, angered at the insolence of the Black grocers at the Peoples' Grocery[30] walked in with a police officer, ordering him to arrest his competition in what culminated in the lynching of the Black shop-owners Thomas Moss, Calvin McDowell, and Will Stewart. In the "White Man's Country" Kenya Colony, 1923, two askaris[31] showed up at the door of a white settler, Ms. Rainbow, attempting to serve a warrant. She answered her door with a shotgun and told the officers to serve it "if you want to lose your life." She informed them that "a black man could not execute a warrant on a white person"[32] speaking aloud the, at times, unspoken rule of colonial law. Fifty years later in 1970 "vigilantes"[33] in Blackface associated with the Ku Klux Klan raided a student center and burned a cross at the University of Delaware. They left posters reading, "We support the police and we will teach you to before we are through with you" and "The Supreme Court may have, tied the hands of law enforcing officers but they will never tie ours. We are here to stay."[34] A declaration that the Black-led social agitation, misnamed the Civil Rights movement,[35] that led to *legal* restrictions in the arbitrary use of police violence, would not be allowed to supersede the supreme law of the colony: the burning cross of white power. The police, Ms. Rainbow, the white grocer, the "vigilantes," and John recognize, are not law enforcers but their enforcers. It is an unforgivable audacity for Ms. Rainbow that the officer would imagine that power turned back against her—as it was for the lynch mob on January 6th, 2021, who during the demonstration of white supremacist strength, beat police officers with flagpoles while stating they love police. Colonist media disingenuously claimed to be stunned at this hypocrisy—it of course was no such thing. The lynch mob knows the police is their attack dogs, sent out to do their bidding, that they had to be beaten was due to the reprimand necessary as punishment for their, at that moment, standing in the way of the lynch mob's power. Ms. Rainbow in Kenya Colony understood the rule of "The Supreme Law" as well as the Jan 6 mob did, as well as did Louisiana's Knights of the White Camelia, who in their secret manifesto said explicitly that the colony was to be the white supremacists' apparatus and their "main and fundamental object is the MAINTENANCE OF THE SUPREMACY OF THE WHITE RACE in this Republic."[36] A law inscribed in the centuries-long trail of "insolent" Black people's corpses left on trees and on the streets of the world in settler white supremacist defiance of the liberal administration and scholars' efforts to present the rule of law as the imperfect but well-intentioned equalizer.

In the settler-colony, the colonial police are in the pocket of settler white supremacists. They are their cudgel, the repressive apparatus of the white settler mob, not its foe and not its restraint. As the settler's fort, they were and are organized to protect against slave insurrections and dispatched to catch fugitives of enslavement. In summer 2020, during yet another peak of the cyclic anti-Black pogrom, they were deployed in riot gear to deter and intimidate the colonized's revolt, to quell "native unrest," while taking photo ops with white supremacist organizations and turning their backs at state administrators who provide politically calculated verbal support to protests against the pogrom. Where it is a hindrance to the lynch mob, as in the relatively rare case that law calls for fully punishing the perpetrators of white supremacist violence—even for the greater good of the stability of colonial rule—it is cast by the mob as a betrayal. The mob expects the police to be unable to discover the culprits of the 1900s lynching despite their presence in the mob. It expects the District Attorney to shield the lynchers of Ahmaud Arbery, and if by chance evidence spills out to the uprising, it expects the state to delay the trial as much as possible.[37] The police are tasked with the maintenance of the white supremacist social order[38] and, like Lieutenant-Colonel Penn, exist to do the white supremacist's bidding. In fact, considering the convergence of interests between the colonial state and the settler mob, the mob's theater of trials and arrest, the frequent exchanges and double-duty in personnel, and so on, it is better to abandon the differentiation between the mob and the constabulary force. To consider instead that they are a spectral mixture:[39] a mob state and a lynch mob society. That the colonial encounter was a race riot, invasion was mob rule that developed secret societies tasked with holding the land and controlling the colonized and these secret societies donned blue uniforms. They became the "thin blue line," the outer rim of the flood of lynch mob power that disorderly "blacks" and "natives" must obey lest they face the "rough justice" of the "raw settler."[40]

In the popular imagination, as well as histories of enslaved and anti-colonial insurgency, secret societies, cults, and anti-government conspiratorial groups are politically against, and even at war with, the police. In the settler-colony, conservative secret society groups tend to be supporters of them—because they are of them or at least the distinguishing line is academic. The settler-colony is not "a country"[41] based on laws as colonists represent; rather, the "country" is the effect[42] of the long-standing white supremacist organizing that is colonialism. Its forces of order cannot be separated from the project of settler-colonialism, that is, the perpetual reproduction of an order of political, economic, and social white supremacy and the subjugation of Indigenous and guest or "inferior races." Whether this order is of a character that is self-aware, such as in Kenya Colony's "White Man's

Country" and in Americanism's[43] America where the African "had no rights which the white man was bound to respect; and that the negro might justly and lawfully be reduced to slavery for his benefit"[44] or the order is refined so that law is presented as blindfolded and befuddled as to why it produces racist effects, will be determined by the exigencies of the colonial occupation and racial control of that particular locality.

Adam, despite finding a rare favor with the magistrates, was not freed from the clutches of the slave driver. The magistrates told John he should abide by his promise to set Adam free, then John returned with the police. It is this recognized, if not admitted, power that Amy Cooper relied upon when she threatened Christian Cooper in Central Park, New York, 2020.[45] Christian Cooper, the Black bird-watcher, with the audacity of a Kenyan askari asked a white woman to submit to the law requiring her to put her dog on a leash. "I am going to tell [the police] that there is an African American man threatening my life," she told him while looking directly at him. She communicated that she intended to bring lynching violence to him. The threat was communicated, implicitly, via her warning that she would say "African American man" to the police. The price of his insolent attempt to have her submit to "the rule of law" would be the mob, in uniform, rushed in and prepared to visit "extralegal" violence onto Christian Cooper, as was long-standing tradition in the US for Black men accused of threatening white women. Christian Cooper would recognize this threat as he lived in the world. A world in which at that very moment George Floyd was being suffocated in another state for the lesser crime of allegedly using a counterfeit $20 bill to buy cigarettes. But Amy Cooper's plan was foiled as Christian Cooper filmed her call. The video presented Amy Cooper's intent to use the police to lynch Christian Cooper for insolence and demonstrated a clarity of intention to lynch and to put on white women's distress in service of that lynching. Lynching generally requires a claim about an offense committed, no matter how implausible. It is crime that mob assembles to punish, which fuels the frenzy of Black bloodlust no matter how transparent the justification. Even when laws protected the master from destroying their "estate" in the enslaved, the killing was couched in the language of correction and punishment.[46] Wanton murder of those one enslaved, when not supplied with a defense, was often criminalized, even if the penalties were trivial. Amy Cooper, in spelling out her intentions while being recorded, destroyed the benefit of the doubt offered to white supremacists. The advantage she ordinarily expected to possess, of her white word against his, was neutralized by the cellphone video recording—a technological reality to which the contemporary lynch mob, which has for centuries depended upon being given the benefit of the doubt, no matter how thin the veil of denial and smirkingly the protest of innocence, has not completely adjusted. The performance of a white woman in distress and vulnerable to the whims of the lurking Black male aggressor, a staple of scenes in "American classic" Ku Klux Klan propaganda films *Gone with the Wind* and *Birth of a Nation*, was muddled by her communicating that she intended to perform. Christian Cooper's video blocked the performance, made it impossible for the liberal media to ride to her rescue, and thus the unspoken social contract between contemporary conservative white power which promises to refrain from articulating its power as white, and the liberal white power which in return sows doubts about the nature of state power as settler power, was broken. Malcolm X once remarked regarding the images of police dogs attacking "Civil Rights" protestors, "If a dog is biting a black man . . . then that black man should kill that dog or any two-legged dog who [*sicced*] the dog on him."[47] But the chain of command does not end there. Amy Cooper, an embodiment of white settler power like John, the white Memphis grocer, and the "Karens" before her, that is to say, the lynch mob, sics the police on the insolent Black rascal too much in leisure, walking saucily in the park.

Adam, Black people, exist surrounded by this Confederacy of white power—police, lynch mob, colonist apologists. Even when an unlikely victory in liberal-minded white supremacist courts is won, one cannot escape from the private army of police power that can at any time be deployed by a settler racist. Thus, the white conservative in the settler-colony may both express love for the police (unless they act against white power) and hatred for "big government overreach" and intrusion despite the fact that the police are if not the most invasive at least the most violent form of government control in citizens' lives. If the police were indeed as liberal depictions have them: a flawed but nevertheless necessary, inherently respectable institution charged with objectively (that is, in a way that is race-neutral) keeping the peace and good order, white supremacists might be expected to hate them. The police, for them, would be a continuation of the hated government agents deployed during Reconstruction to foil the slave owner's right to Black torture, or even, as those who would give them the benefit of the doubt might argue, the rogue agents of the Ancient Regime, officers of the king returning to subdue Republicanism. Certainly, the Ku Klux Klan would not say "we support the police" if it were an institution striving earnestly to deploy color-blind, fair, and race-neutral justice. Conservatives support the police because the police are not as they are presented in criminology textbooks—as the imperfect but necessary institution of public safety. They are the handcuffs in the back pocket of lynch mob society. No reform or anti-bias training will transform this fundamental nature, and the hope that it one day might is a more effective weapon against protest than the water cannon.

The Court-Theater

With Adam in custody again, John was able to use his political influence to delay the case until he could get himself appointed judge and put his tenants on the court as jurors. It must be underlined that the slave owner's influence on the court system does not reflect "corruption" of an otherwise ideal court system. The court, like the police, is an instrument of mob power whether coming to the aid of a white supremacist president or deciding the innocence of Emmett Till's murderers for sixty-seven minutes inclusive of a coke break.[48] The settler-colonial court, with its rituals, patterns of language and dress, elaborate gestures and dramatics, is a theatrical performance of erudition, deliberation, and justice used to render abstract the operation of colonial force. Racial control, both the master's and that of colonial "justice" which supplanted it, requires theatricalization,[49] a theater of logic and causality, rendering practices of torture and kidnapping as predictable, measured, rational action, that is, arrests and sentences, consequences, measures taken for the good of the public. The court, the police, and the master require fealty to fiat. Of its targets, the demonstrated deference to authority and patient audience before its magic show. Among the services the court provides colonialism, three stand out. The maintenance of white rule through the reproduction and expansion of original settler and settlement derived law. The fiction of neutrality and justice which provides plausible deniability for liberal white supremacists who deploy the possibility of an eventual equal justice as a bulwark against charges of the institution's predictable racist treatment. As well as providing a convincing spectacle of justice that eases the courts' victims into the acceptance of carceral violence: the sentence, the arrest, custody, incarceration, harm, and death by captivity. Finally, for John and individual racists, it offers the reins to class power as well as the ability to launder white supremacist force via legal fictions, references to morality, and the fiction of objectivity and ethics.[50]

John, the slave master who became a judge, was too eager to regain his role as a slave master to maintain the performance of the majesty of the court and so once it was settled that Adam was to remain in his custody until the next trial, John in open court ordered Adam to immediately go to Boston and work for his tenant Timothy at the castle. In later centuries, liberal social scientists would argue that the court is independent of the ruling class and any undue influence or dovetailing of interests is a mark of imperfection or corrupting influences. But in these early days of the colony, such illusions were underdeveloped, and the theater of the separation of powers between the enslaving ruling class and the "justice system" did not even ask of John a costume change.

Adam found himself in this time, at the turn of the eighteenth-century Atlantic world, at a moment when the codification of the white supremacist totalitarian order of the slave system was reaching mere adolescence. The "Christian" of colonial and legal texts was becoming "white" and the slave-for-life was becoming identified with the African, concretizing the caricature of the Negro as the being-slave, the cursed of Ham and natural servant of the superior white race. At the same time, the Barbados and Virginia slave laws had by then been well established and were on the cusp of being entrenched (especially in 1705) during Adam's life. Indeed, in several societies of slavery, the enslaved were already banned from testifying against the master.

Adam lived at the birth of racially explicit times, a period when the theater of colonial power was less ornamental, when white power had no need to hide behind the opaque and learned language of court opinions and phrases like "equal justice under the law" but on the contrary, white power was on full display through the court's threadbare fanfare. It was a time when one could witness in daylight the white supremacist exoskeleton of colonial power, long before it evolved and improved in ideological technology with the grand performance of "justice," and the separation of class rule from the plantation, or slave society, into the departments of economics and finance, policing, and the legal profession. In eighteenth-century Jamaica, for example, enslaved people were tried in Slave Courts composed of three landowners and two magistrates (also landowners) and could not bring a case against any master. There, as Diana Paton shows,[51] they were tried in hastily convened courts and were sent off to the "common Whipman" in the open market. Slave owners were also officially delegated to punish slaves for misdemeanors, and while they often could not (legally) "wantonly kill" their slaves, if one happened to die in the course of punishment, the overseer was not to be held responsible. In this scene of bucolic justice, the planter is one and the same with the judge and also delegated himself as the executioner of punishment when the Black offender was not sent off to the commonly agreed-upon Whipman. The court was a ramshackle performance that in its hastiness and without the illusion of the "separation of powers" reveals the Jamaican court as not a deliberative body but a conspiracy of white nationalists against the African in order to facilitate the African's exploitation and repression. Thus whether a disheveled planter with a makeshift powdered wig claiming he had the right to correct runaways in an eighteenth-century Jamaican cane field, or a Justice in the US Supreme Court with calculated gestures and lofty language extolling the virtues of Qualified Immunity for police, the colonial court is a show put on to facilitate the execution of white supremacist power. The special privilege granted to slave owners and settlers in legislation, in crafting laws on everything from the banning of enslaved people hunting and being armed to the banning of Indigenous ownership of cattle in Kenya[52] was testament to the fact that even when judges did not spend the majority of their time shouting the N-word to the enslaved in the courts[53] as they did when they returned to their farms, the justice system is less about equality under the "rule of law" than it is about racial control. Where it is seen to have reformed and has "progressed" to being interested in more color-blind justice and equality, it should be assumed that the theater has gone from a rudimentary nickel minstrel show to a full ensemble performance. Its purposes, race, and class interests remain the same, as will be seen in its outcomes.

The State-Theater

The police, the law, the courts, the entire infrastructure or repressive apparatuses of the state, as it was experienced by Adam, were the continuation of his enslaver's power. It was the outer rungs of the white farm, secondary concentric circles of control radiating from his capture at the center of John's totalitarian farm. Whatever fictions of separation of powers are touted now by the apologists of colonialism, or then, from the contemporary theorists of the modern state and police power, for Adam, for the captive of white supremacist power, all colonial institutions, as fictive as they might be, colluded in his targeting and facilitated the totalitarian exploitation of his body and ending of his freedoms.

Adam's story, as part of the enslavement of Africans in the Western Hemisphere at a moment before a particular province of colonialism was rebranded as the United States, is important also because it gives the

1. "A Certain Negro Man Named Adam"   31

lie to the myth that Black life suffers under or within America. America is but one episode[54] of the plantation. Despite utilizing that nationalist claim to permanence, it is a nevertheless transient narrative framing of a region of white supremacist settler-colonialism. Adam's life was lived on a farm on land that had yet to be misrepresented by colonialism's cartography as America(n). That colonist fictions of the nationalized land, land interpellated as a national subject, attained hegemony at all is itself a testament to the totalitarian nature of settler-colonialism. It holds the power to breathe life into a portion of earth, call it forth by the colony's name, and have it be seen through and through not as earth but America, earth remade in slave society's image. What Black life undergoes on the Indigenous land elaborately misidentified as American, for example, the supremacy of law, the political supremacy of whiteness, the organized slave catcher and settler lynching violence into a standing army branded the constabulary, and so on, is colonialism. It is the constant practice of colonizing that invents the nation. That constantly speaks an image of the nation into fictional existence. Land, like the enslaved African, is taken into total possession, de-spirited and renamed. Ongtupqa becomes the Grand Canyon, and the awe it inspires is credited to the beauty of the colony at the same moment Jazz becomes America's music and African musical traditions become "country," the music of white nationalism and the romance of settlement. So that victims of colonialism now associate colonized land and the art of the colonized with the colony, hesitating to move away from white America for fear that the Delta Blues will go with it and that it is "all they know." Colonialism institutes a mass forgetting that all that is known and loved in life is not its gift but exists despite it. That Blues[55] is in a death struggle against it, not its amniotic fluid. Settler-colonialism is a parasite that declares its intention to erase its host. It does this even, especially, when it offers land acknowledgments, and diversifying and including. It does not give land back. It does not release the ex-slave from the master's grip. It desanguinates, leaves the husk of its victims, parades its spoils, and allows white power to present as modern cosmopolitanism, like a cop in a boubou.

America is an artifact of colonial violence. Performed into existence, the nation is personified as an entity that is flawed, imperfect, guilty, possessed of a particular "spirit" and personality. The ongoing onslaught that is settler-colonial anti-Black violence is then transferred to this fictional entity, attributed to America the person, a good man but a sinner who is striving each day to atone for its "original sin" of slavery— the atonement named racial progress—and who must be forgiven.

Present anti-Black, anti-Indigenous atrocity that is colonialism becomes America, the flawed personage—not a structure[56] of constant attack but Christianity's universal problem of fallen Man. But colonial violence outlasts every transitory narrative of the nation and every state that is said to supplant the previous one, and for whom colonial invasion was merely a tragic founding event at the birth of the nation. The invasion endures. Colonial violence precedes, runs through, and outlives the "nation" because colonialism is the generative practice of anti-Black politics—the fiction of the nation anti-Blackness' personification. It is the methods of plantation production, however abstracted and developed. The colonists' fiction reverses cause and effect. Anti-Blackness *happens in* America as opposed to America being one of several expressions of anti-Blackness. This inverted framing of the colony as encapsulating racism coupled with nationalism's pretension of permanence offers colonialism protection for its chief conceit that its child, the colony, is eternal rather than on its way out, be it by natural causes or forced out by anti-colonialism. But for all colonialism's deception, the land, like the anti-Blackness it witnesses, never changes and will outlast state and nation. It is not a nationalized subject, it remains the land. What changes are the icons, symbols, and language referring to the "new order," imposed upon it. Settler nationalism being the collective brainwashing project, always and in every way buries the old order of still operating machinery of the plantation with the sparkling dust of the "country." In some ways, America, even if the concept existed in his lifetime, for Adam would be irrelevant. What existed was the sustained racial control, the totalitarianism he experienced under white supremacist power, the colonialism that kept him captured from birth to death regardless of the vagaries of colonial nomenclature or the shuffling of individuals or techniques of colonial administration. The nation is settler theater. Adam's problem was the unchanging brunt of colonial power.

Karen Society

Adam did not only face the white supremacist totalitarianism that was the condition of being enslaved, and under the slavemasters' apparatus of the courts and police, law, and the colonial state. He was also closed in at all sides by white society. His working experience was not at all one of comrades working together under the tyranny of the big man with capital. His "proletarian" buddies, maids, tenants, and security guards were, in their actions toward him, deputized officers of the settler-colony. Black Twitter has, since the late 2010s, popularized the term "Karen" to refer to white women of any class who like Amy Cooper threatened or followed through on threats to call the police on Black people for the offense of their existence in public space. Especially existing in a way that displeases or challenges them in space they regard as the undeclared (after the fall of codified American apartheid, all "white spaces" must be undeclared) exclusive property of white propertied people. Adam found himself held captive among Karens of any gender. White working-class people who cooperated with the authorities and the land-owning elite against the African, despite being exploited, although qualitatively less violently, by this class. He was encircled by the casual white supremacy of the everyman. Workers who informed on Adam and would, witnessing his resistance, lead him into the hands of the police.

John was able to collect the testimonies of white tenants and neighbors as to the "wicked behavior" of the negro. In addition to Benjamin Rice, the man residing in the family of John's tenant Thomas who testified Adam raised an ax to Thomas, John's neighbor Joshua Finney testified that Adam came up with his hand to Thomas as if he was about to strike him. Hannah, Thomas' wife, testified that she feared Adam would do "some bodily mischief" and that he had a knife and threatened to cut off Thomas' head. Sarah, who worked the horse and plow, testified that Adam struck her and gave her ill words and disobeyed, mocked, and derided her mother. Adam, remanded to John's custody and sent by John, to work for his client at a castle in Boston, again got the devil in him. It was the entirety of the farm workers present who cooperated in restraining Adam from attacking Timothy with the shovel and who, linking arms with the garrison soldiers, worked as a team to carry Adam off to the dungeon.[57] Thus the Black man's anger was policed at every circle of slave society, including that of the white working-class society who, at least in the presence of the African, aligned their interests with the planter and helped carry the African off to prison. The memory of Bacon's Rebellion had already faded out of existence.

The witness and tenant statements, the Karens' depositions collected by John, were assembled and framed in such a way as to pull on the white nationalist heartstrings of the colony. Poor slavemaster John was turned into a "mere vassal to his slave," cowering before the unarrested Adam who walked in defiance of his master and threatened to revenge himself upon him and all those who offended him. It was not the Black man surrounded by a society holding him against his will, isolated in the midst of a white master and his peers, weighed down by years of torturous violence and forced labor, confronted with the impossibility of justice, and a neighborhood and authority in cahoots to hold him captive and carry him off to jail for self-defense that was the victim. The network of white power, piled onto him at every level from the discursive to the police, to keep him beaten, in captivity and forced to develop their "country" and make profit for them is, in John's narrative, the victim—the innocents made vulnerable to Adam's criminality. The insulted maids, white women, and children struck by an African hand, the threatened men, are the vulnerable and the abused and the courts must lend a sympathetic ear to them. Not the man forced to spend his life at the beck and call of his enemies. The man who was expected to be cheerful as his sinews and mind were soldered to fixed capital without anesthesia, and whose past, family, loves, fears, and desires do not appear in any record. Indeed, the only fear recorded is that of those who are heavily armed and who fear Black insubordination, and who expect the courts to exonerate them and act in their interest as they abuse a man. Just as the armed members of state repression today, expecting exoneration and paid leaves for murders, collecting complaints of brutality[58] like lapels and free to kidnap the poor from the streets or line them up at a wall and publicly fondle them for trespassing in public space, are empathized with to the point that the response "I feared for my life" has become as routine as putting up the yellow tape. The travesty for them, then as now, is not the beatings that were Adam's life but the situation in which the white man "feared to strike [Adam] . . . for fear he should do him or his Children some mischief."[59]

    The world in which a mob surrounding and beating a Black captive is often presented as the tragic past world of a "country" lost in the "original sin" of slavery. Colonialism is bifurcated; forms of anti-Black atrocity no longer permissible belong to the past, a world of tragedy, a foreign country. The continued presence of atrocity, an atrocity defining white supremacist colonialism, is presented as legacies. A white supremacist massacre of Black shoppers in Buffalo is not what colonialism produces and has produced in Katrina, in the race riots of Tulsa, and in the Zong or the genocide after Nat's Virginia, but due to the stubbornness of "racism." But colonization continues and remains the world we inhabit. Race riots are now more efficient with AR-15s and less shooters. Segregationist governors are now Nazi-sympathizer presidents. The specter of the noose and the Confederate battle flag has returned to the Capitol and to musicians' and conservative politician's tongues.[60] "Negro hounds"[61] still rip the flesh of Black fugitives, and vermin and pestilence

1. "A Certain Negro Man Named Adam" 35

devour Black captives in their slave dungeons.[62] Shackles remain on wrists, the concentration camps multiply. The minstrel theater survives in memes, tokens, and Louisiana prison rodeos. Rent and gentrification have driven another great migration, scattershot, in multiple directions. Some forced back to the rural counties with the governors who once defied Yankee voting laws are now experts in gerrymandering. Some migrating deeper into the city and into the homelessness. A Black vagrant flood. Surrogate for traditional European anti-Roma hatred, despised, criminalized, and blamed. Disposable and disposed of, shouted at as dirty and shot at, and the colony's native quarters faces the European quarters in envy, as Fanon says. A "disreputable place inhabited by disreputable people. You are born anywhere, anyhow. You die anywhere, from anything. It's a world with no space; people are piled one on top of the other, the shacks squeeze tightly together." Colonial society is the only one in which crime, often full-throatedly said "Black crime," continues to be successfully presented as the central threat in a society of spontaneous mob and organized negrophobic killings, and in which the organs of police power are cheered on by anti-Black groups who in concert with them brutalize Adam's population. It is the society in which it is possible to feign worry about Black peril and the illegal escapes and resistances to the straits capital and colonialism have put on Black life, to share Nazi websites or police-generated statistics of violent Black crime, and at the same time, no thought is given to the compilation of an encyclopedic and record-clarifying account of the torture of people like Adam. Even as some perpetrators for whom there is photographic evidence of their criminal participation in mid-twentieth-century lynch mobs recline in tranquility in homes and nursing facilities. Indeed, even the present reader might be tempted to feel sympathy for the enslavers, and the insulted and struck maids, the mistreated torturers and captors, drunk as so many are on the punch of the presumption of white innocence. Colonial society, Karen society, is one in which sympathy is shown to a thousand versions of Ariel Castro, a man who kept three women enslaved in his home for over a decade, while his victims are tarred as the inherently evil, violent, unreasonable, and lucky to be so well-treated ingratiates. A place where the mandated schoolbooks and primetime news personalities speak of the experience of happy or "well-fed"[63] enslaved as part of the "plantation family" that could be expressed by that slaveholder Castro, "We had a lot of harmony going on in that home."[64]

These colonial apparatuses, handcuffs fastening to Adam's noncooperative wrists and legs, make up the totalitarian control that is his arrest in settler society. In Frantz Fanon's sense of spatial confinement, police repression followed by the making of the colonized the quintessence of evil, or however totalitarianism is understood. If totalitarianism is Orwellian mind erasure and a government where truth is inverted and all life is controlled, this is the obvious condition of the African enslavement. For a man sent to the dungeon for resisting the guards of white power, a man deprived of a patronym and with the master's *Saffin*, thrust upon him and, again, the English first name thrust upon him. A man misnamed, misnationalized, misaged as boy for reasons of the state to say nothing about the misgendering inherent in colonial gender schema, that is, where do we put "a man" who lives between cattle and castration? Is Celia of Missouri recognized as woman or breeder in her "being allowed" to give birth before being hanged? It is not so much that totalitarianism is perfected in Black slavery, but that it is the West's projection[65] of a feared, arriving totalitarianism is derived from Black slavery. That such an unthinkable thing may await them in the future dressed in fascism or Hannah Arendt's Stalinism is the fear of being reduced to Black life in settler-colonialism,[66] be it John's farm or the Angola prison farm, or probation, or the arrangement of checkpoints at every mile of Black life, what is feared in "totalitarianism" is the generalizing of the life Adam, and of Sandra Bland. We must add on to James Baldwin's claims that "white people carry in them a carefully muffled fear that black people long to do to others what has been done to them" that the dystopian future, the apocalypse warned about in all political stripes of the West, is the fear of being colonized and enduring colonization. That Black life in settler-colonialism is not immediately referred to when speaking of police-states and totalitarianisms is no mystery, but the only possible outcome of the racially organized disposability at the heart of these systems. Adam in his stubbornness, to the chagrin of John and tenant Thomas, made it so that he was not so easily disposed of. A stubbornness mirrored here in the refusal to make his life match other experiences of totalitarianism; rather, Adam's life on the farm, Black life in the plantocracy, that is, life branded, chained, and owned, is the central locus from which other experiences of totalitarianism must be measured. And the enslaved's survival and rebellion against the colonial order are the only roadmaps out of the apocalypse worth charting.

The Intestine Maroon[67]

In March of 1701, after Adam decided he was free—even according to settler law, he refused the summoning of the former owner, John, to meet him in Bristol to be carried to Swansey to be abused by someone else. Adam, of course, was never John's slave. People do not possess property in men,[68] if they can be said to possess property at all. The slave is a narrative fiction. First, a fiction of the master. Or rather, the fiction of the person who through collusion between themselves and the slaveholding society invented the categories of chattel people and masters and placed himself in the latter. Second, the fiction of historians. Adam was not a slave, nor was he a negro or "a black," a caricature inextricably bound up with enslavement, settler-colonialism, and the narrative practices of white supremacist totalitarianism. Instead, he was an African captive placed under a net held jointly by a private landowner and the colonial police state. The act of enchaining, the illegality of auto-emancipation, the promise of arrest and return by public power to private seem, in concert, the state of things: slavery. The captive African, each day held, shackled, and so each day subjected to another kidnapping assault, has this constant experience of assaults masked under the fiction of "the time of slavery." The African has their being, as survivor of these daily assaults, converted—in colonist-narrated history—into the "slave." Not a person assaulted every moment of their life, but a type of thing. As if a man whose house was robbed daily for years was not an unfortunate man subject to several constant attacks, but a new type of being altogether: a "robbed." The robbed is a fiction invented by a state of a band of robbers organized to facilitate and collectively benefit from robbery.

The ubiquity of white supremacist assault, in the narrative of "slavery," becomes a *time*—the time of slavery. Abstracted, the individual perpetrators blur together, the individual acts of violence merge, and both become a tragic time in which there are no individual perpetrators and no one can be held accountable. Unlike a band of serial bank robbers caught in the act and forced to make restitution, slavery is when there are so many perpetrating acts of racist violence that the perpetrators are blameless. And in any case, things have happened so long ago that everyone who experienced it or perpetrated it is dead. The horrid period of anti-Blackness is past, no one *back then* is alive, and so we need to come together and work to repair the wrongs. Colonialism is then suited with revolutionary moments: the Emancipation Declaration; *Brown v. Board*; African, Caribbean, and Latin American Independence; "the 2020 Racial Reckoning." Baptismal waters that we are told have transported the nation and world into an entirely new temporality. But if it looks like there is still the suctioning of minerals to the same metropoles, and if there seem still to be massacres of Black people in the cities and mass confinement and Black labor, it is to be understood not as the unchanging same but as *neo*-colonialism and the tragic "legacies of racism." Anti-Blackness, however ubiquitous, however planetary, is always long ago, culprit-less, and being fixed. Thus, the concept of the slave and slavery, not too surprisingly, protects colonialism. The innumerable frames of settler anti-Black violence are drawn through a colonist narrative so that what appears is a being (the slave), and a state of affairs (slavery). Always neatly divorced from the present. We are not being colonized, we are told, we are merely witnessing an imperfect nation moving in fits and starts toward freedom for all. But in truth, we who have not run far enough away and are still in earshot of colonist discourse are captives of a colonial temporality. We, today, inhabit the anti-Black past the future colonists will wash their hands of. "The 2020s were a time of police brutality and open fascism, the legacies of which are still felt today." And so on and so on until either colonialism or the colonized come to an end.

In his insolence, Adam escaped John's attempt to make of him a docile, supplicating "slave." It is not as clear, however, that he escaped the concept of slavery. In Adam's decision to live out his extra seven years in captivity, enslaved by John but hoping he would keep his promise of manumission, there may be read evidence of his internalization of the illusion of the slave and a trust in the law of slave masters and belief in colonial categories of freedom. Of course, totalitarian control on the farms by definition meant that every escape was a mixture of genius and luck, and Adam may have been biding his time, waiting for his opportunity to set a permanent distance between himself and their society. But John's promise of manumission, and the prospect of being free from his hand, may have kept Adam in place. Both in the sense of being on John's properties as well as in the sense of being within the internal logic of colonial law. In hoping that he would be granted freedom, he risked internalizing slave society's concept of freedom as a legal status—rather than the absence of abuse. The emancipated slave, in being emancipated, is never as free as the runaway—even as the runaway is never as secure, however false that security, from re-enslavement as the emancipated. The runaway cannot be weighed down by any gratitude to their former abusers and in their auto-emancipation upend production and deny the master's, law's, and the colony's sovereignty. This is why the captured maroon is, and has always been, more of a threat to colonial society than the African who believes they were emancipated. In being manumitted, one leaps out of the fire but into the frying pan of a legal freedom, subject to the vicissitudes of colonial law to say nothing of the fact that freedom for Black people in colonial society, as Adam's life after John's farm shows, is no freedom. In marronage, every piece of paraphernalia of colonialism, law, master, and flag, are irrelevant, defunct if not burnt. They belong to the maroon's and anti-colonialist society's "long ago" of slavery. And in that society, there are no Confederate countrymen.

The internalization of colonialism, its categories of legal freedom and slave, its police power did not of course disappear with the dissolution of codified chattel slavery. I have witnessed the internalization of police power while walking down 125th Street in Harlem. Black people speaking about a certain "crime" "getting" people three to five years in prison. As if there is a causal relationship between performing an act deemed criminal and suffering the pain of captivity. Carceral violence, however naturalized and carefully orchestrated to seem predictable and consequence, remains initiated by the aggressor, whether person or state institution. The work of ideological police power, as is the work of corporal parenting, is to represent state violence as rational, measured, and an outgrowth of the victim's action rather than the initiative of the attacker and wielded by them. Punishment is the naturalization of police force. When perfected, it seems to emanate not by the author of the violence but by its victim: "I did this. Of course there are now fetters on my wrists and I am to be shuttled off to a dungeon for years." The epitome of this internalization is achieved when the survivor of incarceration says, "I did this to myself." Better technology than the whip, the prison hides the master's hand and thereby convinces its enslaved that it is a force of nature. It is inevitable and generated by one's behavior. It would be as if the runaway were to believe the mutilation of his body was due to their illicit, immoral hunger to be loosened from the master's grip. That they, ungrateful, robbed the master of his property in running and they themselves generated the welts now opening across their back. It would be as if Adam began to believe that he was indeed a criminal and the dungeon he was sent to for standing up for himself was developed to train him into better behavior. Totalitarianism being not merely the ubiquity of the police but the internalization of "the law" and the transformation of the insolent and insurrectionist into a police station. In 2010, G. Dep[69] said he felt tortured by his conscience after his shooting of John Henkel in 1993 in front of the James Weldon Johnson Houses, and so he decided to come clean, do the right thing, confess, and turn himself in to the twenty-fifth Precinct. What is telling is not that he felt guilty for taking a life, that is understandable, but that the way to cleanse his soul was to give himself up to the state. The state became, in his mind, the confessional, the assistant redeemer, and fate catching up to him, rather than accoutrement of invasion. Similarly, in his skit "How not to get your ass beat by the police," Chris Rock, witting or unwitting conduit of this ideological police power, presents as common sense that that which John called "sawcy and surly" behavior and suggests it would inevitably be met by police violence. A beatdown which might also be read as corporal punishment. The lesson in Rock's skit is that the Black person who is insolent, who disagrees with the etiquette of subjugation and, even worse, demonstrates opposition to police power, would get, as inevitably as a coin to a magnet, the violence of the state and society put upon them. His skit, since 2016, has been shared on social media each time the banality of police violence is upset by radical uprising.[70] As comedy, the skit fulfilled the additional colonist interest in deriding and mocking Black insolence and the instinct to counter colonial authority while affirming the norm of Black subservience.

Considered an especially angry brute of the angry brutish race by the master, Adam existed in a society where the man who called himself his master was also a judge in his case for freedom, directed his arrest, was accused of tampering with the jury in his case, appealed to the legislature to preserve his enslavement, and as will be seen in the following chapter, held the power to fabricate his nature and make of him a caricature. Adam was presented on the center block of white supremacist totalitarianism, surrounded by the wolves of white power who, although tearing at his flesh nevertheless possessed the power to present themselves as the torn. John appealed to every colonial authority that would hear him out that Adam's insolent freedom and his remaining out on the lam was not only a danger to himself but to colonists everywhere. His slip out of the colonist's hand was a travesty of the natural order and reason enough to appeal to his fellow white nationalists—the colonial court is always presumed to be sensitive to the white nationalist cause—to restore Adam to his custody and so right the world. But Adam, as John's tenant Timothy complained, was so proud and surly that he was scared to even speak to him and ask him where he had been. Even though he could beat him he was scared as "he that doth not value his own life, can command another's." Adam lived in the midst of white supremacist society, where he was everywhere threatened with violence and being cast out of the province and into the bare life of the other slave states, more advanced in the biopolitical extractions, forming plantation economies, militarizing their patrols into military police and codifying slave codes. His strength of his conviction, to not accept colonial sovereignty over him made the overseers scared to strike him. His break from the master's will to make him supplicant reminiscent of a more famous runaway (who similarly could not quit, entirely, the colony). Frederick Douglass paints the aftermath of his fight with Edward Covey, a poor man and farm renter famous for his "negro-breaking" who wanted to break Douglass.

> I seized Covey hard by the throat; and as I did so, I rose. He held on to me, and I to him. My resistance was so entirely unexpected, that Covey seemed taken all aback. My long-crushed spirit rose, cowardice departed, bold defiance took its place; and I now resolved that, however long I might remain a slave in form, the day had passed forever when I could be a slave in fact. I did not hesitate to let it be known of me, that the white man who expected to succeed in whipping, must also succeed in killing me.[71]

Adam, too, maintained his insolence and his commitment to be rid of the master's power over him that was more dear to him, it seemed, than life itself. In this, he was a maroon of one, traipsing about the city of white supremacy and police and state power, the jail, the totalitarian cell of white power—"at his pleasure in defiance" of the man who, according to the conspiracy of slave society, deemed him to be his master. Even though he could beat Adam and "lay him at my foot," Thomas decided to suffer the "vile Negro" fearful of what he might do. Thus, Adam, in giving zero fucks, opened up a maroon settlement within the city. He chipped out a space for Black and free existence in white supremacist totalitarianism that by its very nature was an anti-colonial threat, as well as a possible contagion and "evil example of all Negros both in Town and countrey."[72] Surrounded by the society arranged for the purpose of his exploitation, where he could be disposed of without much fuss, a slave in form, he was never a slave in fact. He was no captive of the system that explicitly attempted to train him into servility, into admiration of and partnership with his exploiters and their state, and the belief that they were the good. He was not trained away from the instinct of rebellion and into sheepishness. Whip and sermonizing, repressive and ideological apparatuses of the colony all failed, and he was not felled entirely by colonialism. The state of being absolutely outgunned, the brainwashing and depressing condition of his situation, the concerted nature of his attack from white neighbors, magistrates, slave owners, garrison soldiers, all was not enough to depress his rebel spirit or force him prostrate. Intestine marronage, marronage in town, requires such irrationality. It strives for a future of escape in a land where you remain surrounded. It is much more practical to plead, to supplicate, to acquiesce and develop Stockholm Syndrome and identify oneself and one's interests with the colony. To be nationalized in a series which included lakes and streets. But marronage is a sovereignty of its own that does not permit of colonial practicality and decisions based on the odds of a permanent escape. The runaway is sovereign in running.

Chapter 2

KILLING THE MAROON, BIRTHING THE SUPPLICANT NEGRO

[the] first fears were concerning our Slaves, those irreconcilable and yet intestine Enemies of ours, who are not otherwise our Subjects than as the Whip makes them; who seeing our strongest houses demolished, our arms broken and hearing of the destruction of our greatest dependency, the town of Port Royal, might in hopes of Liberty be stirred up to rise in Rebellion against us"—that is, "kill and slay all the whites, men, women and children"—combined with the "forcible invasion of our Enemies," who see "our hearts are low, our arms broken, our forts lacerated and useless.

The Truest and Largest Account of the Late Earthquake
in Jamaica, June 7, 1692.[1]

"Wal, now, just think on 't," said the trader; "just look at them limbs,—broad-chested, strong as a horse. Look at his head; them high forrads allays shows calculatin niggers, that'll do any kind o' thing. I've, marked that ar. Now, a nigger of that ar heft and build is worth considerable, just as you may say, for his body, supposin he's stupid; but come to put in his calculatin faculties, and them which I can show he has oncommon, why, of course, it makes him come higher. Why, that ar fellow managed his master's whole farm. He has a strornary talent for business."

"Bad, bad, very bad; knows altogether too much!" said the young man, with the same mocking smile playing about his mouth. "Never will do, in the world. Your smart fellows are always running off, stealing horses, and raising the devil generally…"

Uncle Tom's Cabin[2]

A specter is haunting the Western Hemisphere—the specter of the maroon. Always present, hauntingly present, in the colonies of the Americas is the African who was never "broken" into a loving relationship with masters, masters' rule, nor the masters' country. The first settlement in the Americas to hold Africans captive was also the site of the first slave revolt.[3] The tradition of radical distancing from the settler-colony being older, more innate, and universal in Black political culture than the singing marches and placard-holding made to represent it.[4] African practices of refusing colonialism defied the forced-labor extracting overseer and defy the contemporary liberal historian attempting to press African histories of devil-raising into settler nationalist histories of "Black contributions" to America.

An Obscured War from Obscured Places

In 2023, testifying on the witness stand during Alex Murdaugh's trial for the murder of his wife and son, Buster Murdaugh, the surviving son, was asked about[5] his family's plantation-style "Moselle property." He described the estate as large, about 1700 acres, in Colleton County, South Carolina, with deer stands, dove fields, and ponds, a gun collection, and significant areas covered in wild hog-filled swampland. Before the collusion between capital and colonialism remapped the land as "Murdaugh property," that land, or land very near and similar to it, contained the swamp to which, in 1766, more than one hundred enslaved people fled, joining the maroon community established in Colleton County.[6] The assembly of free, rebellious Africans being immediately recognized as an existential threat[7] to the colony the governor of South Carolina,[8] unsuccessfully, sent the militia and hired Catawba[9] to search the swamp and destroy the maroon community. Maroon presence meant the threat of war and the support—emotional and material—for enslaved people's rebellions. Settler-colonialism, which would one day provide Alex Murdaugh his crime scene, in the latter half of the eighteenth century infested Indigenous land with slave patrols in its anti-Black, anti-Indigenous occupation fictionalized as a country. It also, quite literally, eviscerated opportunities for traditional marronage. As John Hope Franklin and Loren Schweninger note,[10] settler expansion to the West in the 1820s and 1830s—and with it the expansion of settled space, violence, land "clearance," destruction of outlaw camps and swamps—destroyed would-be fugitive slaves' chances of refuge in "Indian country" and the safety of the Indigenous "hostile tribes" who often joined forces with the runaways to attack colonialism.[11] Settler-colonialism destroyed Black chances to be free from the slave master's reach at the same moment it destroyed Indigenous space.

Like the jungles and hills of the Caribbean and South America, the "obscure places" of swampland surrounding plantation estates of the Southern United States provided cover for runaways and "outliers" as the British called them[12] as well as improved their chances in defending against raids and search parties. Runaways congregating in the woods and obscure places were a feature of enslavement and indenture from the first moments of colonialism and before the invention of whiteness could be deployed to break off connections between European indentured servants with their fellow exploited people sharing the yoke under the European landowners, the Indigenous and African.[13]

Some writers, sensibly, distinguish between the act of an individual running away, slave revolts,[14] marronage and fugitivity,[15] and African anti-colonialism. For matters of historical clarity, these distinctions are necessary. For purposes here, however, they are interchangeable and all fall under the banner of marronage. Indeed, for every enslaved person who was not broken on the wheel of patriotism to the plantation,[16] and was convinced neither that they were a belonging nor belonged, the hope was to escape the power of the whip and the master's power and, if possible, permanently incapacitate it. Enslavement was a condition of a maroon still captured. Revolt and running away were the means to activate radical autonomy and return to the natural state of freedom from colonialism. A condition that has forgotten even the psychic and discursive reach of colonists, not merely the fact of being unchained bare life within the permanent probation that is life in colonial society. What is important, here, is this move toward radical autonomy and forceful opposition to the colonial power wielded over them as well as their disinterest in identification with the community of settlers. The point is the break with colonialism. The placing of one's hopes anywhere but in the masters' redemption and the casting aside of those propagandizing fellows preaching to hold on a bit longer, "change gon' come." The traveling into obscure places is the eluding of both being captured by colonial police power and by colonial knowledge—indeed the process of inventing the supplicating negro is exactly the project of manufacturing a knowable and docile object prepped for the uses of power.[17] The maroon is its opposite. Where the Supplicant Negro entertains or is forced into conversation with the master, the runaway is auto-ex-communicated. Where the Supplicant Negro is a joke authored by colonist imagination the maroon is unknown to it—haunts and threatens it. Where the Supplicant Negro is a fiction and perfectly policed, the maroon is reality and crisis. The maroon is the breakdown of colonialist totalitarianism in every one of its directions. It is precisely for this reason that its existence necessitated the Supplicant Negro which is itself at once a feeble attempt to push the maroon out of reality as well as an effective means to produce and disseminate the colonialist narrative on Blackness.

The slave never existed. It was the runaway who was enslaved. Captured in what they understood to be a temporary condition that would be escaped through the feet or through death—be it theirs or the masters'. For three centuries everywhere in the slaveholding Western Hemisphere, maroons cut down slave masters, poisoned them,[18] burned their houses, looted masters' property, conspired and plotted against slavery, and encouraged and assisted those still under the whip to escape and fight back.[19] Their actions, taken collectively, reveal an obscure(d) war of African peoples against the colonies in the Americas,[20] launched from obscure and obscured places. Deployed from the overgrown swamplands of Virginia and the Blue Mountains of Jamaica, threatening in the coded secrecy of the "slave conspiracy," hidden as a permanent undercurrent underneath the conspiracy of colonist historians' manufactured memory that has replaced, nationalized and *civil*-ized Black uprising so that modern Black lumpen rebellions from Watts 1965 to Minnesota 2020 seem not the latest developments in the war against colonial society but spontaneous, surprising, spatially, and temporally isolated "riots." Despite being preserved by Black historians, writers, and maroons, maroon war is obscured from popular consciousness which has represented hemisphere-wide Black anti-colonial war as the time of enslavement with some radical, violent opposition at the margins. A framing which throws the rug of Black suffering over the omnipresence of the slave revolt.

While Adam was being put to work in New England, in 1686 across the pond in Whydah (Ouidah, Benin) Africans killed all the white men on a slave ship.[21] In 1695 near Accra, they massacred their would-be enslavers before boarding.[22] In the colony referred to as the United States, an instance understood to be one of the earliest references to racial slavery—as distinct from indentured servitude—began with a runaway. John Punch, an African indentured servant in 1640, ran with two white indentured servants, a Scot and a Dutchman, into the woods. They were eventually caught and given thirty lashes, but it was said that John Punch, being Black, would be a slave for life.[23] Racial difference thus born as a means of instituting a targeted space for totalitarian control and to bifurcate the threat of escape and freedom from landowners.

The enslaved person, opposed to their enslavement, was an "intestine enemy" of the colony. Impossible to assimilate seamlessly into white

2. Killing the Maroon, Birthing the Supplicant Negro   47

supremacist society, impossible to be rid of without damaging the economic foundations of the colonial economy, and desirous of ruining property and those who thought of them as such. In 1649 Barbados, plots to eliminate the planters and reverse the conditions of enslavement so that planter families became the slaves post-revolution were uncovered. In 1673, Bermudan authorities discovered a Christmas Day plot and so expelled free Africans as a precaution. In 1682 on the same island, people enslaved previously in Jamaica "devised a far-reaching plan to organize brigades and murder leading planters during Sunday religious services—then flee via the highway that was the vast sea."[24]

Generally, escape was done in secret as opposed to en masse in the US colony. In the second decade of the 1700s, what is likely to be the first and only recorded case of collectively aiming to leave the plantation and plotting to destroy any of "her Majesty's Subjects" who opposed occurred in James City, Virginia.[25] The plot was betrayed by a plantation patriot named Will, and the principal contrivers of the plot, Scipio, an African and Salvador, an Indigenous man (who were considered rude and insolent), were given exemplary punishment. The head of the African, along with "one of his quarters" and some other body parts, was placed in public places to deter similar inspired acts.[26] Another leader, Peter, escaped and was "lurking in or about the said county or the county's of James city prince George or isle of wight." The snitch, Will, was given his freedom and his identity kept secret until it was discovered and "Several [Negroes] Laid Wait for his Life." He was then sent to other counties on a snitch tour to encourage the enslaved to tell on other enslaved people's conspiracies of freedom.[27]

Informants on the maroons have always been the lifeline[28] of slavery and settler-colonialism. Plantation loyalists and Black patriots were able to use their Blackness to sneak into rebel spaces and carry information back to their masters.[29] Historically, Black "pick-me's,"[30] today attempting, ironically, to refashion themselves as advocates for leaving the "Democrat plantation," were, as the following letter from a loyal enslaved person indicates, one of the most important instruments in keeping the enslaved on the plantation.

> White pepil be-ware of your lives, their is a plan now forming and intend to put in execution this harvest time—they are to commence and use their Sithes as weapons until they can get possession of other weapons; their is a great many weapons hid for the purpose, and be you all assured If you do not look out in time that many of you will be put to death. the sceam is to kill all before them,

men, women, and children. their has been expresses going In Every direction for some days to see all the negroes they could this holladay, to make the arrangements and conclud what time it was to commence and at what plasis they are to assemble. watch they conduc of your Negroes and you will see an alteration. I am confident of the leaders and can not give you my name. I am also a greater friend to some of the Whites, and wish to preserve their lives. I am a favorite Servant of my Master and Mistis, and love them dearly.[31]

The "favorite servants" of white supremacists today are no less committed to assisting in putting down the insurrection. Whether the Black liberal playing "devil's advocate" about abolition, the Black patriot anti-Black xenophobe fitted in settlers' flag, the Black conservative decrying "loud-mouth Black women," or the "Blincel" yapping from the sidecar of Andrew Tate, those supplicating to the settler subscribe to a colonial morality which must always orbit around ending Black freedom.

A City's Near Death by Fire

So you have two types of Negro. The old type and the new type. Most of you know the old type. When you read about him in history during slavery he was called "Uncle Tom." He was the house Negro. And during slavery you had two Negroes. You had the house Negro and the field Negro.

The house Negro usually lived close to his master. He dressed like his master. He wore his master's second-hand clothes. He ate food that his master left on the table. And he lived in his master's house—probably in the basement or the attic—but he still lived in the master's house.

So whenever that house Negro identified himself, he always identified himself in the same sense that his master identified himself. When his master said, "We have good food," the house Negro would say, "Yes, we have plenty of good food." "We" have plenty of good food. When the master said that "we have a fine home here," the house Negro said, "Yes, we have a fine home here." When the master would be sick, the house Negro identified himself so much with his master he'd say, "What's the matter boss, we sick?" His master's pain was his pain. And it hurt him more for his master to be sick than for him to be sick himself. When the house started burning down, that type of Negro would fight harder to put the master's house out than the master himself would.

But then you had another Negro out in the field. The house Negro was in the minority. The masses—the field Negroes were the masses. They were in the majority. When the master got sick, they prayed that he'd die. [Laughter] If his house caught on fire, they'd pray for a wind to come along and fan the breeze.[32]

Malcolm X, 1963

On a Sunday morning in 1741 in New York, a Mrs. Earle, while looking out of her window, overheard a Black man laughing, "Fire, Fire, Scorch, Scorch, A LITTLE,—Damn it, by-and-by,"[33] The man then lifted up his hands and "spread them with a circular sweep over his head." In the mid-eighteenth century, the Atlantic Ocean was foaming with sperm whales fighting the whaling ships looking to extract lantern fuel from their bodies. Sharks tracing the trail of slave ships awaiting the bodies of Africans thrown over by pirates employed by the Western powers. These pirates, renamed "privateers," and their vessels were commissioned by colonizing powers who had not as yet "ruled the waves" nor formalized piracy into "navies." They carried with them letters of marque commissioned as licenses to attack the ships from rival nations they discovered on the water. A cross between seaborne bounty hunters and mercenaries, these private agents of the colonial powers captured the ships and the booty of the enemies, brought them to the Vice-Admiralty or like court and, once judged "Prizes," the booty was sold, enriching the "privateer" ship, the courts, and countless middlemen. In the Western Atlantic, as many as half the seamen on board were Black (whether enslaved or free). A captured ship meant the capturing, in addition to other booty, the "Prize Negroes" found aboard.[34]

In one such Britain-commissioned raid against Spanish vessels, some Black Spaniards were taken as a "prize," after which they were then condemned as slaves in the Court of Admiralty and sold. A Captain Sarly purchased several of these "Spanish negro prizes," at least one of which was known to protest that he was free in his own country and to be angered that he was to be enslaved in New York. The fire, celebrated by the Black man outside Ms. Earle's window, was lit on each side of Captain Sarly's house. Upon learning of it, "there was a Cry among the People, *The Spanish Negroes; The Spanish Negroes; Take up the Spanish Negroes*,"[35] the idea being that the enslaved Africans, who grumbled "at their usage of being sold as Slaves" and behaved insolently when asked about the fires, were responsible for the fire at the master's house.[36] As

Mrs. Earle "didn't know any of the negroes," she couldn't tell who it was who laughed at the fires, but she thought it was suspicious enough to report it to the authorities. The man turned out to be Quaco[37] enslaved by a Mr. Walter. Quaco was arrested, and during his imprisonment claimed that he only said it in patriotic praise of Admiral Vernon's taking Porto Bello from the Spanish in Panama eighteen days before.[38] He was eventually freed from the prison.[39] But as Daniel Horsmanden, Chief Justice in the trials of the alleged insurrections, its court recorder, and author of the Journal of its proceedings indicated, however, "many of [the Negroes] have a great deal of Craft; their unintelligible Jagon stands them in great Stead, to conceal their Meaning." Five suspicious fires broke out in that year one after the other, consuming houses, stores, and forts. The enslaved man's phrasing and laughing about the fires outside Mrs. Earle's window would later be interpreted as evidence of a conspiracy among the enslaved to burn the entire city of New York and rise and cut the throats of all the whites and masters in what came to be known as the "Conspiracy of 1741."

It was thought that the Spanish Negroes, of insolent behavior, out of vengeance for being held as slaves and who were overheard saying that if they were not allowed to return to their country they would ruin all the City, were likely the culprits behind the masters' house fires. Indeed, it was easily assumed that the Spanish Negroes dissatisfied with their transformation into "mere slaves" subject to the violence of slavery were the culprits. Sabotage is closely associated with the Black radical tradition which as Sarah Haley writes, demonstrates the will to break rather than ameliorate or tweak anti-Black systems.[40] Africans who planned to burn the master's house were heard, according to court testimony, to say that "they did not care what they did" . . . and "D—m that Son of a B—h [master], they would make a Devil of him."[41] Whether "pretending to be free" as Daniel alleged, or unaccustomed to the regime of enslavement in the Americas, captured and unswept up in the totalitarian power of chattel slavery, the Spanish Negro, the Black man was angry enough at his condition to attempt to light at least one house on fire—and possibly, the entire city of New York alongside a Black slave-revolting gang.

Caesar and Prince, other supposed confederates described as very wicked and idle fellows, were earlier tied to a whipping post and publicly tortured after being accused of robberies. The whipping post, like stop-and-frisk in later centuries, was not merely a tool to police and "regulate" the enslaved in the interests of colonial order, nor merely to intimidate those who expressed their hatred of the slave condition against the property of the masters in acts deemed "crime," but the site of the Black person tied to the whipping post was at the same time a site of white master gratification. Frederick Douglass opens his autobiographical *Narrative* describing this site of white pleasure.[42]

> [The master Anthony] was a cruel man, hardened by a long life of slaveholding. He would at times seem to take great pleasure in whipping a slave. I have often been awakened at the dawn of day by the most heart-rending shrieks of an own aunt of mine, whom he used to tie up to a joist, and whip upon her naked back till she was literally covered with blood. No words, no tears, no prayers, from his gory victim, seemed to move his iron heart from its bloody purpose. The louder she screamed, the harder he whipped; and where the blood ran fastest, there he whipped longest. He would whip her to make her scream, and whip her to make her hush; and not until overcome by fatigue, would he cease to swing the blood-clotted cowskin. I remember the first time I ever witnessed this horrible exhibition . . .[43]
>
> Mr. Severe was rightly named: he was a cruel man. I have seen him whip a woman, causing the blood to run half an hour at the time; and this, too, in the midst of her crying children, pleading for their mother's release. He seemed to take pleasure in manifesting his fiendish barbarity.[44]

These conditions of the masters' society were the conditions of which the enslaved were said to be ungrateful. Colonial life meant and means being arrested at a whim, publicly humiliated, kidnapped, tortured, and forced to work for and strengthen one's enemies for the entirety of one's existence. Into such a world, Diana, "Mr. Machado's Negro," in an action that master society thought as unthinkable as it was evidence of the inhumanity of the Negro to the apologists of slave society, "took her own young Child from her Breast, and laid it in the Cold"[45] so that the child froze to death. As Jennifer Morgan points out, both infanticide and the birthing and mother's rearing enslaved children were acts of resistance. Diana was not given space to explain why she killed her child. Unlike the women spoken to by naturalist Maria Sibylla Merian, who in 1705 wrote that the Indians and Africans used peacock flower to abort their children so they would not become slaves like they were. Destroying fetuses and children were acts of maternal love and expressions of spitefulness against the masters. As the womb in slavery was an incubator and means of production of slave owner's commodities—enslaved women, as Jennifer Morgan argues, developed "critical knowledge about the workings of power" on enslaved bodies. They both resisted being made "breeders" and protected their babies. As they were conscious of the economic meaning of childbirth, the destruction of offspring must also be understood, as Morgan argues, as part of Black collective resistance.[46] Diana herself would later be accused of being a fellow conspirant with the Black slave revolt, plotting with others in a shady tavern full of the disreputable lumpen people making up the "Confederates" who conspired to burn New York City to the ground. She would later set fire to the shingles of master Machado's house, give the master four shillings, and tell him to "hold his tongue."[47]

In these seedy shebeens, the white tavern owners regularly broke the *Act for the Better Regulating of Slaves* and *Act for the More Effectual Preventing and Punishing the Conspiracy and Insurrection of Negro and Other Slaves* and other slave codes intended to organize, accumulate, and systemize class power against Black people. Instead—and to the chagrin of officials—they sold dice-playing, loud-talking enslaved Africans and freemen Penny Drams of rum or as many gallons as the negro "could steal money or goods to pay for."[48] Upwards of thirty to fifty Black people were accused of meeting in these houses of disrepute, unwatched, drinking and dancing to all hours of the night, in menacing quasi-freedom against the city as a consequence of masters who were "too lenient" and allowed them free time. They were taken up, slavery advocates complained, in the idleness that was in the work of the devil's hands instead of the forced labor of their own. In these lumpen spaces, Black people, for a moment freed from the drudgery, pain, and distraction of having their bodies transformed into instruments for white people, began planning revolution.[49]

During the trial for the conspiracy to burn New York, Kerry, the "Newfoundland Irish Beauty," who according to Daniel was a prostitute of the worst sort, that is, a "prostitute to negroes," testified that during a Christmas while she was living with a Free Negro in New Battery, she saw a white couple, the Rommes, living a few doors down, meet with the ten or eleven Africans. The husband, John Romme, showed them how the rich lived. He encouraged them to—under his leadership—"set them all a light Fire; burn the Houses of them that have the most Money, and kill them all, as the Negroes would have done their Masters and Mistresses formerly," meaning the 1712 enslaved African revolt in the city. John was to stand by them and send word to the other negroes of the country who could read, and if anything foul happened, he would leave to the Mohawk country where he had friends. If the fire did not achieve its purpose and crush the city, the Africans were to steal everything they could. He promised he would then take them to another country and give them their freedom. John Hughson, another white comrade to the planned revolt, was paid twelve pounds by Cesar for eight guns, three pistols, and four swords which he was able to hide under his floorboards for the revolution. A white betrayal especially maddening to the courts. These white allies were the worst of all characters in the conspiracy to burn New York for Daniel as they were the ones who were ultimately responsible as they seduced the satanic negroes into revolution, leading the charge. In this accusation, the advocate for racial slavery and some contemporary historians find common ground: the impetus for freedom derives from white leadership. For the slavery apologist, the plot is dreamed up from pesky, disreputable Publick House owners in the eighteenth century, race-mixing houses, and later the carpetbaggers and Freedom Riders interfering with "our blacks." For some contemporary historians, the fight for freedom was not inspired by the desire not to have one's child sold or be broken on the wheel for escaping the farm dungeons; on the contrary Black hearts were stirred up by seeing the French and American Revolutions and the ideals of *Liberté, Égalité, Fraternité* or received with gaping mouths the trickling down of the ideas of the Enlightenment. Every Black revolt is inspired by American Democracy and European Republicanism, even, especially those that existed before them in which case they were always in anticipation of them, we are told. The colonists chain the history of Black revolt to the teleology of the metropole or settler state.

Uninterested in the revolutionary ideas of Europe, the commodified people developed, independently, their own hatred of masters and masters' society. Cuffee—who believed a great many people had too much money and wanted to murder all the rich—on seeing the fires breaking out in New York reportedly huzzah'd and poured the water he was tasked to use in extinguishing the flames onto the ground. When he was asked if he feared Quack and Caesar would snitch on the revolt, he said he knew they would rather burn on the stake as they took an oath to damn their blood if they would tell. August and Fortune burned their master's house, and Fortune and Sarah were going to burn the Meal Market and all took an oath "that the first thunder that came, might strike them dead, if they did not stand to their words." Quack was always cursing white people. Although he knew the price of rebellion was burning on the stake he still promised "With ash or hang I will burn this town, kill all the white people as they come to extinguish it."[50] Despite knowing they would be put into gibbets, have their heads put on stakes and burned alive the uprising's hatred of masters' society was absolute—as it was for many in every colony in the Western Hemisphere. The murder of African rebels then, and the spectacle of their murder to intimidate the other Africans, serves the same function as the memory-holing of the slave revolt today and its replacement in popular consciousness with the prostrate African. African anti-colonial war in the Western Hemisphere's colonies is muted and in that silence it could be said that Black people have always attempted to force America into democracy and to live up to its ideals, suffering for the greater good of a more equitable colonialism. The maroon is killed so that angry Black children can be trained in the belief that their ancestors were supplicating Black slaves who, with their eyes welled up, have been heroically laboring to pull the colony back from the brink of self-destruction. A myth to obscure Black historical reality which has more often been Diana laughing at the first hint of empire falling into the abyss.

It is still an open question whether the slave conspiracy in New York was overblown, based on a genuine plan, or some admixture of white society's paranoia of a Black uprising and enslaved people's big chat. Of course, there was reason to fear the burning of the city and the Black uprising. In addition to Black people burning down New York in 1712, in 1740, the year prior to the conspiracy, there was a "negro plot" discovered to poison the water supply in New York.[51] In Charleston, South Carolina, that same year, it was ordered that enslaved people were to be better fed and clothed and not forced to work over fifteen hours.[52] This was not long after an enslaved woman was condemned to death for arson and an enslaved man was burned to death[53] the same year, accused of having the "evil intent of burning down the remaining Part of the Town." Improvements were ordered, and bounties for the scalps[54] of runaways were offered in an attempt to stem the tide of fires sprouting up in the city that were no longer able to be attributed to accidents but to the "negroes." In Montreal, Marie-Joseph Angelique was tortured and hung, accused of burning down Montreal's merchant's quarter in 1734.[55] These individual acts of arson were reminders that the war of settler invasion had not been settled and that the desired idyll of the White Man's Country, with co-operating slaves and disappeared Indigenous person could not be achieved. Every fire or rumor of fire meant Stono[56] was not, in fact, put down in 1739, nor were the Yaqui anti-colonial raids in 1740. It was as if, after twenty years of fighting the Maroons in the "First Maroon War" and the British signing the peace treaty with Nanny in Jamaica, Sarah in New York replied with, "this shit ain't over."

Arson, for a population that was often strictly prevented from owning or being seen with arms, provided not only a weapon easily enough obtained for the disarmed but also the possibility of escape if it was deemed accidental. More than this was the sight of the colony burning. Fire is not merely the destruction of property and city centers of the slavery-condoning social order. The sight of the burning of the slave condition provided a view of a time outside of it. A window into the moment of the end of colonialism no matter how transitory and illusory it might be. Just as the burning at the stake of the enslaved arsonists was a window into the perfection of white control and the elimination of the rebellion for the enslavers. The reforms that rebranded the plantation as the prison or the native quarters renamed "the black ghetto"[57] did not stop enslaved people's revolt which, in turn, was re-imagined as the riot. Watts 1965, Detroit 1967, Attica 1974, Los Angeles 1992 cannot be separated from maroon war in the colonies nor can they be reduced to "the language of the unheard." Just as the anti-colonial guerrillas who, when criticized by imperialism's sympathizers as cowardly and barbaric for their choice of ambush and guerrilla warfare reply with "give us planes and we will use planes," fire and sabotage demonstrate the resourcefulness of a disarmed Black army. In 1900, Emma Yates, Roxie Collier, and Lethie Beech conspired with a white fellow inmate to burn the female prison farm at Milledgeville, Georgia—and escape. They managed to cause $4500 in losses and burn the house of warden F. M. Allagood who lived on the farm "which allowed him the greatest sexual access to imprisoned women whom he was reputed to have coerced and harassed." They did not manage to escape and Allagood was not in the house at the time of the fire; still, the action, as Sarah Haley argues, represented resistance to sexual terror in captivity. Black feminist fugitive work in Southern prisons produced an "ontological field in which a rejection of rape and black sexual objecthood is constitutive of black radicalism."[58] The fire is an end in itself.

That revolt is not the pleading language of the unheard but enslaved people's anti-colonial insurrection is known implicitly, despite liberal narrative reframing which attempts to alienate Black war from its meaning and the quest for radical Black autonomy. Mark and Patricia McCloskey knew what they were looking at when they pointed guns at protestors in the uprising against anti-Black killings in Missouri 2020. It is equally clear, and equally unadmitted, why they were pardoned by the conservative governor and are celebrated by white nationalists. After being obliged to testify that they feared for their lives and were threatened by the protests, Mark McCloskey, in a run for political office, announced on the white nationalist Fox News channel that they must take their country back. The second amendment, crafted for militias to help put down slave insurrection, was modeled in this white conservative couple aiming at the angry Black people—the good settlers against Black anti-colonial insurrection. The country is always at risk of being lost, which is to say the ongoing project of colonization in the Western Hemisphere and with it the colonial way of life that includes the African as permanent servant and the Indigenous as disappeared, is always at risk of being ended by anti-colonialism. Lynch mob society must do what it can to hold onto settler-colonialism by all means neccessary. By baton and book. Settler flags in churches. The elevation of anti-patriotic sentiment to the level of heresy. The commemoration of colonial order-preserving white supremacist violence whether in the making of souvenirs from the bones of the burned insolent Blacks in the 1920s or in the erection of plaques today. For example the state of Texas through the *Texas Historical Commission* commemorated the fire in Rusk County, Henderson, Texas of 1860, unsurprisingly from the perspectives of Texans (read white society) in a 2014 state monument which reads:

> Texans were becoming afraid and angry that their towns were burning at the hands of Northern Abolitionists and slaves.
> By the time the fire in Henderson burned the entire business district of the town, people all over the state were ready to fight for their way of life. This fire is argued to be what ignited Texan secession. From New York City to San Francisco, Fifty-Two citizens were selected in Henderson to investigate the fire, and they hanged Green Herndon and his female slave for setting the fire. Evidence of guilt or innocence is unknown.
> Louis T. Wigfall wasted no time using the fire to rally Texans to the banner of secession. "The secession flood in Texas" was too strong for leaders like Sam Houston to resist . . . the delegates . . . listed the burning of Henderson first [in the chronology of events], as the end of the union in Texas.[59]

The "war of secession" to keep the planter's way of life was a valiant war begun as a response to an enslaved arsonist firing the colonial city and a lynching, according to this contemporary reading. The fear of the Black *riot*, and the non-peaceful, unpoliced protest is the fear of the insurrection of the enslaved, the fear of maroon war, the fear of lost "property" and human property's return. It is the fear of the felling of settler cities and their replacement with a world in which cultures of radical Black autonomy are hegemonic.

Evading Capture

Despite the efforts of liberal historians to return the freedom work of the maroon and slave revolt into the service of the slave state, African histories of marronage have survived this forced integration—if not in their books then in the streets and the uprisings that flank and haunt the police-escorted, city-approved protest. It is, of course, no compliment to call the work of marronage, which is by definition the work to escape colonists' power, a contributor to American history, or to present the runaway slave or slave revolt as the first liberty-seekers in the "long, complicated story of America." On the contrary, this attempt to try to snatch the work of marronage back into the service of the slave state is slave-catching at the level of discourse. Malcolm X's parable of the House Negro and Field Negro, one of the most important parables of modernity, has proven one of the most effective sentinels against these efforts, underlining the rebel enslaved's distance from the colonial "we." A rejection of the propagandistic and ahistorical argument that enslaved Black people were actually attempting to force America to live up to its ideals, X highlights what Black liberal American nationalism seeks to erase.

> Whenever the master said "we," [the house negro] said "we." That's how you can tell a house Negro.
>
> If the master's house caught on fire, the house Negro would fight harder to put the blaze out than the master would. If the master go sick, the house Negro would say, "What's the matter, boss, we sick?" We sick! He identified himself with his master, more than his master identified with himself. And if you came to the house Negro and said, "Let's run away, let's escape, let's separate." The house Negro would look at you and say, "Man, you crazy. What you mean, separate? Where is there a better house than this? Where can I wear better clothes than this? Where can I eat better food than this?" That was that house Negro. In those days he was called a "house nigger." And that's what we call them today, because we've still got some house niggers running around here.

This modern house Negro loves his master. He wants to live near him. He'll pay three times as much as the house is worth just to live near his master, and then brag about "I'm the only Negro out here." "I'm the only one on my job." "I'm the only one in this school." You're nothing but a house Negro. And if someone comes to you right now and says, "Let's separate," you say the same thing that the house Negro said on the plantation. "What you mean, separate? From America, this good white man? Where you going to get a better job than you get here?" I mean, this is what you say. "I ain't left nothing in Africa," that's what you say. Why, you left your mind in Africa.[60]

Sandy, a snitch on the conspiracy to burn New York, testified in front of the grand jury that

> upon [Sandy's] coming into the Room, they gave him Drink, and then asked him to burn Houses; and he not giving a ready Answer, *Sarah* swore at him, and the Negroes did also; and with Knives in their Hands, that they frightened him, and he was afraid they would kill him; and upon it, he promised he would, and would burn the Slip-Market; and soon after he went home.[61]

Not only did he refuse to separate from the abusing institution, but in testifying against the conspiracy, in his obedience to the rule of law and will of the masters, the plantation patriot was an instrument in the execution of those who sought to live unmolested. The good slave lending credibility to colonial violence—thus a participant in it.

The possessive pronoun "we" is rejected by 1960s Black separatism. It is rejected in David Walker's 1829 warning to "the Americans."[62] It is rejected by Sarah. Masters feared and hated the runaway, colonists fear and hate the anti-colonist, because the runaway and anti-colonist are not captured by colonialism's "we." They are not beholden to colonialism, nor do they entertain the possibility of any eventual adequate reform that will dress that "we" up enough to be inviting. Nor do they accept to be harnessed by the master's "we" and consider it their God-given responsibility to make the "we" better and more equitable through their suffering. They choose the path of Cassy—the old, abused, quadroon returned to field work after the master cast her out of his bedroom for a younger, newly purchased "negro wench." Decidedly not the path of the forgiving, selfless in suffering Uncle Tom laid out by the white abolitionist novelist.

Stung to madness and despair by the crushing agonies of a life, Cassy had often resolved in her soul an hour of retribution, when her hand should avenge on her oppressor all the injustice and cruelty to which she had been witness, or which she had in her own person suffered.

One night, after all in Tom's cabin were sunk in sleep, he was suddenly aroused by seeing her face at the hole between the logs, that served for a window. She made a silent gesture for him to come out.

Tom came out the door. It was between one and two o'clock at night,—broad, calm, still moonlight. Tom remarked, as the light of the moon fell upon Cassy's large, black eyes, that there was a wild and peculiar glare in them, unlike their wonted fixed despair.

"Come here, Father Tom," she said, laying her small hand on his wrist, and drawing him forward with a force as if the hand were of steel; "come here,—I've news for you."

"What, Misse Cassy?" said Tom, anxiously.

"Tom, wouldn't you like your liberty?"

"I shall have it, Misse, in God's time," said Tom. "Ay, but you may have it tonight," said Cassy, with a flash of sudden energy. "Come on."

Tom hesitated.

"Come!" said she, in a whisper, fixing her black eyes on him. "Come along! He's asleep—sound. I put enough into his brandy to keep him so. I wish I'd had more,—I shouldn't have wanted you. But come, the back door is unlocked; there's an axe there, I put it there,—his room door is open; I'll show you the way. I'd a done it myself, only my arms are so weak. Come along!"

"Not for ten thousand worlds, Misse!" said Tom, firmly, stopping and holding her back, as she was pressing forward.

"But think of all these poor creatures," said Cassy. "We might set them all free, and go somewhere in the swamps, and find an island, and live by ourselves; I've heard of its being done. Any life is better than this."

"No!" said Tom, firmly. "No! good never comes of wickedness. I'd sooner chop my right hand off!"

"Then I shall do it," said Cassy, turning.

"O, Misse Cassy!" said Tom, throwing himself before her, "for the dear Lord's sake that died for ye, don't sell your precious soul to the devil, that way! Nothing but evil will come of it. The Lord hasn't called us to wrath. We must suffer, and wait his time."

"Wait!" said Cassy. "Haven't I waited?—waited till my head is dizzy and my heart sick? What has he made me suffer? What has he made hundreds of poor creatures suffer? Isn't he wringing the life-blood out of you? I'm called on; they call me! His time's come, and I'll have his heart's blood!"

"No, no, no!" said Tom, holding her small hands, which were clenched with spasmodic violence. "No, ye poor, lost soul, that ye mustn't do. The dear, blessed Lord never shed no blood but his own, and that he poured out for us when we was enemies. Lord, help us to follow his steps, and love our enemies."

"Love!" said Cassy, with a fierce glare; "love such enemies! It isn't in flesh and blood."

"No, Misse, it isn't," said Tom, looking up; "but He gives it to us, and that's the victory. When we can love and pray over all and through all, the battle's past, and the victory's come,—glory be to God!" And, with streaming eyes and choking voice, the black man looked up to heaven.

And this, oh Africa! latest called of nations,—called to the crown of thorns, the scourge, the bloody sweat, the cross of agony,—this is to be thy victory; by this shalt thou reign with Christ when his kingdom shall come on earth.[63]

Cassy has had it with thorns.[64] She rejects the logic of colonial morality which holds that it is better to be nonviolent and lead the master through forgiveness and that it is a noble calling to sacrifice oneself on the altar, to do what one can and wait until better things come around. Instead, for her, the destroying of the master is the selfless act, an act in defense of the poor creatures. In taking the deathly risk of running away and revolt, the anti-colonialist disables that part of the colonist machinery, reducing its capacity to harm and at the same time fashions a world the inverse of colonial oppression. The long-suffering hope of Uncle Tom did not result in persuading the master to change but increased his capacity for harm. His suffering, his throwing himself before Cassy, assuming the supplicating form to protect the master from her, is the easy road of complicity, and if there is a kingdom of peace to come, he will be cast out of it. As will *Lamont* in *American History X*, the Black inmate who laughs off the Neo-Nazi Derek's racist threats and performs buffoonery which after winning a smile eventually leads to Derek's rejection of racism. Showing kindness to negrophobes does not lead to the end of racism as it does in the movies. It makes one an accomplice to colonial violence. Black forgiveness has wrought nothing other than playing sidecar with the devil. Grin-washing[65] colonial violence. A balm on the still striking horsewhip. A moralizing of the rehabilitation of plantation culture and thereby assisting its export around the world. It is Cassy who is murdered at the end of Stowe's novel rather than Uncle Tom, who suffers the Christ-like death spectacle by the hands of the "cruel" master Sam Legree. Murdered by Harriet Beecher Stowe. In giving faithful Tom a piteous death, Stowe ensured that that figure, and his message of Black long-suffering and forgiveness, would continue to live beyond her novel as Tom and Africa continue to reign with Christ. Cassy, who decides not to kill the master after being persuaded by Tom lives happily ever after. Cassy is Stowe's attempt at fading maroon anger, which she so perfectly portrays, into oblivion.[66]

The runaway's ability to shove off the master's possessing "we" is aided not only by a hatred of masters and masters' society and the desire to see it burn but positively by a frame of reference in identity that is not born of the colonial state. Unpersuaded by the masters' enticements to see the plantation as home or the white supremacist state's enticement into the nationalism of second-class citizenship, there endures this dream—Cassy's not Martin's: to separate, to set the Africans free, and find an island "to live by ourselves." The African Diaspora's orientation toward Africa, rather than to colonial nationalism, has been essential for the Black imaginary of radical freedom. Often presented as a look toward the past and to salvaging retentions, the Diaspora's African identity has always been directed toward the future in freedom and an impetus to movement. Sengbe Pieh escaping the shackles of the Amistad slave ship's hold, freeing the other Africans, leading to a revolt on board, forced the navigators to return them to Africa. Enslaved people in the Caribbean refrained from eating salt as they believed it would enable them to fly back to Africa. Queenie, a keeper of Kumina, protected the secret language which was Kikongo, ensuring the connection with the homeland would not be broken.[67] Kumina, Myal, Shango, Santeria, Vodun, the Nation of Islam provided a sense of peoplehood and cosmology at a distance from master's society and were instrumental in Black radical politics essential to revolt. Several Black separatist organizations in the US colony state African identity clearly. MOVE[68] members added Africa to their names, the Nation of Islam X'ed out the slave masters' names. The UNIA, Garveyism, and Pan-Africanism, especially of the subaltern,[69] imagined and built a planetary Africanity not only intended to be a refuge from white power, a permanent swamp where all Black people could be runaways, but an Africa strong enough to intimidate every lynch mob away from their rope as they would fear the wrath of a Pan-African world power.[70] A belief in a radical elsewhere. An identity and belonging outside of what is offered by colonial nationalism: a place we were and where it was possible to could go again, sustained Black revolt. It took a torch to the enslaving patronymic and an Amistad sledgehammer to the hyphen chain in African American. As *Dead Prez*, perhaps the most explicit or self-aware continuation of the runaway slave into Hip-Hop (made especially clear in stic.man's "I'm a runaway slave") put it: "I'm an African never was an African-American."[71] Or *Sister Souljah*, in perhaps the clearest continuation of the slave revolt into Hip-Hop, put it, "I am African first. I am Black first. I want what's good for me and my people first. And if my survival means your total destruction then so be it."[72]

It has always been in the interests of colonialism that Pan-Africanism[73] be ridiculed. Pan-Africanism itself is a cumbersome term for the organizing and collectivizing of colonialism's most hated into a self-reliant body ungoverned and independent from the haters. Relatedly, it is in the interest of colonialism that Africans should have their African identity, the basis of this organizing, crushed and replaced by loyalty to the masters and a pledge of allegiance to the flag. If this were accomplished in totality, Nat Turner's slave revolt may not have begun as there would be no rumor of hope in comrade reinforcements from Haiti. Revolutionary Haiti is a vision, not of improved race relations and intersecting anti-racisms, but a pinnacle of utter freedom and a seriousness of both marronage and revolt that has reverberated across every corner of the Black international. It is what Sarah and Kwaku dreamt in 1740.

Toussaint L'Ouverture to Jean-Jacques Dessalines, 1802
LIBERTY ... EQUALITY ...
Governor-General L'Ouverture to General Dessalines.
February 8, 1802

HEADQUARTERS GONAIVES
There is no reason for despair, Citizen-General, if you can succeed in removing the resources offered to the French, especially at Port Republican [Port-au-Prince]. Endeavor, by all the means of force and address, to set that place on fire; it is constructed entirely of wood ...

Watch the moment when the garrison shall be weak in consequence of expeditions into the plains, and then surprise the city with an attack from the rear.

Do not forget, while waiting for the rainy season which will rid us of our enemy, that we have no other recourse than destruction and flames. Bear in mind that the soil bathed with our sweat must not furnish our enemies with the smallest aliment. Tear up the roads

with [cannon] shot; throw corpses and horses into the fountains; burn and annihilate everything, in order that those who have come to reduce us to slavery may have before their eyes the image of that hell which they deserve.
Salutation and Friendship,
(Signed) TOUSSAINT L'OUVERTURE[74]

The slave masters themselves knew of the danger of Pan-African identity and worried that news of a successful revolt in Haiti could be a contagion that would inspire the enslaved stationed at their pillow. Maroon Haiti's promise that it would be a sanctuary for every runaway put every enslaver's blood and treasure at risk. It may be true that Haiti today is in part being punished for standing up for Black freedom, just as the caught runaway was led to the center tree and whipped to death as a warning to the others. Although, rather than only being a conspiracy of France, Canada, the United States, and their Caribbean overseers engaging in permanent vengeance at the victorious slave revolt, Haiti's torture is also practical. A free Haiti would be a free maroon state still capable of inspiring Black revolt and a future outside of white power. It would be dangerous if it inspired more maroon states—to be an example of a dream of freedom that was not about agitating to sit at the table of brotherhood. Instead of thinking of Haiti the poor man of the Americas, a small island beset by eternal tragedy, a maroon state might wake other Black communities in the Western Hemisphere into putting away colonial nationalisms and alliances with masters' societies in favor of an identity forged in Black revolt. "Our" countrymen will no longer be our countrymen. We might no longer feel obligated to see as fellows half the electorate who still shout at Ruby Bridges. Or listen to the other half who baits us to reconcile with them for the sake of solidarity in the colony. To lure us to work together with those busy stuffing 1890s minstrel imagery into memes, globally distributing them while salivating at the possibilities of the third Ku Klux Klan in administration. A maroon state might mean options. The citizen of the slum whose feet are sore from all those years ordered to stand with their hat in their hands at the door of the racist might turn, curious about the lights from the Black city. Maps might all of a sudden be imagined differently. The Caribbean, the slave coast of Colombia, Bahia, Brazil, and further might be seen as the even deeper South. Jackson, Mississippi, and New Orleans, cornered by white supremacist policies, might present as less isolated as the dissolution of the bordered imaginary is immediately the multiplying of the Black population. Indeed, the entire

Western Hemisphere may be revealed as a disarticulated metropolis of hoods, of Southside Chicagos, Tivoli Gardens, and Rocinhas not to be separated from Lagos and Peckham. Broken free of the settler census, a greater sense of peoplehood might emerge, one strong enough to have colonial authorities at least second-guess whether instituting apartheid policing[75] or leaving dirty water in Flint, Michigan is prudent. And with Haiti regaining its position at the helm of a revolutionary, subaltern Pan-Africanism full of Black societies waking up to the fact that they have white supremacists surrounded—and that they should come out with their hands up.

Identifying with Africa also made it difficult for white supremacist totalitarianism to produce the supplicating individual, the minstrel caricatures of the "negro personality," due to long-memory.[76] It was long known to enslavers that the African-born enslaved were the most dangerous because they had clearer memories of freedom in Africa and so could envision it more easily than those raised in totalitarianism, as well as envision returning to a life not bordered by slavery and white power. African-born enslaved people were assumed more dangerous and with a greater tendency to become runaways because of their desire to return to Africa and reuinte with their people. In 1705, the Virginia legislature had a law on the books concerning runaways who didn't "speak English, and cannot, or through obstinacy will not declare the name of his or her master or owner." Both the inability and the insolent disinclination to declare the name of "one's master" increased the potential of danger and noncompliance in the African. It is unsurprising that Malcolm X's removal of the "slave master's name" as well as declaring that Black people are African and not American is the same X of "stop singing and start swinging." The break from colonial patriotism meant that enslaved people and runaways took the opportunity of the 1775 settlers' revolution in the colony to offer to fight for the British against the patriots in return for their freedom.[77] On July 8 of that year, a snitch told authorities "an insurrection of the negroes against the whole people" was to occur in the evening in North Carolina—threatening a widespread Black movement against the colonist' patriots.[78] Black freedom being a betrayal so wicked it was immortalized in the third verse of *The Star-Spangled Banner*.[79] The runaway has been evading capture by American nationalism before July 4th, 1776, unswayed by the flag or other paraphernalia of colonial patriotism. Indeed, if Frederick Douglass gave his famous address "What to the slave is the Fourth of July?" not to the Rochester Ladies'

2. Killing the Maroon, Birthing the Supplicant Negro 65

Anti-Slavery Society but to fellow runaways, the question might be differently inflected.

As the African unprostrated, the maroon is an existential threat to the settler negrophobe's and white abolitionist's way of life. The maroon is the African not "broken in." Not trained into a harmlessness useful to the reproduction of the colonial state. A society of people not sated by anti-racist charity—and dictatorially ungrateful. They loosen screws in the thresher of white supremacist settler-colonial sovereignty where they do not burn it down altogether. They undermine the plantation idyll and throw off the leash and the reach of law, their freedom and independence a declaration of war with the colony. At times this was explicit, for example, enslaved people breaking out of a jail in Prince George's County, Maryland, and linking up with a maroon community to launch a war against the colony.[80] Or in North Carolina in the early 1800s where an attempt was made by "six stout negroes, mounted on horseback" to liberate enslaved people incarcerated in Elizabeth City Jail—one of several events in this apex of maroon war in the US colony that foreshadowed Assata Shakur's liberation by the Black Liberation Army from the Clinton Correctional Facility for Women in Union Township, New Jersey.[81] Shakur's escape, one of the most daring acts of marronage in the US colony of the contemporary period, escaping not only policing but both the reach of the epitome of the Black liberal turned bounty hunter in President Obama on one hand and the white nationalist in President Trump on the other. An 1830s report on Bras-Coupé or Squire, another rebel enslaved person and hell-raising desperado turned into legend, spoke about his death at police hands like this,

> This demi-devil has for a long time rulled as the "Brigand of the Swamp." A supposition has always found believers that there was an encampment of outlaw negroes near the city, and that Squire was their leader. He was a fiend in human shape and has done much mischief in the way of decoying slaves to his camp, and in committing depredations upon the premises of those who live on the outskirts of the city. His destruction is hailed, by old and young, as a benefit to society. . . . It is hoped that the death of this leader of the outlaw negroes supposed to be in the swamp will lead to the scouring of the swamp round about the city. This nest of desperadoes should be broken up. While they can support a gang and have a camp, we may expect our slaves to run away and harrowing depredations to be committed upon society.[82]

The existence of maroon society was both a danger to settler life and a hope and inspiration of the enslaved unchained to masters' consciences. Like the always concurrent Indigenous insurgency, the African who managed to escape the hold of the masters and join with bands of other runaways at any point could pose a mortal threat to slave masters and had as much, and often even more, reasons for vengeance. The maroon was, in being free, not subject to the "rehabilitation" and educative, legal, and policing handcuffs of settler-colonial totalitarianism and the machinery that attempted to produce Africans into supplicant, docile, obsequious half-children. The runaway was not granted freedom; they took it—as they were of it. Maroon society, by definition, was not interested in folding back into the regime of colonialism and trusting in its reforms for better race relations and reconciliation under the banner of white power that in Adam's time and place was rapidly becoming the stars and stripes. Because slave revolt, marronage, Indigenous anti-colonial revolt, and other anti-colonial responses to settler-colonialism are an existential threat to the project of colonialism, it is important for colonists, even in contemporary colonialism, to declaw these always-present forces and present them as mere historical facts where it is presented at all. Equally important, they are presented as uprisings at the outskirts of the time of slavery. Chattel slavery being the historical period and marronage on its margins, haunting colonist periodization like it haunted the plantation. But the perspective which locates marronage far in the obscured margins of history while the state, policy, and slavery are at the center, is the perspective from the plantation. For our purposes, it may be better to be rid of the "antebellum" period conceived of as the time of slavery and instead, centering anti-colonialism and the view from marronage, reflect on this period of chattel slavery as a time, the apex, of maroon war. A war that continues despite being effectively rhetorically relegated to the past.

If in Europe the history of punishment can be separated into two periods, the first, the punishment spectacle, birthing the second, disciplinary and surveillance institutions,[83] in colonialism's totalitarianism, all forms of punishment are deployed at the same moment. Incineration of live bodies, and the display of slave conspiracists' heads in gibbets or on spikes, floggings as well as the strictures of the everyday in racial control, the forced dances of the coffle and auction, the panopticon of the overseer, the whipping house, forbidding independent farming.[84] It is always the specular dismemberment of Sam Hose as well as order by slave bell. It is the spectacle of the first-of-its-kind experimental robot killing of Micah Xavier Johnson for the unforgivable crime,

2. Killing the Maroon, Birthing the Supplicant Negro   67

in the colony of copacide[85] the highest crime being a Black person murdering the police officer.[86] As well, it is the moving coffle that is arrest. The everyday, non-spectacular events such as the firing of James Humphrey,[87] wrongly accused of stealing at his workplace and, once removed from handcuffs and leg restraints, volunteering to the officers who intended to "document the hell out of" the case so that it "won't fall back" on the business a "thank you for your service." But colonists soon discovered more effective ways to kill the runaway rather than through torture or the murder of their bodies. They would find a more effective confinement than the prison. These were not effective deterrents for the conspiracists to burn New York as Quaco said, he would have burned slaveholding New York even if it meant he burned too. The white abolitionists and pro-slavery racists discovered that to properly kill the violent runaway, the anti-colonialist, you could not rely on intimidation, torture, and destroying the body—especially from women and men who expected to be tortured for their actions. You must also stamp out their acts with the caricature, the minstrel, the loving and happy slave. And thus they fabricated the Supplicant Negro. Replace the devil that haunts with the child.

Half-Devil and Half-Child: Fabricating Adam

> The colonist and the colonized are old acquaintances. And consequently, the colonist is right when he says he "knows them." It is the colonist who fabricated and continues to fabricate the colonized subject.[88]
>
> —Frantz Fanon

> Take up the White Man's burden—
> Send forth the best ye breed—
> Go send your sons to exile
> To serve your captives' need
> To wait in heavy harness
> On fluttered folk and wild—
> Your new-caught, sullen peoples,
> Half devil and half child
> —Rudyard Kipling, White Man's Burden (1899)[89]

In his diary, Samuel Sewall, one of the magistrates who would rule against the slave owner John in his case against Adam, said that he wrote *The Selling of Joseph: A Memorial* in 1700 as a general questioning of slavery after being "much dissatisfied with the Trade of fetching Negros from Guinea." The interest in writing it wore off, but it rose again after he received a petition from a Mr. Belknap to free a Negro and his wife held unjustly, which was very likely to be in regards to Adam and his case with John.[90] Using the biblical story of Joseph, Sewall set out to question the morality of Transatlantic human trafficking.

Instead of recounting Adam's particular history of violently resisting almost every rung of white supremacist totalitarianism that had him bound—a story the details of which, as a presiding magistrate in the case against Adam, he was intimately familiar, his lasting abolitionist legacy is a story about "the negro" in general. Adam, shovel raised, ready to strike John's tenant before being jumped by slave society, Adam threatening to cut heads off in a bid for his freedom, and finally walking saucily about town like a runaway in the middle of the city, is nowhere to be seen in *The Selling*. Sewall instead acknowledges "the negro" as part of the human family by way of considering them, like all other mankind, sons and daughters of the "first Adam" and brethren and sistren of the last "Adam," the Christ. "These Ethiopians, as black as they are; seeing they are the Sons and Daughters of the First Adam, the Brethren and Sister of the Last ADAM, and the Offspring of GOD" and thus "they ought to be treated with a Respect agreeable."[91] As part of God's children, Christians are obligated to treat the Black person, whom he relates to the "Ethiopian," with respect. Instead, these Black brothers and sisters in Christ have arrived in the colony as the mistreated enslaved in "great Crouds of these miserable Men, and Women"[92] calling into question Christian love.

At the same moment that Sewall humanizes the downtrodden and tragic Africans as human beings capable of suffering, however, he also otherizes and alienates them. Treating these pitiable Ethiopians with respect is the Christian thing to do, but they must also be excluded from the settler nation delicately forming in vitro in the colonies. These "Ethiopians" are not up to the task of autonomy. As enslaved Africans, they are disruptive and would only ever be the colony's "internal foe."[93]

> Few can endure to hear of a Negro's being made free; and indeed they can seldom use their freedom well; yet their continual aspiring after their forbidden Liberty, renders them Unwilling Servants. And there is such a disparity in their Conditions, Color & Hair, that they can never embody with us, and grow up into orderly Families, to the

Peopling of the Land: but still remain in our Body Politick as a kind of extravasat Blood.[94]

Indeed, Sewall's may not have been best described as the first progressive anti-slavery document, as the *Colonial Society of Massachusetts* celebrated it. It may have been in the main, as Lawrence Tower suggests, a puritan response to the problem of the increase of the slave population which grew rapidly after the break in the *Royal African Company's* monopoly.[95] Sewall shares John's worry about the prospect of the formerly enslaved, free and not deported, and the havoc they would create in the colony. This problem made so much worse, in Sewall's perspective, as this minority was an abused minority, a problem for every imagining of a Christian republic. Their phenotype a problem for the imagining of a white nationalist republic. Added to this the very rational fear of the newly emancipated, aggrieved, and unchained in proximity to their aggressors—Black vengeance being not yet unimaginable. Sewall's acknowledgment that the African can "seldom use their freedom well" on the other hand can be seen as a necessary nod to negrophobes in order to win their ear. He must show that he is not impractical or unreasonable as he too recognizes the obvious inferiority or at least infantile and irresponsible nature of the Negro race. It is just that this inferiority is no excuse for ill-treatment. Possible eventual expulsion may be the only solution, but if it were to be one day imposed the continuous importation of the "numerousness" of unhappy slaves would be a hindrance. Chattel slavery was a problem not only for Christian morality but it also impeded the crafting of a white nationalist settler-colonial society. Thus, even in this first document hinting at abolition, the humanization of the Black person is tempered with the impulse to expel them from the white supremacist colonial-national project, both for security (he suggests it would be more conducive to have white indentured servants for the "Welfare of the Province"),[96] and for settler society's social cohesion.

Sewall presents the tragic picture of the slave trade and slavery itself.

> It is likewise most lamentable to think, how in taking Negros out of Africa, and Selling of them here, That which GOD has joyned together men do boldly rend asunder; Men from their Country, Husbands from their Wives, Parents from their Children. How horrible is the Uncleanness, Mortality, if not Murder, that the Ships are guilty of that bring great Crouds of these miserable Men, and Women. Methinks, when we are bemoaning the barbarous Usage

of our Friends and Kinsfolk in Africa: it might not be unseasonable to enquire whether we are not culpable in forcing the Africans to become Slaves amongst our selves.[97]

The *Blackamores*,[98] subjected to the unsanitary and murderous conditions of the slave industry, are to be sympathized with and advocated for, and are deserving of Christian humanity and pity. In addition, their mistreatment may be at the root of the "barbarity" their "kinfolk" might experience on the continent. Black people appear as the alien inferior in Sewall's tract, but also as men and women suffering great tragedy at Christian hands and subject to misuse and violence. The "sullen peoples" being part devil, but mostly child.

John's Reply

John could not countenance the interference of *woke*, bleeding-heart liberal magistrate, Sam Sewall, in his efforts to regain control of his chattel, Adam—worse, Sewall's implication that his conduct and decision not to free Adam was lacking in Christian morals. He wrote a reply to Sewall's pamphlet entitled *A Brief and Candid Answer to a Late Printed Sheet Entitled the Selling of Joseph*,[99] using common sense white supremacy to effectively counter Sewall's "first abolitionist tract." John asks what Sewall would see done. Would he have all the Black people be free and have their former owners be compensated out of the public treasury? (Which would be costly for taxpayers). And if this were to happen, would it not be required to then send all the Negroes out of the country? If not, this remedy to the supposed ill of slavery, Black free people in the settler-colony, would be "worse than the disease." Free Black people, "if there be not some strict course taken with them by authority, they will be a plague to this country."[100] It was commonsense to John and his audience that if you remove Black people from the totalitarian control of the slave masters and private authorities, you would necessarily have to place them under the totalitarian control of the police and public authorities. Black people must always remain under white power's totalitarianism. A settler-colonial truism that has left its indelible mark on conservative thought—which is always the survival of the slave owner's thought. With these and similar counterpunches, John, in his time, was often thought to have won the argument. Even some of those who were for the abolition of the slave trade would argue for it based on the inferiority of Negroes as "thieves, liars, and [eye servants,]" arguing for the importation of white indentured servants instead which Sewall agreed were preferable.[101]

John needed to destroy Sewall's depiction of the piteous Ethiopians abused by enslavement. Instead, he presents Black people more directly in the conservative' negrophobic tradition. He ends the first section of his reply to Sewall's *The Selling* with an original poem.

The Negro's Character

> Cowardly and cruel are those blacks innate,
> Prone to revenge, imp of inveterate hate.
> He that exasperates them, soon espies
> Mischief and murder in their very eyes.
> Libidinous, deceitful, false and rude,
> The spume issue of ingratitude.
> The premises considered, all may tell,
> How near good Joseph they are parallel.[102]

Giving the lie to the early abolitionist's depiction of the unfortunate men and women ripped from parents, wives, and husbands, abused and in need of white mercy, is the slave owner's depiction of what he argues is the Negro's true being. A coward, cruel, vindictive, murderous, libidinous, and, as importantly, an ungrateful being. The poem is an almost perfect list of the main features in the negrophobe's traditional caricature of the Black person. Nothing like the slave Joseph of the Bible, to whom John argues Sewall disingenuously compares them. The pathetic brothers and sisters of the First Adam, even who might fail to use their freedom effectively if it were to be given them, disappear, and (proto-)Americanism's *nigger* appears in their place.

> As if to illustrate the totalitarian nature of colonial exploitation, the colonist turns the colonized into a kind of quintessence of evil. Colonized society is not merely portrayed as a society without values. The colonist is not content with stating that the colonized world has lost its values or worse never possessed any. The "native" is declared impervious to ethics, representing not only the absence of values but also the negation of values. He is, dare we say it, the enemy of values. In other words, absolute evil.[103]

Not content to reduce the African to farm equipment, or perhaps because of the failure to do so, the slave master and colonist, and his society, attempt to beat into the African's mind, and into the mind of those witnessing his exploitation, that they are evil. John makes "the negro" both Adam—and his kind "the blacks," that is, the colonized, largely enslaved African population, the "extravasate blood"—out to be absolute evil and the "imp of inveterate hate." This devil was not the pure force of evil, an unintelligent power but, as John writes of Adam earlier in his text[104] they possess a "cunning, serpentine genius." Thus, not Sam Sewall's piteous Ethiopians incapable of self-control, for John, the African enslaved were crafty, cruel imps. Not requiring education or Christian teaching, they required police control. It is as if, before Rudyard Kipling invented a more nuanced colonist's picture of the native as half-child but half-devil, Sam Sewall thought of them as mostly child—and John as full devil.

The dehumanizing language accomplishes at once the association of Adam and his rebellion against white supremacists' fetters as the quintessence of evil as well as the bestialization[105] and demonization of the man and race. Blackness is represented as evil to make it the target of law and police violence, as well as the legitimate target for white or "civil" society, from which it is positioned externally. Blackness, in its capacity to revolt, is the legitimate target of slave owner, lynch mob, police, and societal violence[106] and despite what the coddling abolitionists might say, is always scheming against the "citizens" and the entire settler-colonial "way of life." The colonist carefully excises the human from the representation of the enslaved and produces a narrative about their nature reminiscent of Europe's werewolf,[107] a cunning beast external to society that has moved into it and can be killed, and yet human enough to be derided and judged, and imputed with reason and thus made sinful (an inferior part of fallen Man as the slavocracy's religious instruction would have it). Negrophobia, the hatred of the negro, being bound up with the settler-colony's required theriocephaly.

Of course, neither this evil being, enemies of white values, or in the American settler vernacular "the nigger," nor the piteous Ethiopian are anything more than caricatures. They are two sides of the same colonist imagination. The first preferred by the conservative, the second by the liberal. What John's poem describes was not the innate nature of "negro's character," of course, but rather the presence and position of the maroon (marronage being the only reasonable, thoughtful, and moral position to take when confronted with settler-colonialism and white supremacist totalitarianism). The only moral position to white supremacist settler-colonial totalitarianism is that of the slave revolt that may very well be prone to revenge, cruel, murderous, and show ingratitude to the benevolence of sadists who have kept them in bondage, wield violence against them unprovoked, and convinced themselves through an elaborate system of ideological reinforcement that they are masters.

Engraving the Supplicant

A Black specter was pounding against British abolitionist Josiah Wedgwood's late 1780s workshop window. There was trouble in the colonies. A constant stream of news of conspiracies, violent insurrections, and attempts at revenge by the tortured Black populations of the "New World" reached the metropoles. The counter-revolution for slavery had been decided in favor of the American colonists and performed into law in the Treaty of Paris 1783 which established the settlers' "United Colonies" now rebranded the United States of America. The cessation of hostilities between their allies of convenience, the British, on one hand, and the masters, now styled "American revolutionaries," become official, the African formerly enslaved guerrillas fled to the swamp to continue the attack and flee, continuing the war against the masters and newly birthed masters' society along the Savannah River. As the Spanish province of Louisiana was being rocked by African American holdouts under maroon leader St. Malo from 1782 to 1784 it was complained to James Madison that fugitive slaves and white people were uniting against plantations, threatening life and property. Still fresh in memory were fugitive slave wars and slave revolts, *Tacky's Maroon War* in Jamaica, the *Stono Rebellion*, and New York enslaved people's revolt and conspiracies as well as constant streams of murmurs of slave unrest, arson, masters turning up poisoned or stabbed, stirrings in St. Domingue, the first embers of what would become the Haitian Revolution, and the maroon war under Flore Bois Gaillard in St. Lucia.[108] These arguably were the best of times for maroon war and the worst of times for the sadists and their hold on their human machinery. Against this tumult, at the crest of an apex of slave revolts and maroon war misrepresented as the time of enslavement, amidst increasingly humanizing reports of the fates of people under white supremacists, burned and hanged in America, thrown out of ship cabin windows into the sea to collect cargo insurance, sculptor Henry Webber labored in Josiah Wedgwood's factory. Like the first Geppetto in his wood-shop crafting Pinocchio, Webber and jasper specialist William Hackwood modeled what would become a Josiah Wedgwood original, the world-famous "slavery medallion."

This medallion, to be worn as jewelry, was crafted for the Society of the Abolition of the Slave Trade in its inaugural year, 1787. The Society was an abolition organization for which the prominent businessman Josiah Wedgwood served on the committee. This medallion was a deliberately "emotive" anti-slavery ceramic cameo featuring a Black man on one knee, his chained hands clasped in a plea, his head upturned, supplicating to a force standing outside of the picture with Wedgwood's words "Am I not a Man and a Brother?" forming a rim over him. Art historian Mary Guyatt argued, "the silhouette effect heightened the slave's shadow-like existence and depersonalized [the slave figure] to the extent that he could represent his entire race and thus remind the audience of the scale of the 'crime' abolitionist felt slavery to be." While the enslaved man was supposed to evoke pity and thus persuade society to the abolitionist cause, the figure of the Supplicant Negro was selected because it kept the slave at a distance. An other, supplicating to liberal society, a non-threatening object and submissive party. "If, on the one hand, the slave was to be pitied, it also appeared that the abolitionists wished to present him as an eminently dignified figure: rather than breaking out of his chains through his own brute force, he is shown patiently waiting for his white master to liberate him via an act of Parliament."[109]

The piece was a hit. Upper-class men and ladies wore them in bracelets and pins. It became a symbol of solidarity with the abolitionist cause in English society and beyond in an early and more visceral signaling of solidarity against racism and racist violence than perhaps even the colored ribbon and Black Lives Matter sticker campaigns of the twenty-first century. Almost universal, it also had the function of etching the moment of abolition in collective consciousness. It framed it as one involving a supplicant, chained slave tugging on the heartstrings of a society with a conscience that was called to lift him up into the community of brotherhood and human enlightenment. White abolitionism was decidedly not the practice of reflecting the fires of Black anti-colonialism in search of radical autonomy. On the contrary, it was the gesture of solidarity by a superior white empathy and progressivism—a quest for legal reform.

White abolitionism's appeal to empathy and sentimentality did have some hold on upper-class public opinion. Apologists for slavery were no longer relying, as John Saffin had, on their invention of the negro imp, the brutal savage that stole and was ungrateful. Instead, conservatives began to argue on abolitionist terms, attempting to show that slavery was in fact a humane act, saving Africans from the human sacrifice and

2. Killing the Maroon, Birthing the Supplicant Negro 75

violence of Africa into the civilization and order of the West. In 1786, Mr. Gordon Turnbull, who described himself as a man who resided with the slave owners and so knew the condition of slavery more than the elite foreign abolitionists who made decisions based on rumors, published *An Apology for Negro Slavery: Or the West-India Planters Vindicated from the Charge of Inhumanity*. In his attempt to do what the title pledged, he argued that enslaved negroes were actually happier than the free Black people. The latter, he said, were often forced to "assist [the enslaved] in cultivating their little plantations, play on the violin ... at their dances, or serve them in some of the most menial occupations, in order to gain a bare subsistence."[110] The quality of life under racial discrimination, a society that forced several free African Americans to go about life groveling, is proof, for him of the more humane condition of slavery. Seventy years later, George Fitzhugh in his 1857 pro-slavery *Cannibals All!* would try to speak to present the conservative, that is, slave owner's position as the truly empathetic one. In fact, he argued that abolitionists should turn their eyes to the suffering poor white people instead of the relatively content slave in an early white nationalist's "charity begins at home." (Home being constituted more openly at that time as the white race.) The suffering and exploitation of the white working class being mobilized by the exploiting classes to defend prolonging anti-Black policy being not a new feature of what has been deliberately misframed as contemporary "populism" but a central feature of racial capitalism. Appeal to sentiment also found its way from back to center stage in 1850s blackface minstrelsy. The outlying, violent fugitive slave and later the "uppity" and scorned, rebellious Northern "free black"[111] characters were being replaced with faithful "uncles" and "aunties" on stage as blackface minstrelsy expanded from crude, white working-class culture to middle-class entertainment. The "Black peril" began to fade and blackface songs began to feature characters like Uncle Ned the "good slave." Uncle Ned, an old, arthritic Black man who lost the wool from head and died after a life of faithful service to "white folks." For his prize, he went "where de good darkeys go,"[112] off to find his place on the doorstep of a segregated heaven.

In 1884, one hundred years after the anti-slavery medallion featuring the pleading slave adorned the clothes of the British elite and was engraved in liberal consciousness, when news came in of "explorer" caravans losing men under a flurry of "the most troublesome and intractable"[113] Indigenous Africans of the region as they pushed into Nairobi, Mark Twain, celebrated American writer and white abolitionist, commissioned a noted caricaturist of African Americans,

Edward Winsor Kemble, to illustrate his *Adventures of Huckleberry Finn*. In the second chapter of *Adventures*, which would become one of the most beloved and representative classics of American literature, we are reintroduced to "Miss Watson's big nigger, named Jim."[114] This black thing appeared briefly in Twain's earlier 1876 novel, *The Adventures of Tom Sawyer*, but it is promoted to second stage as a central character in *Adventures of Huckleberry Finn*. Twain based Jim on the celebrated abolitionist's formerly enslaved butler, George Griffin who he described as "wise, polite, always good-natured, cheerful to gaiety, honest, religious, a cautious truth-speaker, devoted friend to the family."[115] The performances of servitude and good-humoredness as necessary for that office as service, Twain was able to exact impressions from a man with permanently doffed cap, forced into servitude by the meager opportunities offered to the "emancipated," and use them to build upon the figure of the Supplicant Negro already well-established by the mid-nineteenth century.

The second chapter opens with the white boys Tom and Huck mischievously hiding out in the woods. "We went tiptoeing."[116] An act presented in the American classic as one of the mischievousnesses in a romance of boyhood. In his preface to *Adventures*, Twain stated that "part of my plan has been to try to pleasantly remind adults of what they once were themselves, and of how they felt and thought and talked, and what queer enterprises they sometimes engaged in."[117] These queer enterprises are the province of white boyhood. For Black boys, the act remains—in the settler-dominated societies of today—trespassing, a crime. In fact, not a mere crime, but it is the charge used to rationalize and justify lynching as the case of Ralph Yarl shows. Yarl, a Black sixteen-year-old was shot after ringing the doorbell at the wrong address in the reality of the Missouri from which Twain extracted his fictionalized, whitewashed impressions. Ahmaud Arbery was afforded no "boys-will-be-boys" narrative after going "tiptoeing" through a construction site. His lynching by two men in pickup trucks and their cameraman, who shouted the N-word at him, was defended by some of the most powerful institutions in media and personalities in politics. Black children would fare no better in the time of Huck. Indeed, in *Adventures of Tom Sawyer*, Jim, who is described as "the small colored boy,"[118] cannot be of service to Tom and carry out his punishment of whitewashing the fence for him because the Missis would see it as skylarking and tear "de head off'n me."[119]

After tiptoeing, the white boys spy the adult Jim sitting in the summer kitchen. When the boys accidentally make a noise by stepping on a branch, Jim is alerted and "got up and stretched his neck out about a minute, listening," asking, "who dah?" Going to investigate and moving nearer to Tom and Huck's hiding place, Jim, the dutiful slave, said aloud, in comical minstrel-speak, that he would sit down and listen until he found out who made the noise. He then, as comically, promptly fell asleep near a tree. On seeing this, Tom Sawyer decided he wanted to play a prank on him and, despite good Huck having his reservations, the rapscallion boys tied Jim to a tree and slipped off his hat, placing it on a branch. Jim, upon waking, would come to believe a witch took his hat and made up lies, which he told to the other "niggers . . . come from all around" about witches who put him in a trance and rode him down to New Orleans. The stories giving him immense pride and almost, according to Huck, ruining him as a servant.[120] The easily tricked, superstitious negroes—upon which the early Klansmen would play the trick of dressing up as the white-clad ghosts of Confederate soldiers in order to scare them into submission[121]—are also, in their essence, the clownish, pathological liar and trickster.

Later in the novel, Huck runs away from his abusive, drunk of a father and comes across Jim, who was a new runaway. Hearing that Huck was likely murdered, Jim is frightened at the sight of him. He immediately calculates that it is Huckleberry Finn's ghost and prostrates himself. Huck, like Hamlet's father, peers out of the woods and serves as a ghost for the quivering Jim.

> But by and by, sure enough, I catched a glimpse of fire away through the trees. I went for it, cautious and slow. By and by I was close enough to have a look, and there laid a man on the ground. It most give me the fan-tods. He had a blanket around his head, and his head was nearly in the fire. I set there behind a clump of bushes, in about six foot of him, and kept my eyes on him steady. It was getting gray daylight now. Pretty soon he gapped and stretched himself and hove off the blanket, and it was Miss Watson's Jim! I bet I was glad to see him. I says:
>
> "Hello, Jim!" and skipped out.
>   "He bounced up and stared at me wild. Then he drops down on his knees, and puts his hands together and says:
>   "Doan' hurt me—don't! I hain't ever done no harm to a ghos'. I alwuz liked dead people, en done all I could for 'em. You go en git in de river agin, whah you b'longs, en doan' do nuffn to Ole Jim, 'at 'uz awluz yo' fren.'"[122]

And so Jim, speaking in a language that is to serve as the inverse of Hamlet's language, responds not to his father but to his Huck. Inverting Hamlet's *sang froid*— "Why, what should be the fear? I do not set my life in a pin's fee; And for my soul, what can it do to that, Being a thing immortal as itself"? It waves me forth again; I'll follow it." Jim in his *negro-trembling*, follows his Huck.

One way of reading these figures of supplicant African enslaved people on their knees begging the omnipotent white power for mercy is to seem them as racist, unfortunate depictions by well-intentioned but often misguided abolitionists. The sort of charitable reading that is given to white blackface performers who were also contributing to black communities. And to "non-racist" filmmakers and historians who cast Black people in an eternally supporting role.

Another, perhaps now more ascendant, reading pushes back against conservative apology and says that these depictions are unforgivable and require elimination for the benefit of anti-racism, or at least a serious placing into context. Often, the speed of removing racist literature, like the felling of statues, covers the scene of the crime and helps dress up settler-colonial space as something less violently anti-Black than it is. The revolutionary act, in the ongoing project of colonization, skirts the borders of reform.

Still another reading is possible. Jim, despite being entirely an invention of Mark Twain's mind, exists. Although, unlike Twain's telling, he did not drop to his knees, clasp his hands, and beg the child runway Huckleberry Finn not to hurt him. Jim, since Huckleberry Finn was born, had wet dreams of killing that child by his own hand. Indeed, one does not have to rely on the untold and rumored legends of Jim spoken in the hush arbors and by captured maroons orbiting the "slave quarters." Even in *Adventures of Huckleberry Finn*, Jim was suspected of killing Huck, murdering him for the $6,000 the white boy came up upon hidden away in a cave.

> The nigger run off the very night Huck Finn was killed. So there's a reward out for him—three hundred dollars. And there's a reward out for old Finn, too—two hundred dollars. You see, he come to town the morning after the murder, and told about it, and was out with 'em on the ferryboat hunt, and right away after he up and left. Before night they wanted to lynch him, but he was gone, you see. Well, next day they found out the nigger was gone; they found out he hadn't ben seen sence ten o'clock the night the murder was done. So then they put it on him, you see; and while they was full of it, next day, back comes old Finn, and went boo-hooing to Judge Thatcher to get money to

hunt for the nigger all over Illinois with. The judge gave him some, and that evening he got drunk, and was around till after midnight with a couple of mighty hard-looking strangers, and then went off with them. Well, he hain't come back sence, and they ain't looking for him back till this thing blows over a little, for people thinks now that he killed his boy and fixed things so folks would think robbers done it, and then he'd get Huck's money without having to bother a long time with a lawsuit. People do say he warn't any too good to do it. Oh, he's sly, I reckon. If he don't come back for a year he'll be all right. You can't prove anything on him, you know; everything will be quieted down then, and he'll walk in Huck's money as easy as nothing."

"Yes, I reckon so, 'm. I don't see nothing in the way of it. Has everybody guit thinking the nigger done it?"
"Oh, no, not everybody. A good many thinks he done it. But they'll get the nigger pretty soon now, and maybe they can scare it out of him."[123]

Jim ran away the same night that it was suspected Huck was murdered, leading to an organized hunt in which the white man who could bring Jim to "justice"—which in settler-colonialism is without exception always a synonym for making him suffer white power—was to be paid $300.

Jim, an escapee of Mark Twain's pen, was nevertheless haunting his imagination, outlying in the dark, overgrown scrub of his subconscious. Twain in a self-soothing act had to misrepresent him and fictionalize him into the dopey "Nigger Jim." In the same way, Stowe had to make the "goblin-like," plaited Topsy—the wicked enslaved girl and "one of the blackest of her race," who said she just did things because she is evil—saved and redeemed by Christian kindness.[124] An effort to stave off premonitions of Celia of Missouri. In the same way, Josiah Wedgwood had to force the enslaved to their knee through imagery not only in order to win the sympathy of a racist society but to calm the storm of Black anti-colonial war that pulled up on his imagination. The slave was on bended knee before the good master abolitionist so that he could not be jumping horseback to horseback in Indigenous African anti-colonial revolt, or in leafy ambush waiting for the Red Coats, or with a moonlight machete gleaming in the master's bedroom. "Miss Watson's Jim" is encountered by Huckleberry Finn as he runs off. He comes upon Jim resting by a fire with his head wrapped up in a blanket and foolishly too close to the flames. An image that the reading white audience in the era of the maturing minstrel show was primed to imagine as the comedic leaping about in flames, because of his characteristic, innate stupidity. Better the flames burning the stupid negro than to remember the flames burning the sugar colonies and cotton fields and the settler mothers with babes in arms and the makeshift fire brigades shuffling to put out the flames of the slave-fed white supremacist cities. Racism may be distraction[125] but it is also a lullaby, lulling the racists into a false sense of security.

The playful runaway Huckleberry Finn encounters the marooned runaway Jim in the woods, and Huckleberry demands to know why old, dopey Jim is outside.

"He looked pretty uneasy, and didn't say nothing for a minute. Then he says:
"Maybe I better not tell."
"Why, Jim?"
"Well, dey's reasons. But you wouldn' tell on me ef I uz to tell you, would you, Huck?"
"Blamed if I would, Jim."
"Well, I b'lieve you, Huck. I—I RUN OFF."
"Jim!"
"But mind, you said you wouldn' tell—you know you said you wouldn' tell, Huck."
"Well, I did. I said I wouldn't, and I'll stick to it. Honest INJUN, I will. People would call me a low-down Abolitionist and despise me for keeping mum—but that don't make no difference. I ain't a-going to tell."

At Huckleberry Finn's mercy, Jim is able to become Huckleberry Finn's dutiful and devoted friend and follows him through the rest of the novel on his adventures as faithfully and long-suffering, perhaps, as Twain imagined his butler George Griffin to do. But the master seldom fathoms what is in the servants' hearts and what is expressed in hushed tones in the maid's quarters and summer kitchens. The Daltons of Richard Wright's *Native Son* ask Bigger Thomas if they treat him well, and he says yes, and they take his smiling word for it. The liberal is always in willful ignorance of Black plight and eager to accept that the Black lumpen youth turn worker is content with their low station. This self-soothing lie, that the Black person is simple, happy with their lot in life, is precisely why they are so often surprised or feign surprise at the colonized's indignation. "O why did Bigger kill her? O why are

2. Killing the Maroon, Birthing the Supplicant Negro 81

Minnesotans burning their own prison-neighborhood? Surely this is not the way to start a dialogue? Surely the police killed him by accident?" But no one is simple. Huckleberry Finn encountering a runaway in the woods would be more likely to encounter a Jim that was waiting for his day. The slums of the colonies are not in bucolic peace—despite their silence. We don't squeeze our caps and bow our heads before past due notices and empty refrigerators.

There certainly was a fear of the other Jims. The "outlying negroes" who led white men to barricade their doors at night and sleep with pistols under their pillows.[126] The bands of Black fugitives hiding out in woodlands and swamps who inspired white men led by James Madison to craft *the Second Amendment* to raise white militias to put down the enslaved's panafricanist revolts.[127] Their Founding Fathers, frightened that every howl in the night might be the harbinger of Black anti-colonialist warfare, bidding them beware of the Ides of the Black revolt's march. White abolitionism, however genuine in its commitment to ending slavery, was often at least as committed to containing Black anti-colonial abolitionism, that is, the abolition of white power. It sought to save the baby of the slave society from the bathwater of the institution of slavery in a time when many enslaved were still reading constellations, refraining from eating salt, and dreaming of the day when they would "fly home to Guinea." Praying that a strong wind would advance the flames over the master's whole house by-and-by. Again, some of the first white abolitionists called for the abolition of the slave trade not because of some Exeter Hall-forged charitable feelings toward the Africans, but because they feared, rightly, the dangers of a population they enslaved. The anti-slavery medallion, like the anti-slavery novel, soothed the national consciousness by quarantining the vengeful runaway and transforming them into the manageable, pitiful "darkey." A useful fairytale that transforms the monster under the bed into the black docile lab. The devil of the coming Black uprising into the jester, the supplicant, the wise in his own native way, and the harmlessly devoted saint-prince.

In polite academic company, the rejoinder to the critique of white abolitionists producing and trafficking in the image of Black supplication and idiocy tends to be some version of "they were men of their times." Twain, it might be said, had little to work with. His heart was in the right place; indeed, he advocated for and praised the emancipation of the enslaved, but he was operating in a time when his audience expected to be entertained in literature as they had been in minstrel theater, and there were, at the time, few examples of Black humanity from which he could draw upon to fashion his characters. Twain's chosen illustrator,

Edward Winsor Kemble, created racist illustrations, it will be conceded, but it would be a mistake to judge the nineteenth-century ideas by our relatively enlightened twenty-first-century, post-Obama lens. But the "men of their times" argument is always unconvincing because there were other men in those times. And women. Other people who at the very moment the image of the dejected piteous slave taking a knee was being chiseled out from the rock of the settler imaginary, were using what meager weapons they had to bring about the abolition of the colony and every master in it. People these men of their times were keenly aware of and to whom they were, through their fabrications, reacting. The minstrel was invented not because there was no knowledge of Black thoughtful humanity but because it was ubiquitous. Nigger Jim was invented because of the knowledge of the maroon whose name was unknown in the swamplands or, worse, hid out within the body of the shifty-eyed house servant who went by as he was told to. George, who smiled faithfully when called but on more than one occasion was caught in a suspicious, furtive glance. George, the happy and loyal servant, who could not be completely trusted not to have poisoned the children's drinking water. Those who speak of "men of their times" are trained only to count white men. It is the same universal "men" in "all men are created equal" in the settlers' "Declaration of Independence," the universal man of the settler's white national universe, where all others are servants and ghosts. The enslaved who disagreed that he was "Nigger Jim" shared residence in "their times." Captured maroons, who in their very being held the truth as a foil against the Supplicant Negro and scribbled that truth in fire and destruction against the colony, in anti-colonial publication, as Black discourse. Black people, in their millions, the living discourse on Blackness, are imagined to be invisible by apologists for the minstrel-age literati. Even as it is clear that these men of their times were neighbors to the constancy of slave revolt and thus in closer proximity to a Black humanity not neutered by patriotism, not knelt in deference to the settler flag, but raised up and moving toward a futurity unsettled.[128] Of these men who, too, bar their doors and worry that the militia would not be enough, it is said they knew nothing about Blackness but Jim. The claim that "the men of the times" were ignorant of Black humanity is in fact an admission of an imagining of a past where slave plantations were full of actual minstrels and caricatures. Where the fictional Jim actually existed, and the writers and illustrators had no other reference from which to construct their images. Imagining the existence of Jim, or of writers who did not notice Black humanity, is more telling of the liberal white supremacist imagination and the hold eighteenth- and nineteenth-century white supremacist production of the Supplicant Negro has on it than it is a persuasive defense. It is a devolution in the perception of the white abolitionists, not progress. Men of our times rely on an imagining of history in which certain people speak, and certain others have not. Its use reproduces that discourse where white male voices are privileged and in so doing it reproduces white power in historical memory—forcibly displacing the subaltern from "time." There were other people speaking beside the men of their times despite the herculean colonist project to continuously deny them.

Moreover, they were not ignorant; they were deliberate. Twain's illustrator, Edward Winsor Kemble, was commissioned to illustrate an 1891 edition of *Uncle Tom's Cabin* and was able to depict the enslaved Tom with neither minstrel effect nor ogrified, even if it was pathetic. In 1881, before the publication of *Adventures of Huckleberry Finn*, William Henry Shelton came up with the engraving of *Discovery of Nat Turner* depicting the fugitive's capture. The piece which depicted a standing, armed, soldierly Nat Turner (even with hints of the devil in the facial features)—no minstrel in capture, was available to Mark Twain for a reference but he chose the cartoon. The progressive writer and the illustrator possessed the skills and the references to make non-racist images of Black people when called upon. They chose to produce images of Black supplication as they took pleasure in it, found comfort in it, and had and have a vested interest in engraving the image of the Black supplicant into colonial society. An image that cannot be divorced from the white supremacist hatred of the African. Following the portrayal of Black people as supplicating negroes in Mel Gibson's film *The Patriot* (2000), the uncanceled star's telling his girlfriend that if she got raped by "a pack of niggers, it would be your fault" was not far behind.[129] Like the "Five Points Riot" in New York who beat Black people and burned churches while singing Blackface songs[130] in 1834 or the chocolate syrup poured on the Black men who visited a white woman in a white Mississippi suburb in 2023[131] the pop culture and literature of Black supplication is of a piece with beating Black people back into "their" place.

The disarmed, vulnerable, pleading slave figure does not inspire mercy in colonial society. On the contrary, it is the preferred target of violence. Appeals to white liberal sympathy in a colonial society ordered by white supremacist logic only deliver temporary reforms when they deliver anything at all. The white supremacist discursive field, in both its infantilizing liberal and dehumanizing conservative guises, deployed the figure of the Supplicant Negro to blot out the threatening image of the rebel enslaved person and the *swart gevaar*, anti-colonial Indigenous Africanity. In doing so, it aimed to produce Black people and Black life as passive subjects at the mercy of white power. Black people's protection and existence became white society's prerogative. Rather than tugging on the heartstrings of white supremacist society until it released Black people into the "brotherhood" of equality and full citizenship, representations of the Supplicant Negro helped concretize a logic of Black disposability. It taught white power that for the slave burning on the tree, or the dead in a Buffalo Tops supermarket, there will never be a collective out there interested in vengeance. There is no price to be paid for what is done to "the blacks." The slave whipped to death will use his last words to whisper "Give my love to Mas'r, and dear good Missis."[132] Four little girls bombed in churches? Feared-for-my-life executions? After the anchors shake their heads and regretfully speak of "a tragedy," "the legacies of racism in our country," and "senseless violence," the news cycle will churn on, things will be forgotten, the night will come. The negro has an exceptionally strong hide. The African American has an exceptionally large capacity to forgive. Sleep well. It is safe in the colony. That was just the wind.

Chapter 3

THE MUZZLE OF CIVIL RIGHTS

Lift Thine Eyes to the State

The ossification of supplicant Blackness in the colonial imagination—whether pathetic minstrel or kneeling slave—set the stage for the narrative of Black supplication to migrate from kneeling before the masters, the master race, and the masters' society to—in the "Civil Rights" instead, kneeling before colonialism, that is, the state for justice. With the slaveholding master class collectively demoted after the war, Black obedience and performed devotion needed redirection—Black autonomy and self-possession being unthinkable and then, as now, the culmination of every apocalyptic nightmare of colonial chaos. A Black statolatry to the Civil Rights order, the other "great Emancipator," was required of Black people. Alongside the (eventually dearticulated and internalized) slave codes of performed subservience to white law and white people[1] a second Black code of the peaceful protest and discipline of bodies, actions, and ideas in "Civil Rights" began to emerge. The demand that Black protest must be peaceful and disciplined to the point of absurdity, and that servility must be performed before ex-masters and masters' society, follows neatly from the representation of Black campaigns for justice as the supplication of the downtrodden slave. The activist, like the slave, is a being who is never to be armed,[2] on bended knee, and always to have their body regulated, language ventriloquized, and spirit contorted into performances of obsequiousness. The liberal moral framing of colonialism as a "nation" marred with bad racism but blessed with good, Black long-suffering leads to the presumption that colonialism can be corrected. Racism can, with linked arms, be "overcome," and the nation set on the path of that peaceable colony the founding generation always intended it to be as they removed Black bodies from their teeth. The view is a sharp departure from the slave revolt which did not take up the question of "racism," an early twentieth-century concept that blossomed into a fixation as it was discovered to hold properties that could set aside the colonial contradiction and present the suffering resulting from the general practice of colonialism as its tragic excess. The slave revolt instead took up the question of power and therefore did not concern itself about whether or not racism was a moral failing but about escape and incapacitating their torturers and the totalitarian order. The revolt's view that there was a competition between powers, a conflict where the objective is not to resist, perpetually play defense, and ask for change but to defeat and ruin colonial power was occluded and replaced with the fight for an equitable, more equal, and more just society which is to say a fight for colonial reform.[3] The best achievements of the new Civil Rights resistance keep the reins in the colonists' hands and make any other, border-transgressing, freedom-dreaming seem impractical if they are not silenced outright.

Maxine Smith, a postal worker from Tennessee who became active against racial control in 1960s Memphis, Tennessee, refused to be called a Civil Rights leader.[4] Malcolm X, who famously pushed for a transnational human rights[5]—in opposition to civil Rights—is still bound by the ankles to Dr. King in a lazy, reductionist "Civil Rights" dyad. Kwame Ture departed the *Student Nonviolent Coordinating Committee* for Black Power declaring the thesis of the present work more succinctly and effectively:

> Dr. King's policy was that non-violence would achieve the gains for Black people in the United States. His major assumption was that your opponent will see your suffering and be moved to change his heart . . . He made one major fallacious assumption. In order for nonviolence to work, your opponent must have a conscience. The United States has none.[6]

Nonetheless, he—like the others, is posthumously, through the historical revisionism of AI and Google searches, remembered as a "Civil Rights leader." They, like many others involved in the uprising against white supremacist totalitarian racial control, sitting-in, boycotting, escaping, and envisioning the overthrow of American apartheid, had the Civil Rights label retroactively foisted upon them. Black people's revolutionary labor is domesticated by Civil Rights. It is nationalized, privatized, alienated from Black liberation, and handed over in bales to the state. The instinctive work to free oneself from the fetters of colonial totalitarianism is taken from the Black imagination of radical autonomy and given over, through the Civil Rights concept, to the imaginary of colonial reform. Whatever radical ideas individual activists possess are rarely recorded. Whatever the anti-colonialisms of the subaltern, unpublished Black masses rarely find room in the canon. Rarely do they survive the power of the Civil Rights concept and be left alone to be remembered as in radical opposition to colonial culture. They instead are tethered to that lofty, white abolitionist program of government outreach forever. The Black masses against mid-twentieth-century apartheid and colonialism are not permitted to speak outside of the muzzle of Civil Rights, and when they do, it is presented in defense or support of Civil Rights. Allowed to speak to demonstrate—usually in the presence of rising anti-colonialist sentiment—how radical Civil Rights can be. Black anti-colonial thought is beaten back in Civil Rights; a Claudette Colvin sat in the shadows behind Rosa Parks. Except for a few who have survived the power of the Civil Rights concept like Fannie Lou Hamer still imagined with a shotgun in every bedroom, scores of the laborers of Black freedom have fallen to the misremembering that disarms the colonized and presents them to public consciousness lobotomized and garlanded with peace and a nonviolent imagination.

Civil Rights begin as colonial law. First drafted by famed abolitionist lawyer and Illinois Senator Lyman Trumbull as the *1866 Civil Rights Bill*, the bill survived as Congress overrode President Andrew Johnson's veto; the president claiming that capitalism would be a better guarantor of equality for the newly emancipated Africans than government interference. The bill went on to become the *1866 Civil Rights Act*, leading to the *Fourteenth Amendment*. The supplicating negro was brought "up from slavery" only so far as they could be brought to kneel in praise of Reconstruction and the promises of the postwar colony. In the 1860s, in the wake of Civil War, that battle of white supremacist brother against white supremacist brother, the Union, the relatively progressive victors who captured or retained hold of the administrative state—proposed a reformed colonialism and offered a false invitation for the enslaved to join with colonists as "citizens" in the building of a racially plural, more inclusive, and equitable society. With the enslaved now "freed," it was then no longer seemly for the new Jims to go about begging the old Huckleberry Finns, pledging to follow them to the end of the earth faithfully. Just as unseemly, as both liberals and conservatives warned, was the sight of a masterless class of Black people going roving by the light of the moon. The Civil Rights era—a period we are constantly reminded we currently inhabit as it is forever "unfinished"—in order to meet the requirements of its disingenuously imagined fantasy of colonial post-racial citizenship, needed either the destruction of slavery and all its legacies, attitudinal and social, and a radically "new negro." Or, alternatively, a new, more appropriate master to govern the blacks.

The settler-colony elected for an evolution in masters. The Civil Rights state stepped in to replace white abolitionists and masters, and laws and Union soldiers (at least for a time) became the new wards. The emancipated were expected to clasp their hands in thanks to Lincoln, as some no doubt did,[7] and hope in the new Americanism. The savior of the "negro race" now cast as a white supremacist society, eventually enlightened and more sympathetic and not, as argued by the practice of the slave revolt and runaways, the day in which the masters' society was in ruins. Black people were now to fall prostrate before the state—a position that is expected to this day as there has not yet arrived, riding in on a Juneteenth horse, news of our emancipation from "Civil Rights."

Of course, supplication to white masters and society was still expected in the new relatively liberal order. "Freedom did not abolish the lash," but subjected the newly emancipated to police and legal power, strictures of the Black Codes and other corrective terrorist violence of white society "to restore relations of master and servitude."[8] The slave was sold to a "kinder" master and then returned. Reconstruction eagerly collapsed into white Redemption and slave masters who a decade earlier had stripped off their gray Confederate uniforms had got back on the horse. Several masters donned Ku Klux Klan robes as the private totalitarianism of plantation custom was codified and urbanized as Jim Crow society. The ashen tree where the disobedient enslaved were to be burnt to death in the quiet of the plantation was relocated to clearings in the woods where tickets were sold and the once secret execution places given a carnival atmosphere.

Audience as Overseer

David Walker and/as the Hostile Native

In the late nineteenth century, in British East Africa, the protectorate was busy. It was attempting to transform Indigenous anti-colonialists, the so-called hostile savage—who, through the flurry of poison-tipped arrows, provided an existential threat to their European-led caravans traveling with African servants to trade in "Dark Africa"—into a subject population governed by, recognizing, and interpellated by colonial law.[9] The threatening waKikuyu and waMeru were by force and by invitation pulled into colonialism and the emerging colonial project of Kenya Colony, already being thought of as White Man's Country. A similar process was happening at the same moment across the pond.

The enslaved in the Western Hemisphere's "White Man's Country" were invited into a new relation of power with white supremacy. A modernized subjugation to colonialism that bore little resemblance to the violence of the initial colonial encounter made up of the repression of slave ships and the genocide of the African veld. One represented as an invitation to collective nationalism. The rebellious, hostile maroon was to be forgotten; the slave revolt and the desire to burn the fields were to be transformed. Just as the laws that declared East African "natives," and thus subject to the British Monarch and the laws of the colony,[10] via the 1860s Civil Rights laws and the Fourteenth Amendment, a new subject was to be born, the Black citizen. And like Kenya Colony and settler-colonies elsewhere, this citizenship was to be understood as second-class. It was bequeathed to the ignorant blacks out of master society's generosity. The promised land of racial equality and the promised land of national independence held above our heads as carrots to one day brush against our lips as long as we kept faithfully producing for our now-former masters. The slave was to be sold into citizenship, the native into subject-hood, and promised the more genteel dictatorship of the state. Neck shackles became prisons and obsequiousness became patriotism. A more civil slavery. "Post-colonialism" and "Civil Rights" are synonyms marking the same scam.

In every settler-colony, there are holdouts. Nandi resistance in British East Africa tore up colonial railways and expressed their skepticism of the invitation into colonialism by not being induced to give up their "killing habit."[11] Several runaways were similarly uninterested in colonial unity and elected not to return to a white-governed world after Emancipation. Of course, treaties are designed to mislead and sound appealing. Many Black people were sold on the idea of the American state and a new era. Indeed, the international calls for "brotherhood" and liberty for all were likely powerful siren songs for those who despised the lowly status of their brothers of color and were taken with the fashionable new talk of the nineteenth century of Man. Freedmen and monied classes, like the colonized elite in Africa, would be the first to champion and celebrate the possibility of colonial promise. But in every settler-colonial project, however hegemonic, there is a history of refusing incorporation. A history that both the state and the colonized intellectual now attempt to re-envision as an imperfect belonging. But railroads continue to be stripped up; assimilation does not always capture its man.

> Perhaps they will laugh at or make light of this; but I tell you Americans! that unless you speedily alter your course, you and your

Country are gone!!!!! For God Almighty will tear up the very face of the earth!!! Will not that very remarkable passage of Scripture be fulfilled on Christian Americans? Hear it Americans!! "He that is unjust, let him be unjust still: and he which is filthy, let him be filthy still: and he that is righteous, let him be righteous still: and he that is holy, let him be holy still." I hope that the Americans may hear, but I am afraid that they have done us so much injury, and are so firm in the belief that our Creator made us to be an inheritance to them forever, that their hearts will be hardened, so that their destruction may be sure. This language, perhaps, is too harsh for the American's delicate ears. But O Americans! Americans!! I warn you in the name of the Lord (whether you will hear, or forbear,) to repent and reform, or you are ruined!!!![12]

Few texts survive that are as unforgiving of settler-colonists as David Walker's *Appeal to the Colored Citizens of the World*. Perhaps this is because the medium of writing and publishing is too bound up with the centering of the audience that does not deserve further conversation. The secret meetings in hush arbors, in rumor, codes hidden in song and recited poetry, double-entendres in jokes, playing fool to catch wise, (and today, Black social media and the unsigned trap, drill, spoken word, and reggae music)—that is, the orature that imagines a Black audience—on the other hand, can more freely house the unpolished radicalism of a subject people. Anti-colonialism tends to find more fertile ground in prisons, slums, street corners, and enforced illiteracy than in the book talk. Before the white gaze, however supportive, Black writing seems so often to find itself, the world over, on its knees appealing to master's society—even, especially as it claims to speak to "the globe." Asking them to see us as human, demanding this, that, or the other while the rushed, coded, clandestine unwritten literature of runaways, priests and priestesses, revolt conspiracists, and slick-talkers directly address the Pan-African world, be it imagined locally or worldwide. It is a difficult thing to genuinely write primarily for a Black audience. Though it is exceedingly easy to claim this was always the intention—and receive praise and gifts from a primary white liberal audience for so many "exciting, novel" attempts. Walker's *Appeal* is an exception. It calls out to an imagined Black audience to lift themselves from their chains collectively while warning the "Americans" about their coming destruction. As important as his chosen audience is his lack of identification with the nation. An anti-Crispus Attucks in his separating Blackness from Americans, he marks the failure of colonialism's interpellation and attempted creation of the Black patriot. He rejects assimilation-in-chains. Black against the Americans, not a Black American against racism. The ruin he imagines of America is not the ruin of a Blackness within it, but a Blackness happily watching Christian Nineveh burn.

Appeal is partly a diagnosis of colonialism and slavery, as well as an open call for a rising from chains and into insurrection against the masters. This, of course, was unacceptable for the liberals and conservative Americans alike. Police arrested free Black people found with copies of *Appeal* and deployed officers to stop its dissemination. Enslaved people found with it on their person were sent downriver, and efforts were made to stop the "incendiary publication," trafficked by runaway and fugitive networks.[13] Pro-slavery advocates threatened Walker's life, and white abolitionists washed their hands of it. Benjamin Lundy wrote of the text,

> I can do no less than set the broadest seal of condemnation upon [Walker's Appeal] . . . Granting that the colored race have as much cause for complaint as the writer intimates . . . yet this is not the way to obtain redress for their wrongs. The moral, not the physical, power of this nation must be put in requisition. Any attempt to obtain their liberty, and just rights, by force, must for a long time to come end in defeat, if not the extermination of the colored people . . . acrimonious language should not be indulged, and even revengeful feelings should be repressed . . . I am glad to find that some of the colored people have *publicly* condemned the pamphlet in question.[14]

"Not the way" is still a favorite phrase of the liberal who has appointed themselves to a parental role over every Black and Indigenous rebellious youth who, tired of the promise of increased conversations, has picked up a stone or a match. The white abolitionist is always heartened by the Black people who serve and stand with them, and from their porch bark condemnations at the anti-colonialist in the shadows. This function of the colonized intellectual, as Frantz Fanon[15] categorizes them, is present in all settler-colonies and has been for centuries. Handy and often handsomely paid, the Black figure is trotted out to condemn and temper down the spirits of revolt of the colonized. They are celebrated and often ceremoniously given the titles that approximate "noble wise savage." The spokespeople of the settler's peace, that is, the smooth operation and good order of colonized people's oppression, are given a platform, or a seat near the cable news anchor, in order to bring the rowdy lumpenproletariat, the rioting underclasses, the non-colonial law-abiding to heel and set them to work within the parameters set by the Confederacy of white liberal abolitionists and the white supremacist state. Often they do more than mere condemnation, as in the case of Sadie Tanner Alexander who during the 1964 revolt in Philadelphia, asked the mayor to "deputize '50000 responsible Negro leaders' 'to support the police.'" As J. T. Roane argues, Alexander was demonstrating citizenship through a willingness to police poor Black communities, evidence of the "larger relation of mediation envisioned within mainstream Philadelphia civil rights theorizing, organizing, and action."[16] The moral demand for Black peacefulness under oppression being nothing other than the liberal's method of "nigger-breaking."

This notion of compromise is very important in the case of decolonization, for it is far from being a simple matter. Compromise, in fact, involves both the colonial system and the burgeoning national bourgeoisie. The adherents of the colonial system discover that the masses might very well destroy every thing. The sabotage of bridges, the destruction of farms, repression and war can severely disrupt the economy. Compromise is also on the agenda for the national bourgeoisie who, unable to foresee the possible consequences of such a whirlwind, fear in fact they will be swept away, and hasten to reassure the colonists: "We are still capable of stopping the slaughter, the masses still trust us, act quickly if you do not want to jeopardize everything." If events go one step further, the leader of the nationalist party distances himself from the violence. He loudly claims he has nothing to do with these Mau-Mau, with these terrorists, these butchers. In the best of cases, he barricades himself in a no man's-land between the terrorists and the colonists and offers his services as "mediator"; which means that since the colonists can not negotiate with the Mau-Mau, he himself is prepared to begin negotiations.[17]

The world was given a live demonstration of the colonized intellectual's function the night Killer Mike stepped in between the uprising and Atlanta in his tearful conference to temper down the uprising after George Floyd's murder. His mission, whether or not he subscribed to it, was to softly but firmly set the limits on the horizons of Black revolt, despite the putatively Black radicalism in his lyrics which today, despite his closeness with the police, has several white Marxists (of any race) suggesting that he had good songs. The colonized intellectuals, as Fanon writes, are "violent in their words and reformist in their attitudes."[18] Killer Mike, as if pantomiming the text, wears a "Kill Your Masters" shirt while working with authority figures in pursuit, the always permanent "pursuit" of a solution to the negro question. That question, expressed in Rodney King's "Can't we all just get along?" is in contemporary parlance now more often styled "racial justice." As if colonies are in the business of producing justice of any type. As if apartheid's cauldron[19] has an interest in racial equity programs.

Walker, perhaps because he is confined in text and the strictures of that medium, the limitations of audience, and so on, even as he is one of the most distant from colonial mores and hope in the state, nevertheless still hints to a possible day of repentance and reform for the settler-colony, even as he seems not much bothered either way. In this way his work is not the equal to the illiterate texts of plantation arson and escape that did not, as evident in their action, argue for a space left for the colony's reform. And yet the text bumbled along to do its work, perhaps inspiring some otherwise-occupied freed persons and some enslaved to rise up against colonialism in full knowledge of the odds. Things have been degraded since that firebrand smuggled his prophecies under ragged clothes and through shipping ports. The fiery condemnation of the colony has been switched in the nursery for its opposite, a Civil Rights encouragement to call the nation toward its ideals. From the labor of survival, and escape, and returned fire, we are praised for our long-suffering, our blood and sweat in the service of colonial democracy, and our stubborn, never-turned-back pleading for change to come. With David Walker well-muzzled, the Black freedom struggle is now popularly conceived of as associated not with anti-colonialism but the progressive Americanism of Rev. Dr. Martin Luther King Jr.

King's Dream

> Five score years ago, a great American, in whose symbolic shadow we stand today, signed the Emancipation Proclamation. This momentous decree came as a great beacon light of hope to millions of Negro slaves who had been seared in the flames of withering injustice. It came as a joyous daybreak to end the long night of their captivity.
>
> But 100 years later, the Negro still is not free . . . One hundred years later the Negro is still languished in the corners of American society and finds himself in exile in his own land. And so we've come here today to dramatize a shameful condition. In a sense we've come to our nation's capital to cash a check.

When the architects of our republic wrote the magnificent words of the Constitution and the Declaration of Independence, they were signing a promissory note to which every American was to fall heir. This note was a promise that all men—yes, Black men as well as white men—would be guaranteed the unalienable rights of life, liberty and the pursuit of happiness.

It is obvious today that America has defaulted on this promissory note insofar as her citizens of color are concerned. Instead of honoring this sacred obligation, America has given the Negro people a bad check, a check which has come back marked insufficient funds.

But we refuse to believe that the bank of justice is bankrupt. We refuse to believe that there are insufficient funds in the great vaults of opportunity of this nation. And so we've come to cash this check, a check that will give us upon demand the riches of freedom and the security of justice.

We have also come to his hallowed spot to remind America of the fierce urgency of now. This is no time to engage in the luxury of cooling off or to take the tranquilizing drug of gradualism.

Now is the time to make real the promises of democracy. Now is the time to rise from the dark and desolate valley of segregation to the sunlit path of racial justice. Now is the time to lift our nation from the quick sands of racial injustice to the solid rock of brotherhood. Now is the time to make justice a reality for all of God's children . . .

But there is something that I must say to my people who stand on the warm threshold which leads into the palace of justice. In the process of gaining our rightful place, we must not be guilty of wrongful deeds. Let us not seek to satisfy our thirst for freedom by drinking from the cup of bitterness and hatred.

We must forever conduct our struggle on the high plane of dignity and discipline. We must not allow our creative protest to degenerate into physical violence. Again and again, we must rise to the majestic heights of meeting physical force with soul force. The marvelous new militancy which has engulfed the Negro community must not lead us to a distrust of all white people, for many of our white brothers, as evidenced by their presence here today, have come to realize that their destiny is tied up with our destiny . . .

So even though we face the difficulties of today and tomorrow, I still have a dream. It is a dream deeply rooted in the American dream. I have a dream that one day this nation will rise up and live out the true meaning of its creed: We hold these truths to be self-evident, that all men are created equal.[20]

It is difficult to escape the name of Dr. Martin Luther King Jr. or his speech given at the *March on Washington* at the Lincoln Memorial on August 28, 1963, because of their importance to colonialism.[21] Black thought is, one way or another, ball-and-chained to King. Despite the diversity in Black political opinion for the last 500 years, even "within" the fictional borders of Americanism, there is no pass one can be granted to journey off of that particular "I have a dream" farm. It is taken up here and quoted at length, however, not merely in acknowledgment of its force as a fetish object of American liberal nationalism that, with that other talisman the Civil Rights movement, supposedly inaugurated a new era of American justice. It is read closely here because it happens to be particularly telling and representative of the long and "unfinished" transformation from supplication to white masters to supplication to the liberal white supremacist state that defines our contemporary Jim Crow era.

Departing from David Walker, Dr. King places Black people in the category of Americans. He uses the possessive pronoun "our nation's capital" to conduct the revision of American history so important to colonialism, repositioning Black people as shareholders in the American dream rather than its sharecroppers. The chattel, the enslaved possessed by the state, are now dressed up as contributors, if unfairly treated, to the shared project of colonial democracy. Their consent to this offering of their forced labor as contributions is no more asked for in the dream narrative than it was in the fields. The enslaved are made to answer Josiah Wedgwood's question on the anti-slavery medallion "Am I not a Man and a Brother?" in the affirmative. It is now "our nation," we are no longer the nation's things. The Black man is Joseph, weighted down by a coat of racist brutality in the brotherhood of settler-colonists, asking, perhaps more sternly in the twentieth century, for his rightful place in line for the colonial inheritance.

After doffing his cap to the "magnificent" words composed by the racist architects of the colonial state, writing their drivel fresh from chasing their negress o'er hills and fields, after bowing to the "Founders" romanticized in American nationalism as bathing and perfumed powdered wig-wearing savants of liberty, Dr. King complains of not being paid what is due. He presents Black people as being owed. "Yes, Black men as well as white men," the "yes" serving to stave off anyone who might counter with the obvious fact that the enslaving class did not intend democracy for those they enslaved in Virginia any more than they did in Athens. King's depiction of what in the enslaver's mind were crosses between chattel and enemies—half-devils and half-children— as human subjects patiently awaiting freedom, allows him to suggest that the enslaved were robbed of their promised inheritance. His "Yes, Black men as well as white men," is his vehicle of revisionism, his route to push past historical fact. The liberal's inclusivity; King's attempt to integrate Black people into what Walker and maroons dreamed of as burning buildings. It presents the years of anti-Black atrocity and Black unfreedom as an oversight that should have been remedied by now. But as was decided by the Supreme Court in *Dred Scott v. Sandford (1857)*—in a most predictable and typical outcome of the settlers' chief juridical institution—Black people were never understood to be part of the citizenry. It was and is not a matter of "being seen" or "heard." It was not that they were denied unalienable rights as King would have it, rather they were alien to the regime of rights, the pursuit of happiness, and liberty. It was that the negro had no rights the white man was bound to respect. King's "yes" is an insertion of Black life into colonial humanity to plead the case to the state while massaging the state, claiming that it is good and marvelous and not the chief product of white supremacy that cannot be willed into a racial justice machine.

Even in conversations with self-proclaimed Black radicals—among those who do not join the white liberals and present King's word as biblical truth not to be strayed from or if strayed from at least acknowledged as important—one often notices an instinct to save King and interpret the Civil Rights movement in the most positive light. They say of King that he needed time to learn his lesson and that he drew nearer to Malcolm X near the end of his life, stumbling in his faith in colonialism and worrying that he, like a reversed Moses, was integrating his people into a burning house. The "Civil Rights Movement," of course, is an artifact of liberal historians who have collapsed the plural works of freedom and rebellion against racial totalitarianism—be they a brushing off a sicced dog or campaigning for school integration policy—into an attempt to expand rights. The Black people who kicked out at police dogs fossilized as campaigners for state reform, well-muzzled, never to be asked whether they were activists or as disinterested in the state as they were of being bitten by its work-animals. That centuries-long work of uprising against master society and racial totalitarianism—work that predates the "founding" of the colony—is left without a tongue and, like the silent man on bended knee enslaved on Wedgwood's medallion, and then again in Sojourner Truth's "Ain't I a Woman?" is forced to say something that was not necessarily in their language. Black anti-colonialism is muzzled and made to utter in the chorus of the state. To have it be said of it that it was actually a participant in the "long Civil Rights movement." It becomes eternal, a vampire as Sundiata Keita Cha-

Jua and Clarence Lang argue, collapsing all Black liberation movements of every place and time into one narrative, erasing distinctions and the heterogeneity of their often incompatible aims.[22] A narrative that can stretch out to collect even Nat Turner, or forward to wash out the flame of uprisings against the lynch mob after George Floyd's death and leave the ash of "the summer protests for racial justice." Escape from race riots, defending homes from marauding horsemen, healing wounds: all labor of survival is categorized as the work for rights. The runaway is pulled back to the plantation and thanked for their service. The work against the civil[23] and the author of rights, the state, becomes the work for the civil and for rights. King puts a ribbon on the fraud by saying his dream, taken to mean Black people's dream, is deeply rooted in the American dream.

But it is not excusable to say that Dr. King didn't know. Others did. King dreamed wrongly. His faith in colonialism was calculatingly ungrounded. There was neither a check nor promissory note issued. And, as we have seen with John and Adam, if the master issues a promissory note of freedom for those he enslaved, it should not be taken seriously. There has been no failure of "America" to live up to its ideals. These ideals have been, for some time now, liberty and the pursuit of happiness for slave owners and the pro-slavery community, and freedom from the tyranny of abolition. Indeed, patriotism in the colony is developed as explicitly anti-Black ideology. The Abolitionist movement was conceived as British and un-American in the 1830s, leading the Bowery Theatre's owner on July 9th, 1834, to quell a mob angry that an abolitionist meeting was held there by waving American flags and playing Blackface songs. On July 4th of that year, a mob attacked the Chatham Street Chapel due to an anti-slavery lecture held there and then went to City Hall Park "to act out their patriotism in knocking down the black."[24] January 6th's lynch mob's US flags bound up with nooses, Confederate flags, and Auschwitz t-shirts, the 1976 photo—defensively named "soiling" old glory—[25] of a white man spearing a Black man with the US flag are not misrepresentations of patriotism. This is how the lynch mob's creed should be interpreted and how it has been interpreted by settler mobs in settler-colonies globally. It is the straying from the explicit Dred Scott ruling, the *Declaration* of all settler states: "the African has no rights which the white man is bound to respect; and that he might justly and lawfully be reduced to slavery for his benefit," that is currently being brayed against by what the mob aptly terms real America. It is a return to the ideals of settler rule that the MAGA movement preaches. This return is what white Kenyan settlers demanded at the point of Civil War, and is what was achieved in the Nats takeover in 1948 South Africa and Israel's takeover in 1948 Palestine. "America" is not exceptional as the liberal ideologue beats into every podium. It is typical.

King's "I Have a Dream" speech makes an appeal to the state and society, even as it stands and does not necessarily kneel. It states I am a man. It marches on Washington (of course not in the way George Washington marched; the Black "march," if it is to be moral, must be nonviolent). But the horizon it lifts its eyes toward is the horizon of colonialism's—it bears repeating—fictitious borders. It asks the occupier for equal rights in the territory it occupies and in so doing presents the occupier, the enemy, as a benevolent, if slow, master. The captured, worked, and killed who in their songs once identified themselves with the biblical Israelite slaves fleeing Egypt now find themselves recasted in *the dream* as the brother of the masters destined to join in support of the occupation rather than pray for a deluge to drown the empire. Led to the mountaintop of the state, other possibilities of Black action that draw on powers other than the goodness and founding democratic foresight of American society are eclipsed. Even as our help, history has proven, has never come from persuaded US racists but from international pressure be it the promise of a liberated Saint-Domingue, the moral force of the Soviet Union, the avenues of escape opened up during the war against the slaveholding patriots, the reverberations of the anti-colonial victories in Africa and the Caribbean as well as "Third World" decolonization, even Europe.[26] King directs his followers' eyes back toward the masters' society. Colonist morality trumping the fugitive's imperative, King, with assistance of the liberal press, can help mute the swelling danger of those who remained intellectual fugitives to Americanism such as those explicitly stated in anti-chorus with Dr. King, Malcolm X's "I am not American—I am one of the victims of America." King fulfills perfectly what Stowe a century earlier had Uncle Tom do to the runaway quadroon woman Cassy, quieting the riotous Black person and endowing Black suffering, forgiveness, hope, and death under the masters with a saintliness. In a sense, Dr. King is functioning like another white abolitionist, Benjamin Lundy, holding back the ghost of David Walker, now inhabiting the personages of a gun-toting Fannie Lou Hamer, *Ballot or the Bullet* Malcolm X, or a build-your-own-nation-and-leave-them separatist Marcus Garvey. He helps a narrative of "Civil Rights" muzzle the mouths of late nineteenth-twentieth-century Black radicalism just as the presence of the "Am I Not a Brother?" medallions stamped out the shadow of slave revolts.

Conspiring to place the horizon of freedom as coterminous with the state pushes against the latent internationalism of workers, the lumpenproletariat, and the marginalized races. It misdirects away from the weapon of Black internationalism birthed in the slave ship's hold and the early plantations, in the rumors of a solidarity offered in revolutionary Haiti, and the news of help from Black "Canada." It directs the struggle away from linked arms with the global colonized and instead asks us to knock at the neighbors in the European Quarter's door despite the likelihood of being shot. Just as the white supremacists now styled defensively as "the far right" embolden, confer and trade with each other internationally, so can and does the colonized world. But Black people are consistently asked to lift their eyes to the perpetually improving in race-relations state. This while the lynch mob trades pictures of lynchings "across the pond"[27] and white supremacist militants train in Ukraine. This while their billionaire ideologue stuffs a sock in the mouth of Black Twitter and uses South African mineral money to stimulate the sentiments of the next Rhodesia-nostalgic Dylann Roof. But new *Shosholozas* are already increasing in volume in Baas' Tesla factories and on X. Nkosi Sikelel' iAfrika is DJ-blended into *Lift Every Voice* and *Knuck if You Buck*. Anti-apartheid movements in Africa are as much African American heritage as Bob Marley's *Zimbabwe* is the inheritance of the continent. Borderless, Pan-Africanist anti-colonialism, as it is experienced at this second under slum boom boxes and from laptops in project row houses, is our birthright. Where we come from. Not, as we were all taught in their classrooms, *Little House on the Prairie*. "Racism in the U.S.A is as much a world problem as was nazism"[28] to expand on Williams, it inspired Nazism in the 1930s just as it does today. It is no mere strategic mistake to circumscribe Black people's appeal to the planted borders of the hostile colony. It has long been plantation strategy to cut all ties between the enslaved in America and Africa, the African Diaspora, and the world.

Making demands of a racist society is not only negotiating with terrorists, it also conspires with nationalism to pretend that the colony is indispensable when in fact the opposite is true. Emancipation can go nowhere, we are told, without the consent of white power, be it the persuasion of racists or the allyship of less angry racists. White abolitionism is indispensable in the pursuit of Black freedom, as Hillary Clinton in her reprimand to the audience at home during her 2008 campaign against Obama reminded us. "I would point to the fact that that Dr. King's dream began to be realized when President Johnson passed the Civil Rights Act of 1964, when he was able to push through

Congress something that President Kennedy was hopeful to do, the president before had not even tried, but it took a president to get it done," she said. "That dream became a reality, the power of that dream became real in people's lives because we had a president who said we are going to do it and actually got it accomplished."[29] So colonial freedom begins running slowly, leashed to the colonizer's empathetic cooperation, and determined by the president's, the master's, action. Saint-Domingue is disappeared. Algeria, Chimurenga, FRELIMO, the Amistad, MPLA Medusa-struck into silent masks. Appeals to racist society throw themselves at the coattails of the state and to nothing and no one else. As if it is accepted that the state is a permanent feature of Black life, a god, at whose altar we must all learn to get along. But the future—no matter what it looks like—is inevitably post-American. No empire is permanent. This is a matter not only of historical truth but of logic. No human institution stretches out into infinity no matter how loudly it swears by its permanence, how persuasively it performs its omnipotence or how many world bases dance out omnipresence; Rome will fall again. David Walker will have his day. It is not a matter of "if," it is a matter of "when." The trouble is the most astute of the lynch mob sees this as well, and as all their actions indicate, they recognize this brand of liberal-dominated white supremacy as insufficient and have moved to return not so much to the great old days but to further and deepen the Hitlerian trajectory of the settler-colony. Where those communities bled of their manual labor can be seen as a surplus population and with some finality be all thrown over the Zong. Every step in a genocidal direction—migrant bodies trapped in the levees, the metaphor contained in the public extermination of Black Studies— is hallelujah'd over. Movements for Black life are shot at. At least half of the population is openly interested in overt white rule rather than shared governance in the colonial occupation. At least half would burn any promissory note. "America" does not hold the exclusive rights to the pursuit of liberty and is far from a serious candidate in that effort. The dream of freedom, of course, belongs to the runaway, the fugitives hiding from the founder-slave masters. Not the slave masters and not their idolators. It is, however, of course fitting that even freedom dreams have been ripped from the Black liberation tradition and credited to its enemies, repurposed as a negro harness.

Continuing this inversion of David Walker's address, King devotes only a portion of the iconic speech to Black people—the targeted victims of white supremacist totalitarianism and for whom he is seeking liberation. It is as if they are second-class citizens not only in the streets but even in the space of his liberatory oratory. When the intended audience is Black, he turns from praising the marvelous Constitution to an offer of sympathy lined with a reprimand for the temptation toward revolt. He talks down to Cassy. Two years before Dr. King delivered this Sermon on the Colony's Mount, Frantz Fanon, while participating and theorizing from a struggle that would raze similar high and lofty places in Algiers, wrote about the colonized intellectual: that peculiar creature useful to colonialism but dressed in the uniform of a liberatory struggle for the people. Fanon writes that this creature is ambiguous on the question of violence.[30] A hesitant but faithful ally or at least asset to colonial power set up to quell as much as possible the colonized lumpen's rage. In the colony, while the militancy of Blackness was threatening slave revolt, King had to step out and say the struggle must not degenerate into physical violence. Vulnerability and nonviolence, preferred qualities in the prostrate slave, are championed instead. A civil disobedience obedient to civility and carefully calibrated to not move out of certain unacceptable parameters is instructed. And so the speech had the same function of the police dogs, making sure the colonized do not get too free and step out of their place and abandon nationalism's coffle.

It is not explained why Black people must not have their creative protest "degenerate" into physical violence. Especially in a speech beginning with praise for the warrior Lincoln and delivered on a national mall named for George Washington, two leaders of degenerations into physical violence of which the liberal generally approves. Similarly, it is not explained why Black militancy must not lead to a distrust of all white people or descend into bitterness and hatred. And why confronting terrorism and the atrocities of totalitarianism with forgiveness and vulnerability is not outright complicity. Or why we should accept that the state and society are indispensable and necessary partners. In essence, the call to march is a call not to march. To behave in a way that promises nonviolence and no sudden moves. It is a demonstration against the injustice of totalitarianism through the performance of the Supplicant Negro. To be Stowe's praiseworthy Uncle Tom, the faithful servant being whipped to death yet electing not to join the runaways in the liberal settler's heartwarming story. It is no uprising, nor a revolt, but the moral force of the beating heart of prostrate Blackness. This is precisely why Dr. King is so prized, and Civil Rights has been such a powerful symbol in liberal white supremacy. The colonial state is fine to honor him because, despite the perfection of totalitarianism which represents any slight progressive adjustment as revolutionary, he poses no threat to colonialism. Just the opposite. King is the most successful salesperson of colonial reform. An idea bought to this day by the truckload: that colonialism's future is justice. The promise that with enough muster and allegiance to colonialism's founding myths, the slave master's political project can evolve into one in which all men are equal.

Of course, King is celebrated by Black people who are not apologists for colonialism as well, but there is a distance between the state's platforming of a usable native chief to help keep down the always threatening *swart gevaar* and a figure that has been endowed with a meaning beyond himself, embodying the possibility of an off-ramp from the most blatant forces of Jim Crow. In this sense, I might concede that King means different things to different people. But this is not enough. Still, "non-violence emboldens the racists"[31] as Robert Williams observed. The enslaved who did not resist the whip did not, in this show of fidelity, convince the master to end his whipping. That is the promise of slavery, one that was never intended to be kept. Uncle Tom died in Stowe's novel. Several Indigenous people are classified as extinct. Long-suffering on earth and a charitable disposition to the men who believe they are masters do not automatically guarantee one sweet day of redemption and multiracial peaceful cohabitation. The colonized are not christs. Beatings often result in permanent damage. Killings lead to extermination from memory. The Civil Rights millenarianism preached by those who ask us to stay on our knees should be cast out like miracle spring water.

Testifying that Black people are created equal and human did not persuade and inspire settler humanity any more than did our suffering under the whip. Again, Black humanness was never at issue—they have known. An angry Frederick Douglass in his "What to the Slave is the Fourth of July?" speech—one that might have been decried by Barack Obama as exhibiting the damnable pessimism of a Rev. Wright—condemned this constant debate about Black humanness.

> What point in the anti-slavery creed would you have me argue? On what branch of the subject do the people of this country need light? Must I undertake to prove that the slave is a man? That point is conceded already. Nobody doubts it. The slaveholders themselves acknowledge it in the enactment of laws for their government. They acknowledge it when they punish disobedience on the part of the slave. There are seventy-two crimes in the State of Virginia which, if committed by a black man (no matter how ignorant he be), subject him to the punishment of death; while only two of the

same crimes will subject a white man to the like punishment. What is this but the acknowledgment that the slave is a moral, intellectual, and responsible being? The manhood of the slave is conceded. It is admitted in the fact that Southern statute books are covered with enactments forbidding, under severe fines and penalties, the teaching of the slave to read or to write. When you can point to any such laws in reference to the beasts of the field, then I may consent to argue the manhood of the slave. When the dogs in your streets, when the fowls of the air, when the cattle on your hills, when the fish of the sea, and the reptiles that crawl, shall be unable to distinguish the slave from a brute, then will I argue with you that the slave is a man![32]

And yet we are called on to demonstrate our humanity and the high planes of a superior morality to persuade those who have prepared vast networks of nets to catch and keep at bay humans. Again, what power desires of Black people is not the evidence of humanity but the performance of supplication. The liberal proposal for increased conversations gives white supremacists the benefit of the doubt and considers white supremacist violence a consequence of white supremacists not yet hearing the good news of Black humanity. Those who call for our demonstrations of humanness and making our human lives visible to convince racists we are human may be the only ones convinced that Black humanity is not patently obvious. They are the ones who see the problem as one of an error in perception and believe the onus is on the perceived to fix it rather than the perceiver. The solution to torture, however, is never a change in the performance of the tortured. The solution to colonialism has never been an increase in dialogue and conversation and greater, more charitable knowledge of the Other. Indeed, any warming of feeling occasionally perceived in individual white supremacists for Black people is warmth generated by the oppressed in a prostrate position. It is never an empathizing with the disrespected and now disrespectful Black rebel who stands uncompromisingly free. It is a warmth from the Black man who, disarmed, finds his rug. Who sold his soul at the price of a noogie. As a Kentuckian once expressed it in 1857, "I like a nigger . . . but I hate a damned free nigger."[33] The question, "Am I Not a Man and a Brother?" has never been the question of the enslaved and has always been the ventriloquist's imposition. But even if it was it was never a question that could jolt men with the whip handles between their teeth who have sold their own mixed-race offspring into slavery into equity. Fugitivity, marronage, the slave revolt, the poisonings, flight has decidedly not centered debates about humanity and were never around long enough to become models for the white abolitionists' puppets.

The "soul force" and moral superiority of men like Gandhi, Nelson Mandela, and Martin Luther King Jr., in the liberal imagination, are reflected in their calls for nonviolent resistance in the face of colonial systemic atrocity. This is what accounts for their aura, their praiseworthiness. It is their willingness to be lashed, to bleed, and to have their body and the bodies of their people bled into sacrificial lambs in the hope of persuading the omnipotent colonist to be less bad and to share. But neither Black nonviolence nor nonviolent or passive resistance is new. The non-resisting enslaved were pushed to the ground and torn up by dogs before the contradiction in terms "peaceful protest" was coined. Limbs were removed in the Congo for any perceived slowdown in rubber production. Several schools in "former colonies" in Africa and the Caribbean still punish students for speaking in their "nation-languages."[34] Public floggings and lynchings were, and are, punishments for impertinence[35] and disobedience, defensively reconceived as "police brutality" and "police-involved shootings." The refusal to strike back, far from being a novel idea vested with the power to eventually win over oppressor hearts and minds, has been inculcated in the enslaved through master and colonial law. In Virginia's appropriately named *An Act for Preventing Negroes Insurrections* of 1680, Black people were warned to keep their conduct nonviolent centuries before King's admonition. "It is further enacted by the authority aforesaid that if any negroe or other slave shall presume to lift up his hand in opposition against any christian, shall for every such offence, upon due proofe made thereof by the oath of the party before a magistrate, have and receive thirty lashes on his bare back well laid on."[36] Moreover, nonviolence being falsely credited not only as the sole agent of political change but the sole property of the supplicant renders invisible the quiet, non-subservient resistances all throughout colonialism, which were passive out of necessity and under threat of punishments more severe. Nonviolence is conflated with faith in colonists and colonialism, but one does not imply the other. The problem with Kingism is not, or not merely, nonviolence but its appeal to the colonial occupation. The instruction to wait, hand and foot, on the devil. (Even if that waiting has now advanced to the "Bank of Justice's" teller's window.) It is a faith program that has required the depersonalization of the colonized into a Hydra of the noble savage, Lassie the dog, and the long-suffering Christ.[37] Its bleeding, the object of the blood, is but a gift and a lesson for an ignorant and imperfectly Christian whiteness. But the Black woman holding onto the hem of the garment of Christ is not healed. She is imprisoned and called woke. There is tremendous soul force in the beings born as property but who have stolen themselves from it. Moral superiority in the subjects and people who have no interest in bleeding any longer and for anyone. Especially not in service of "reminding America to live up to her ideals" which is to say of colonial expansion.

Rose-tinted speeches from a Black, mustachioed, baby-faced orator at the Lincoln Memorial did not barricade well enough the door from the culture of the mobs who massacred communities at Tulsa, at Colfax, at Springfield, at Elaine, at New York. It did not stem the tide of the eternal *Red Summer*—did not prevent the dragging of James Byrd Jr., the hunting of Ahmaud Arbery, the police rape of Michael Jenkins and Eddie Parker. It did not finally put the Confederacy back in its box and lead to a pluralistic, equitable if flawed, millenarian, racially equal America brought about by the gumption of the liberal, hopeful youth. America is the Confederacy—as both Black radicals and white supremacists see clearly. The liberal white supremacists have only borrowed the administration of its state from "real America" who now, after clamoring for its return with nooses and Viking helmets, have had it peacefully transferred back to them. Settler-colonialism has not evolved into racial justice as King dreamed it would. The slave owner's country did not, as predicted, develop into a light on the hill beckoning the tired, huddled masses yearning to be free. That light has always been a searchlight. An anglerfish. Colonialism does not wither away to reveal an equitable society after being assailed by flowers and native vulnerability. It only "loosens its hold when the knife is at its throat."[38] If it says otherwise it is deploying colonial tactics. The treaty held out; the handcuff locking on the trusting wrist. All that can be hoped, all that has ever been hoped for within the confines of settler-colonialism is that the whipped might not be whipped so harshly for a while. An offer unacceptable to the maroon.

The argument expressed by anti-colonialism and marronage is that even if, after this long Samson-like suffering, the bright day of adequate justice were indeed fated to arrive, perhaps a few years from now, when justice will roll down, scales would fall from racists' eyes and Elysian fields would sprout forth, it is still unacceptable. Even if that day were to come, it would be too late. It was too late from the first day. The anti-colonialist says the colonized do not deserve any more extensions to their sentence—in fact, the aim is to de-seat the parole board. Their answer to "be patient, give it one more day" is no. It is Sister Souljah's reply to Dr. Cornel West, who pled with her to be patient with white racism and unserious allies because "that may be all we can get." "I don't work with 'all I can get.'"[39] The masters do not deserve one more day in power—even if the following day is "Emancipation." No. Liberal gradualism, which surfaces to hush anger on anti-Black atrocity with "well there has been some racial progress we cannot discount this," this sixty years of gradualism, after King's 100 years, is banned. The colonists, the liberals who hold King's words on their breast: "We have also come to his hallowed spot to remind America of the fierce urgency of now. This is no time to engage in the luxury of cooling off or to take the tranquilizing drug of gradualism," recite it day after day, generation after generation—a groaning, long-drawn-out, tiresome, stale now. The liberal colonist's now is never as present, never even as near as the aspiring runaway's impractical "one day I'll be out of here." Even if that latter's day never arrives, it is still more immediate than the urgency of colonial reforms. Or, as another orator powerfully and tellingly branded it, "Change." The slave master who says work well and suffer with a kindly face and you may be set free and the Civil Rights master who says work well, be in good order and suffer, and there will be freedom are recognized as in the same body despite a change in emphasis. The fugitive is not buying the stuff still being peddled by Civil Rights hustlers who would convince the population to wait on the oppressors' racial enlightenment—even on trains to Auschwitz. Who in this late day when governing politicians and country music stars are flirting with bringing back lynching and lynch mob society, feels well rested and refreshed after crowning their own King, when the pogrom continues apace, are still saying hold the line America will change. As the sky falls and the glaciers melt, that three-card monte, that okey-doke, is no longer bought. It is *Civil Rights* that has given a blank check to white supremacist society, and confronting the slave revolt, the colonists have discovered that it has been voided. Less a roadmap that set America on the right course, it would be more accurate to say that King's dream has functioned as the cover-up that excuses and humanizes a society ruled by people who would erect buoys to drown migrants from the countries they destroyed and be allies to genocide if it suited imperialism's world order. It is a way to speak about colonial atrocities, to romanticize every welt across the body of the Black Samson who brutishly pushes his dogged strength against the pillars for the benefit of all Americans. But atrocities are not unfortunate rivers to be crossed on the road to freedom; they are atrocities. King's dream is not the only Black dream; there are other, more worthy dreamers. Even, especially, those who dreamed illegally, who were not permitted to speak and whose actions were not recorded as a matter of security. Americanism and its "imperfect experiment in democracy" is not—for every Black person—a powerful enough concealer to cover the bruises it leaves.

Barack Obama's "A More Perfect Union"

"We the people, in order to form a more perfect union..."—221 years ago, in a hall that still stands across the street, a group of men gathered and, with these simple words, launched America's improbable experiment in democracy. Farmers and scholars, statesmen and patriots who had traveled across an ocean to escape tyranny and persecution finally made real their declaration of independence at a Philadelphia convention that lasted through the spring of 1787.

The document they produced was eventually signed but ultimately unfinished. It was stained by this nation's original sin of slavery, a question that divided the colonies and brought the convention to a stalemate until the founders chose to allow the slave trade to continue for at least 20 more years, and to leave any final resolution to future generations.

Of course, the answer to the slavery question was already embedded within our Constitution—a Constitution that had at its very core the ideal of equal citizenship under the law; a Constitution that promised its people liberty and justice and a union that could be and should be perfected over time.

And yet words on a parchment would not be enough to deliver slaves from bondage, or provide men and women of every color and creed their full rights and obligations as citizens of the United States. What would be needed were Americans in successive generations who were willing to do their part—through protests and struggles, on the streets and in the courts, through a civil war and civil disobedience, and always at great risk—to narrow that gap between the promise of our ideals and the reality of their time . . .

But the remarks that have caused this recent firestorm weren't simply controversial. They weren't simply a religious leader's efforts to speak out against perceived injustice. Instead, they expressed a profoundly distorted view of this country—a view that sees white racism as endemic, and that elevates what is wrong with America above all that we know is right with America; a view that sees the conflicts in the Middle East as rooted primarily in the actions of stalwart allies like Israel, instead of emanating from the perverse and hateful ideologies of radical Islam.

As such, Reverend Wright's comments were not only wrong but divisive, divisive at a time when we need unity; racially charged at a time when we need to come together to solve a set of monumental problems—two wars, a terrorist threat, a falling economy, a chronic health care crisis and potentially devastating climate change—problems that are neither black or white or Latino or Asian, but rather problems that confront us all . . .

Like the anger within the black community, these resentments aren't always expressed in polite company. But they have helped shape the political landscape for at least a generation. Anger over welfare and affirmative action helped forge the Reagan Coalition. Politicians routinely exploited fears of crime for their own electoral ends. Talk show hosts and conservative commentators built entire careers unmasking bogus claims of racism while dismissing legitimate discussions of racial injustice and inequality as mere political correctness or reverse racism.

Just as black anger often proved counterproductive, so have these white resentments distracted attention from the real culprits of the middle class squeeze—a corporate culture rife with inside dealing, questionable accounting practices and short-term greed; a Washington dominated by lobbyists and special interests; economic policies that favor the few over the many. And yet, to wish away the resentments of white Americans, to label them as misguided or even racist, without recognizing they are grounded in legitimate concerns—this too widens the racial divide and blocks the path to understanding.

This is where we are right now. It's a racial stalemate we've been stuck in for years. Contrary to the claims of some of my critics, black and white, I have never been so naïve as to believe that we can get beyond our racial divisions in a single election cycle, or with a single candidacy—particularly a candidacy as imperfect as my own.

But I have asserted a firm conviction—a conviction rooted in my faith in God and my faith in the American people—that, working together, we can move beyond some of our old racial wounds, and that in fact we have no choice if we are to continue on the path of a more perfect union . . .

Ironically, this quintessentially American—and yes, conservative — notion of self-help found frequent expression in Reverend Wright's sermons. But what my former pastor too often failed to understand is that embarking on a program of self-help also requires a belief that society can change.

The profound mistake of Reverend Wright's sermons is not that he spoke about racism in our society. It's that he spoke as if our society was static; as if no progress had been made; as if this country—a country that has made it possible for one of his own members to run for the highest office in the land and build a coalition of white and black, Latino and Asian, rich and poor, young and old—is still irrevocably bound to a tragic past. But what we know—what we have seen—is that America can change. That is the true genius of this nation.[40]

Just as Dr. King opens his speech showing his fealty to the anti-Black Great Emancipator Lincoln as a symbol of his patriotism and fealty to empire, Barack Obama begins his own great speech "A More Perfect Union" with a nod to the opening lines of the US Constitution. The appointed spokesmen for the blacks begin their momentous addresses with this demonstration of kneeling to the king's sword to demonstrate loyalty to the crown above all things before being allowed to speak and lay out the grievances of their people. Obama, however, is more plaintive in his call than King, who in turn, was more forgiving than Douglass was in his Fourth of July address, which was more agreeable than Walker's *Appeal*. Obama pleads with—or, as it is sometimes read, inspires—an imagined American society to remember they are a brotherhood and must live up to the "nation's" founding ideals while at the same time denouncing his pastor, Dr. Jeremiah Wright Jr., and his Walkerian speech that damned America and empire and which led to media investigations that ultimately shamed the reverend into an apology.

Obama, as a voice for the Black tradition represented as voiceless, advances the Supplicant Negro figure. The supplicant, in a magical, state self-affirming twist for the colony, rises to the head of the table of empire. After 2007, it was more forcefully argued that America might be making a post-racial turn as evidenced by the rise of Obama, despite the derision and the "pessimism" of Black radical critique. Obama was helped along by several other Black public figures in this hope-shaming of Black anti-colonialist "negativity" and "idealism" and the sober observation that the settler-colonial empire could not and did not intend to become post-racial. Perhaps most distressingly was the eminent documentarian of Black lumpen New York life, Nas, whose 2008 song "Black President" sampled Tupac's quote, "And although it seems heaven sent / we ain't ready to see a Black President" and immediately fastened to it the liberal correction and Obama's motto, "Yes We Can" as a chorus. It, of course, turned out that no, you cannot remix empire into justice, as proven by Obama's non-post-racial drone strikes and wars that struck down hope for scores around the world and expanded the unchanging same of imperialism. The Civil Rights-inspired "community activist" was promoted to the chief officer of American power through a public denouncing of the Black radical tradition temporally (and perhaps surprisingly) embodied in Rev. Wright. He won his audience by mimicking the language and tone of the "Civil Rights" movement's leaders and flattering the liberal colonists as citizens of an imperfect but always perfecting democracy. One in which a seemingly intractable issue of race is part of a national redemption story on the crest of which he, humbly, stood. The colony's violence disappears in Obama's narrative, and under the top hat is revealed a false equivalency: "both sides." One black, one white, who both, equally, must confront their biases and put them aside to finally sit together at the table of brotherhood that is the settler-colony.

Assata Shakur of the Black Liberation Army and fugitive of American concentration camps, in her seminal autobiography, provides the dictum against Black supplication: "Nobody in the world, nobody in history, has ever gotten their freedom by appealing to the moral sense of the people who were oppressing them."[41] The speech and the entire saga of Obama can be defined by attempting just this appeal to settler society with predictable results. But this attempt is not seen as folly, even in its expected and predictable failure, even in its repetition each generation. On the contrary, in liberal spin, it becomes "Hope." Associating itself with the Christian theme, hope becomes a positive thing in itself. It is not folly, which is cursed; hope in the "nation" is proper and patriotic. Grave robbing the baton from Dr. King, Obama becomes Obama the Good, his Black naysayers the cretins of history that the fate of the nation must push past. Against Black liberal Christlikeness, Black radicalism appears brutish, slow-witted, criminal, and aggressive, taking on all of the stereotypes of Black young lumpen youth against the bow-tie, smiling youth pastor kindness of the Black liberal. In situating radical thought as brutishly pessimistic, the liberal failures of analysis and predictions on "race relations" and the radical's superiority of analysis are not a point in radical theory's column. Sound analysis becomes miserly; the constantly erroneous, the province of optimism. Fugitive thought, cowardly and violent; liberal statolatry equity-minded, no matter how it is linked with white supremacist killers or facilitates the work of killing. Obama ascends to his throne, bowing to the Founding Father gods, the scepter of Hope and freedom in his left hand, the fetters and extradition order for Assata in his right. Both supplicant and slave catcher. Colonialism's best "unifier"; capitalism's best herder.

What Mr. Obama recommends is forgiveness and understanding so that we could move forward together in colonialism. He asks for collusion with that white supremacist function of Civil Rights that casts the story of Black dissent as the plea of the peaceable Supplicant Negro. He wants unity and an end to "divisive rhetoric." But the country is not united. It is not a country. A colony is always a predatory relation, and no matter how the painters paint John's farm as idyllic, Adam was not part of it. Obama, the understudy reverend dreaming of the sons of slaves and slave owners sitting at a table of brotherhood, as is, he often points out, represented in his own body, appoints himself to lead the charge of letting bygones be bygones. As if the past is gone. As if it is not the same forgiveness on the minds of juries and judges who are forced to take up the case of those who dole out the summary justice to the natives on the street and who are now inconvenienced by a trial. A forgiveness that promises no deterrence. That the police keep in their pocket and flash for us if they detect any hesitation in our throwing our faces onto the ground or resistance in being thrust against a wall. Forgiveness is complicity. There is nothing "old" about our wounds.

The most precious offering of Barack Obama's speech to colonialism is the reinterpretation of the constant atrocity that is settler-colonial occupation as an ever-expanding, flawed but not disingenuous, "improbable experiment in democracy." For this take not to be thrown out at the first hearing, it must first hook onto the settler's story, and afterwards, hitch the "Black story" onto the same wagon. For his own great speech, Obama, after observing protocol, bows to the US Constitution and the House of Lords that is the wise Founders and immediately follows with a reiteration of the settler's romance. Like the romances of the Veld of Afrikaners in what was renamed South Africa, the great return in what was renamed Israel, the founding of White Man's Country in what was renamed British East Africa, a tale is told that presents "the native" as part of the flora and fauna, the natural, pristine environment on which persecuted and hardy pilgrims begin their story. The narrative of empty space expands the settler-colonist's clearing of people and land at the level of discourse. Indigenous peoples and extant political systems are cleared from the stage of the *terra nullius* on which the genius pilgrims, through the hardship of tough terrain and tougher Indigenous resistance, begin a novel experiment in society and settle.[42] It is never being mentioned the other experiments that were exterminated or which still lay on the ground on which they built their cities, parched. Obama's great speech on race begins and expands upon the racism of the settler narrative that removes the "lower races" from memory. The bloodletting of the European invasion disappears, and what remains is a haunting quiet on which the good, never genocidal[43] settlement self-erects.

Immediately after showing fealty to the colony's mythohistory, he launches into the big lie:[44] "The document they produced was eventually signed but ultimately unfinished. It was stained by this nation's original sin of slavery . . . " a convenient retelling to legitimize the state birthed in white supremacy for an age when racism is frowned upon. These worthy "founders," the most prominent of whom still had the stench of slave-catching on his breath,[45] are in this praise song for settlement recast as people uncertain about the white supremacist nature of the colonialist republic and were leaving the job of perfecting a racially equitable empire to future generations. Future, greater minds would reckon with the nation's "original sin of slavery," this story goes. In their "genius," the wise founders created not a static society, but one in which there was always room for improvement. It is this blessing they, in their foresight, bequeathed the present generation of Americans—before they went home to tug at the neck irons of the Africans in their bedroom.

But the "country" did not merely forget to include Black people in its vision for "liberty," as the big lie would have it. They did not scan the room for potential candidates of freedom and miss the servants chained to their fountain pens. Colonialism did not plan to get them on the next go-around in the "ever-expanding freedom experiment" that was "America." Americanism is no such thing.

The narrative that "America" is an imperfect experiment in democracy that extends the promise of freedom to more and more folks every generation conveniently leaves out the fact that Americans were the reason for enslavement. In it, the bully is praised as wise and benevolent for planning on ceasing to twist the weaker boy's arm—and the non-twisting of arms is a genius gift bestowed upon the weaker boy by the community of well-intentioned arm twisters. That Obama's narrative is a service provided to white supremacist society is demonstrated every time a white supremacist today counters complaints about colonial anti-Blackness with "actually, America actually freed the slaves," followed with, always in the same tone as the slave master, "the blacks should be grateful."

Crediting Black freedom to the genius of the slave masters' always perfecting state robs the enslaved's work of escape and hands it over to the house of their oppression. The image of the slave owner's republic, with its territory of torture chambers, of forced-labor fields, hushed sexual attack and "alligator bait," of the enslaved assembled and forced to watch as a master chopped a screaming enslaved man up with an ax and cooked body part after body part over fire for dropping a pitcher of water,[46] is, in the hopeful patriot's depiction, inverted. The enslaver becomes the liberator. The institutions he established to protect him are re-envisioned as always en route to being for inclusive justice. The auction blocks were always en route to becoming platforms for the oration of freedom dreams. The slaughterhouse always en route to Animal Liberation. If Obama is correct and America is indeed "an ever-expanding democracy" that incrementally included more and more people each generation, then by that logic we would celebrate a Dachau that every generation reduced its population. The "Boer Republics," the Urban Area Act should be praised as steps toward the ending of apartheid. We should not put away the writings on *White Man's Country* as they should guide us toward improving a multicultural Kenya, which was always their intention despite the kibokos and concentration camps.[47] In this logic, enslavement itself, it can be said, is a project of freedom in that slaves are sometimes freed, thus producing instances of freedom. The plantation is an ever-expanding democracy whenever there is a promissory note of manumission given, never mind the auction block. The state is an ever-expanding democracy with every change to anti-Black laws, never mind the empire. A man for freedom but holding a white man in chains is a walking contradiction. A man for freedom but holding a Black man in chains is a visionary.

Colonists, like Obama, in order to make their Americanist story work, rely on the ambiguity in the concept of freedom in the colony. It is presented as having a positive value rather than being the absence of enslavement. Presented thus as a thing, not the absence of a thing (enslavement), it is therefore presented as a thing that can be bestowed. A granting to the blacks by the Americans. No mention is made that it was they who kept them shackled to the wall. The patriot presents the state as a subject of history, a benevolent emancipator, expanding the realms of their generosity generation after generation. But freedom isn't gifted. Liberty does not expand. Enslavement retracts. Repression pulls back into itself with every push. Freedom is not given; enslavement ends. In fact, it may be a boon if the concept of freedom were abolished altogether (being as it is a term only intelligible in slave societies). Then the abusive might no longer be considered charitable when they stop their abuse.

The settler's narrative, which begins with Black enslavement as the norm and already ongoing, considers, in colonist logic, freedom as gifted and as a testament to the good nature of the masters. In this logic, every chain-pulling slave driver is a celebrated liberator every time they decide to release one of their captives. (Slave master praise is a concept with a popularity entirely unsurprising in a slave owner's republic.) No matter how earnestly the master yelps his revisionism and declares that he was always on the enslaved's side, he is not.

Freedom, however, is innate and inalienable. It was not invented by the slave masters nor the slave masters' country. Neither can bestow it, nor can it be gifted. On the contrary, any person or republic that has enslaved has signed their contract with obsolescence—this law we have codified in plantation fire.

Despite what faithful Obama testified to before the raucous applause of the liberal colonists, racism is not a stain. The idea of racism is in itself problematic and perhaps like freedom, it is time to rid ourselves of it altogether as it presents itself as something that occurs outside of colonialism. Something that colonialism, now the personified country, can one day, with enough goodwill, wipe away. So the colony can be stained with racism instead of the colony being an exercise in racism. Colonialism is racism in action. There is no subterranean country that can one day absolve itself from it. This is a fable constructed for the purposes of furthering the racist act of colonizing. The colony is not perfect, nor approaching perfection, and that occupation that on occasion passes progressive laws is celebrated at all is a demonstration of how deeply colonization has taken possession of psyches. So much so that genocide and slavery are merely a stain on the Constitutional Republic—not the settler's "constitutional republic" a stain on the histories of Black and Indigenous freedom. The violent universe in which Black people were forced to live their entire lives is reduced to a blip, an imperfection, a regrettable mistake of an institution that otherwise had freedom stayed on its mind. Black life is relegated to the slave quarters, a black mark upon the grand landscape and beauty of the Big House and plantation state. Our holocausts are spoken of as imperfections of a perfecting state. Our unfreedom, lives broken on the wheel of colonial totalitarianism, are the flaws of an "imperfect democracy." "Racism" is understood as ignorant and mean-spirited, a deep unfairness in law and attitude and as such it must be addressed with "anti-racism," some psychological tricks and book-learning—not the shoveling soot over colonialism's furnace. "We must come together to make America work." Why we "must," why we are ordered again into laboring for the master, is left unexplained. Why America is so indispensable to a free future, why unity with those who still wave the pro-slavery flags of the South and are louder each day with explicit calls for lynching is desirable is left unexplained. One day, when we have trained ourselves away from the concept of the slave and native, it will be rushingly and immediately clear that colonialism, in its enslavement and displacement, was, for all its gadgets, nothing more than a killing field. Then, espousing settler-colonial patriotism will be as frowned upon as other Holocaust denials.

Obama and his liberal colonists and Civil Rights apologists stand, back toward the state, in its defense, replying to this critique that one cannot judge the founding generation by their ignorance of the humanity of Black people. It bears repeating, however, that the humanity of Black people is and has always been immediately obvious. The claim that it is and was not is the central claim of white supremacy. But if we were charitable, which we are not, and granted that it was ignorance that led to these blood streaks, we remind the colonists and Obama, who has lived a life in defense of colonial law, of the colony's dictum *ignorantia legis neminem excusat*, "Ignorance of the law is no excuse," and present our own in the space of the anti-colony: "ignorance of Black life is no excuse." It doesn't matter what you did or didn't know; your time is up.

Toward the Killing of Civil Rights

The notion of "Civil Rights" converts the work of Black survival in racial totalitarianism into a story about colonial improvement. The rebellion against the white supremacist order is re-represented to the rebellious as a time of peaceful, orderly, and respectable protest in the country. Supplication while standing. Rights discourse implies negotiation and a relationship with the state—not escape from it. *Civil* indicates a life lived within the society, not the overturning of it. It begins, as much as it shouts, well-tamed and well domesticated—far safer for power than the image of any slave revolt. Tamed and taming it thus functions as a muzzle on the Black lumpen-led revolt against colonial totalitarianism. Like the slave muzzle to prevent temptations toward violence and taking more than what is owed, like the spit hood placed on Deobra Redden and Daniel Prude to silence and prevent impertinence and rebellion against the police order, to kill and thus quell the rumors and "prevent the negroes insurrections" it clamps down on Black radical thought. Of course, the immediate liberal response to an attack on Civil Rights will claim the attacker has a misapprehension of what Civil Rights is and was. That the Civil Rights movement cannot be reduced to placards, leaders, or a single King speech but daily struggle that was often violent, radical, and aggressive. But that this radical, even anti-colonial history of Civil Rights is not immediately present in the notion of Civil Rights itself demonstrates the powerful use of the muzzle. Civil Rights must be corrected, stretched to include the afterthought of anti-colonial action that it supposedly contains. The anti-colonial aspects of Civil Rights history exist as an exterior to it, always on the outside, to be shoehorned in. It is domestic. It is critical of the state but offers constructive criticism, not the "criticism of weapons." It openly pledges allegiance to colonialism and is not capacious enough or polices too well, or muffles, the entry of anti-colonial ideas. This alone is reason enough for the muzzle to be cast away.

The concept of "crime" co-opts experiences of harm, naming harmful actions criminal (lumping them in with non-harmful actions that destabilize capitalist order) so as to gin up anger against the criminalized and secure legitimacy for police power, its supposed enemy. Similarly, Civil Rights co-opts the history of Black uprising against apartheid and makes it a nationalist story about injustice that can be remedied in colonialism—legitimating the colony. The term is usefully and deliberately confused with the historical movement against white supremacist totalitarianism which has been a constant of Black life throughout all of modernity, transcending all invented borders. Civil Rights discourse occupying histories of Black activism, an attack against the concept can then easily be made to look like an under-appreciation for that Black sacrifice, just as an attack against the concept of crime positions the critic as a supporter of harm. The police, the state, in both cases quietly assume the role of the good and the necessary. So one cannot remove the slave muzzle without someone accusing you of siding with the masters—par for the course considering colonial ideologies' powers of inversion. Regardless, the muzzle must be removed.

It must be stated clearly that Civil Rights is impossible in settler-colonial occupation. A Civil Rights dream within colonialism requires the disappearing and domestication of Indigenous people. It expects a rights-future in settlement, a logic that denies Indigenous claim to land and space as a right. It reorients the Black struggle away from fleeing into the refuge of Seminole and Mohawk country and toward joining the occupation, joining the Buffalo Soldiers. Civil Rights imagines settler futurity[48] and as such is settler-colonial from the outset. In this settler-colonial imaginary, liberal interpretations of Civil Rights invent the central narrative of Black history as a struggle to fix the colonial house. Mammy is both freeing herself and setting their table. Black people should be praised for "abetting the rise of democracy in the US," they say, or some such paternalistic patting of negro heads for being at the forefront and the first builders of the colonists' project. "We built this country," we demand honor for having erecting of our own whipping post. In Civil Rights, the Black liberation struggle is a valiant brute's attempt to make America great again, to call it to live up to its ideals, instead of the quite specific task of allowing Black people to be hurt less and survive—to be unavailable to auctioneer and misanthrope. It is still impossible to think of Black self-care outside of service and self-sacrifice. It is expunged from public memory that Black resistance to these very patriots[49] who inspired a vengeful Francis Scott Key to celebrate the bombing of "the hireling and slave" in the colony's national anthem.[50] Africans' radical opposition to the colony is well dusted over and high school students are left only with Crispus Attucks—the faithful guard dog of the "American Revolution."

Civil Rights and liberal nationalists' proposed remedy to the "race question," namely the enslaved's forgiving of the master, the colonized forgiving the colonizer, has not resulted in Black liberation nor the abolition of the Jim Crow era. In fact, those reached out to with the olive branches today campaign not for the amelioration of Black suffering but for a return to the apex of open torture, muzzled mouths, banned books, and draconian laws to keep the native, the immigrant, the blacks in their place. Waiting on the Godot of the racists' enlightenment has only given the Confederacy time to regroup. Advocating a day more of waiting, for more hope for society to turn around, is complicity with our being stalled, complicity with the strengthening and emboldening of white supremacy. It has given more time for the silent—yet always heard—colonial majority to speak up boldly again. Again, mainstreaming the denial or minimizing of holocausts and returning to the old aims of Von Trothas and the Hitlers. To play their game of (im)plausible deniability. A "fourteen words" here, a using the 1930s fascist flag's motifs for the new far-right party there. They come to the fore again, with, at best, the appeasement of colonist liberals who despite now having the benefit of the hindsight of these past centuries to see what white supremacy is interested in once in unchallenged possession of the state apparatus, argue there is still room to persuade the hard-liners. But there is no more use in convincing liberals to cease knocking at the racist's door than there is in sweet-talking the racist. And we do not have the luxury of time or the interest in waiting to be saved by the progressing America of the liberal's imagination when the real America has us by the collar.

And every lynching volk song,⁵¹ every banned book, and every hoisted Confederate flag makes their intentions perfectly clear. Again, any person who is still waiting on the enlightenment of would-be slave masters in this era of open Nazism would wait even on the scaffold. Wait even in a noose. There is no point in being in communication or debate with that type of unseriousness. The colony has never discovered racial enlightenment. Or if this is it, it is trash.

The Civil Rights approach, the tinkering with colonial laws and policies, and attitudes should be killed. The bag of goods that "America" possesses some exceptional virtue, spiritual or the fruit of an exceptional wise group of white men, can self-rectify, and one day live up to ideals of equality and liberty it has not for one hour neared should no longer be bought. One might ask whether all countries and all polities that have ever existed are as deserving of hope and are such worthy conduits for inspiration, or if it is just America. And whether unfinished "words on a parchment" are truly a fetish object capable of rousing populations who still fight to keep monuments to kidnappers and child-sellers on state capitols.

Americanism and American nationalism encourage and train Black people from infancy to see their hope in American liberal and white abolitionism and believe the only route to freedom passes through America's change of heart. So many are taught to fear leaving identification with the colony as if Blackness is an inferior home. They are asked to pledge allegiance to the promise of colonialism. But neither Americanism nor the American is the master of Black fate. The future is not decided by them. And there are more people in the world than the American liberal. Even if supplication were to be made, there is no reason to choose such a lowly idol. Civil Rights places the muzzle on, and US nationalism puts on the blinders to train Black thought to the masters and masters' society for refuge. It masks the possibilities of international solidarity and says things are better on the plantation. A lie that says this is all there can be—that this world order is the only one possible, in all universes, and pragmatism is not about burning it away but making adjustments within it. A lie that contains the same hallucinogenic properties as the master's tale that there was nothing beyond the plantation's end, so don't run. But the end of "US racism" will not come from Americans. It will not come from another half-minute "racial reckoning." It will not come from men and women salivating at the prospect of the return of mass deportations but who, after a few jokes exchanged on the factory floor, begin to realize "we are not so different after all." No, it will be made obsolete by the interchange between racialized people the world over who have no interest in waiting at the racists' doorstep.

Americanism has been very successful in presenting to the "domestic" population America as a project of liberty despite the absurdity of the freedom-loving state having the highest incarceration rate in the world. Despite having a Civil War aimed at preserving slavery, where masters and their apologists, half the population, threw themselves into the mud for the right to maintain neck shackles on children. Despite being one of the last to abolish (partially) chattel slavery and having military bases all over the Black world and elsewhere. Americanism being for freedom is not laughed at in the colony, not always laughed out in the rest of the world, as it has been laughed at in the slave quarters, evidence of its status as an ideological superpower. Its ideological power growing more sophisticated and in tandem with its military might, the collapse of rival superpowers and their counter-critique, neo-colonialism's ripping the voice box off of the "Third world," and the Civil Rights effect. Domestic propaganda is not merely a power over the colonized within the colony but the notion of an always-to-be-redeemed America helps imperialism abroad. But however incessant that hum of America the good, it remains the case that colonialism does not improve. There is no possibility of adequate reform in a slave state. What is at the heart of "America" is that black lives don't matter. America is indistinguishable from this central tenet. It is as foundational to it as Indigenous lives and land do not matter. American freedom, always to be read as settlers' freedom, is the freedom to do what you will on the mounds of the dark-skinned and killed.

Civil Rights is a kind of slave bible. It has hints and impressions of moving passages, but it is edited down so that whatever truth is in it serves the purposes of slavery. In it we are trained to obey our masters, to be peaceful, walk orderly, preferably on the sidewalk, and be heard but not disturb the divine peace. We are trained into an imagination that does not permit a quest for the return of our pounds of flesh. Black war, Black resistance is only a further construction of the house of empire. Black rebellion is judo-flipped back into servility. Black anger is hushed into the good order at the heart of a well-policed society, the bargain being, after we are long enough on good behavior, freedom will be granted. But John does not free Adam after faithful service. The famous "promissory note," King speaks of, will never have sufficient funds as colonialism and its settler nations are an instance of white supremacy rather than an entity tragically flawed by it.

It is not said enough, but the people who spat in the face of Black anti-colonialists claiming that America had changed, as evidenced by the election of Barack Obama, were wrong. They were wrong and faced no consequences for that error. No penalty equal to the ones Black radicals received for being correct in their "pessimism." Liberal media continue to pay and appeal to the Black liberal for a type of wisdom of the natives as radicals still languish in prisons or exile and are hunted down by liberal politicians and state agencies fresh off their DEI and implicit bias training. They were wrong about change in America as were the people who believed it had changed after the Civil Rights Acts. As were the people who thought it changed at Reconstruction. As were the people who thought it changed after the end of the Transatlantic slave trade. They will be wrong as long as they personify the process of colonization as the country. As long as they have not departed the cult of nationalism that dresses an abattoir as a friendly giant with personality flaws. A spell that could not be cast on Adam, who saw the state in the nude as his handcuff. Or on Sam, a man severely beaten and forced to wear an "iron collar affixed about his neck" for life as punishment for endeavoring to "promote a Negro Insurrection in this Colony."[52] It was never a powerful enough conceit for those who were possessed by everything and everyone except the colonial "we."

In the liberal colonist spin, every evidence of the intractability of the violence of colonialism is presented as a stubborn and tragic "legacy." Every policy reform doomed from the start to go nowhere, or in a few years to be met with whitelash, every Reconstruction followed by Redemption, is just how the cookie crumbles. In this way, the liberal joins the conservative willingly or unwillingly (and we are not charitable enough to believe intent matters) in the manufacture of the stasis that is the colonial situation. Together, they have groomed a significant amount of Black people into patience with the genocidal. This is also why both are violently against anti-colonialism, the end of stasis.

The propagandist for colonialism, whether styled liberal or conservative, erects self-replicating images of the colony from the settlers' perspective, at the expense of the colonized. Distorting colonial reality, excluding histories, and then inviting sanitized versions of it back under the label of inclusivity. And this continues infinitely, carried on the language of progress and improvement, carrots to move the colonized to draw the wheel of occupied land another and another day—with a promise of the dream—for everyone—just inches out of reach, as long as we keep trucking, pulling the gears of the anti-Black state. It is the same promise that the master always gives the slave. That John gave

Adam.⁵³ The promise of unmolested nationhood given to Palestine, of independence to the colonies of Europe. Keep on truckin'—freedom is just out of reach. Don't mind the whipping—they are tragedies that will one day be represented as histories to be included in the tapestry for the state. Your colonizer is surprisingly your ally, even your compatriot.

It is precisely this misrepresentation of affairs that the maroon has run from. Has shoved that soiled dream off their back like the harness it is. The fugitive says with David Walker "a groveling servile and abject submission to the lash of tyrants . . . are not the natural elements of the blacks, as the Americans try to make us believe."⁵⁴ The runaway says we are not their mules, their hewers of freedom. We are not the errand boys on the road to a more livable colonialism. The Black liberty the master promises he keeps in his fist in his pocket is probably not there, and if it is it is enough of an offense that he does not give it up now. It is the business of long-colonialism to turn everyone into unsuspecting negroes. To work the colonized until they are husks of themselves and primed for the fire. But the carrot of "hope" has too long been allowed to molest the donkey, now finally tired of being beaten and driven nowhere. It is the business of revolt to fork that "dream" into the furnace. A practice fundamentally at odds with the complaint and plea that the dream "did not include me," despite Black liberal obfuscation that claims they are one and the same thing.

The question naturally arises: What would it mean to tear off the muzzle of Civil Rights? To consider Black thought as a vast architectural palace we are free to roam and one is not only to be stationed at the colored fountain of *MLKism*. To be no longer domesticated and apply to our estimation of the colony and our approaches to it Black and anti-colonial traditions not penned in the "Civil Rights tradition." To not accept the devolution sold to us as progress. The slave revolt becoming the general strike, becoming the peaceful protest, becoming the police-escorted parade protest, and now banning the Black literature, banning even diversity, equity and inclusion, banning Blackness altogether so that all that exists is a muzzled acceptance of totalitarian power, dazed and murmuring, "we are all Americans." What might emerge after immersion in maroon and fugitive thought forced into hiding by a well-guarded and well-policed liberal view of struggle? A manifesto of escape, a politics of fence-jumping. And to think of the Herero struggle, the Black European migrant struggle, favela survival, as not Black elsewhere but templates for not resistance but the onward charge against the white supremacist empire. If the muzzle was removed, the blinders cast off, would we not think of employing an anti-apartheid struggle to perennial Jim Crow society? Pick up again Lorenzo Kom'boa Ervin's planned boycott of American businesses?[55] Think of the *Boycott, Divestment and Sanctions* movement not only for settler-colonies overseas but this one. And as the country is nothing but the people who agree with its conceit and conspire to imagine it, would we not boycott the colonial imagination as well? What would it take to see a Soweto Uprising in the Confederate states?

J. Edgar Hoover warned of a Mau Mau in America,[56] what would it mean if his efforts to prevent an anti-colonial struggle to free the land from the "White Man's Country" were not totally successful? It may be time to no longer be had, and to force off the path of the slave revolt into an American fight for Civil Rights, equality, and an end to racism—moribund efforts in a settler-colonialism that still stands. It may be time to set torch to these new and any future Black Codes.

Chapter 4

SUPPLICATION IN THE SPECTACLE

The runaway cannot be arrested. They can only be assaulted. The binding of the free, that has been normalized as arrest and legitimated by the settler-colonial order as part of "criminal justice" has not been convincing to those who reject the planter's authority and the rule of their institutions. The handcuff is still the shackle. The officer is still the overseer.[1]

The colony, for all its post-Emancipation, post-*Brown v. Board* justice, reforms, and rebranding, has still not found it necessary to rid itself of the coffle. For all the "change" that has been promised, in every generation, since the time of Adam and John, settler society has not managed to beat its addiction to witnessing the scene of the disobedient African forced to prostrate themselves on the ground, hands tied, and transported back to the plantation.[2] Colonialism does not change. Despite the sleight of hand of liberal nationalists who use historical periodization to crown every necessary tinkering in its operation as a watershed moment and a step along the ladder of progress, the interests of the slaveholder and segregationist remain paramount. The *White Citizens' Councils* rebranding as *Conservative Citizens' Councils* in order to be "mainstreamed"[3] might have assisted the liberal in holding their hands up and preaching, "Thank God, almighty things have changed!" But this is not enough to draw the anti-colonialist back to colonial nationalism. The runaway has not lost object permanence.

Just as the slaveholding and segregationist interest did not evaporate after *Emancipation* and *Brown v. Board*, marronage did not end after the semi-abolition and evolution of slavery. The politics and practices of marronage have been sublimated into Black and Indigenous anti-colonialism, Black separatism, African Internationalism, and quests for radical autonomy, as the totalitarianism of colonial capitalism, that is, plantation conditions have extended into the present era. Runaways had to survive outside of the licit economy. Considered self-stealing property, labor absconders, and deserters, their very existence was criminal. The methods of survival, liberating other property from slave owners, food, hogs, horses, jewelry, boats,[4] forging free passes and badges (required to be worn by enslaved people away from their plantation),[5] hiring themselves out, and trading with enslaved populations and others were criminalized. To be both designated a slave and not incorporated by white power was illegal, threatening, and sinful. Today, in our post-*Emancipation* period of supposed racial progress, development, and democratization, there is still a class that survives largely on the outside of the licit economy. Who are the subjects of the illicit and "informal economies" of the world, the starving and the unemployed, the "drug dealers," criminalized sex workers, students, undocumented workers, hustlers, and con artists, parolees. The colony's Black lumpenproletariat. A class that Frantz Fanon described as *the* radical and revolutionary class in the settler-colony.[6] Not the workers who—at least in the settler-colony—are relatively privileged despite being for the most part bootless wage-slaves and often disciplined by the workforce into an intellectual detention,[7] but the unemployed, semi and "underemployed," the Black industrial reserve army.[8] This class, born of the colony's native quarters, where you can die anywhere and of anything, and where people are packed on top of people and buildings squeezed together,[9] in the slums, shacks, ghettos, homeless, and migrant encampments of the world, although patrolled and hyper-surveilled, have also, of necessity, developed a form of opacity in the bandos, trap houses, motels, street corners, lamplit project building lobbies, and dark alleys that shield them and their activities from the predatory gaze of settler power.[10] The hood, the garrison, the shantytown functioning partially as the maroon swamp. The danger of the destitute, the threat of the denizens in the unlivable spaces of settler territory, the "other side of the tracks," terrifies and disgusts the propertied classes, and these bounce between requiring the industrial reserve class in existence to provide short-term labor,[11] and discipline workers with the threat of lumpen financial instability on one hand and fantasies of slum clearance on the other.

Just as maroon settlements were constantly raided by military officers and runaway slave-hunters as a fight against their predations on the city, the hood, this new native quarter, is subject to frequent police raids. Just as there were heroic stories of runaways escaping to the maroon settlement, in slums all over the world there are stories of the outlaw escaping police clutches and being hidden in the native quarter by the armed power of gangs,[12] and/or being shielded in the folds of the poor. But the native quarter, being "trapped" within the discursive and imagined political space of the colony, is never as free as maroon space no matter how much more the runaway is pursued. The runaway has never been interpellated by nationalist ideology as a slave. The Black lumpen, escapee of wage-dependence, is nevertheless often arrested by colonial ideas. Often they still consider themselves an American as a matter of natural fact[13]—however qualified, and however distant they are from Americanness. The runaway has shuffled off their master's coils and clothes, the lumpen might sport Dipset's red, white, and blue.

For the Black lumpenproletariat, captivity is a feature of life. Police cruisers shark-circle the block. The sexual and emotional abuse that is prisons and jails is so rampant that the torture of incarceration has, for many, become a rite of passage. Outside, the calls to "free my nigga," however charged and symbolic, are expected to be impotent and never to amount to a call inspiring another Stono rebellion. In the native quarters, patriotism can be bought, shackles are often[14] successfully rebranded as handcuffs, arbitrary fiats of settler interest are accepted as "law," and colonized attack colonized as a proxy,[15] as the architects of their condition are out of reach. And yet, as if the plantation hatreds of the "cruel and incorrigible runaway" were hereditary, settler-colonial society[16] has hated the figure of this denizen of lumpen space, the "Black criminal," the thug and "ghetto dude,"[17] the hoe-Jezebel, and has used these figures to impugn all Black people regardless of class. Like the vengeance brought onto the heads of the insolent enslaved, the trespassers of the color line, and the African Indigenous insurgents, settler white supremacists today still seek to stage the spectacle of murdering the Black fugitive of capital.

Arrest provides settler society, always nostalgic for chattel slavery,[18] the theater of the coffle. A show of putting down "the blacks" who were disrespectful of authority, the capture of the fugitive of normative order. The disobedient black is "caught," forced supine, prostrate, vulnerable and subject to the whims, the mercy and vengeance of the patroller. The pleasure at the sight of stripping, fondling, manhandling, and dragging the African under the guise of security, managing threats to society, and social regulation is dramatized in the "usual suspects"[19] pushed into the cruiser. It is not only the constabulary that has emerged from the slave patrol[20] (which in turn evolved from the need to deal with runaways and enslaved peoples' unrest)[21] but the scene of arrest is carried over from the spectacle of the caught runaway. The yelping negro hounds now disciplined K-9 units sicced on Black people who are resisting capture.[22]

Complementing the scene of arrest, of course, is the scene of summary execution. Slave patrols—both professional as well as with the volunteer slave catchers—[23] were often permitted to kill runaways at will with no fear of punishment.[24] The video of the killing of Walter Scott showed the officer Michael Slager slowly aiming and firing into Walter Scott's back as he was running away after a fight over the officer's taser. The officer, apparently unaware that he was being recorded by a witness, moved over to his victim's body, placed something near it, then called and said he shot Scott after a scuffle with his taser and that he feared for his life. In stating his fear Michael drew out this license to kill the runaway, that is, those "resisting arrest," a colonist's privilege which offers unlimited credibility to the officer and deputized civilian or (vigilante)[25] no matter how stark the video evidence or how unlikely it is that the armed, paramilitary-trained officer feared the unarmed runaway.[26] John wanted the state to catch Adam because he feared for his life, police and slave catchers could be excused for shooting the runaway on sight if they feared for their lives, and the police charged with murdering a Black person can expect a not guilty verdict if they state they feared for their lives. Those who have lived for centuries under the terror of their disposability, under race massacres, negro hound hunts, deaths in custody, those who fear for their lives every day surviving the multidirectional dangers of the native quarter are excluded from this license to kill. Indeed the slave, the black, is to be always unarmed. Those stopped by armed men ordered by gangs with a reputation for anti-Black violence and led by men who wear "white power patches" and train under "killology,"[27] are not allowed to fear. Not only are they not allowed to shoot in self-defense, but they are ordered to make no sudden moves. They must not run. It is unreasonable for them to fear for their lives as they are brought captive into the holds of the cruiser to be processed in the holds of the police station. Into rooms which, as Mark Fuhrman, alleged evidence-planter turned police expert on police procedure, put it, "got the smell of niggers that have been beaten and killed in there for years."[28]

The body-cam footage of the killing of Laquan McDonald showed a Black boy sauntering through the street in defiance of the law before he was summarily shot by Jason Van Dyke. The police said Laquan McDonald lunged at the officer, but after being forced to turn over the video, which disproved this, Jason was arrested in 2019 and got out in 2022 for good behavior. Where Laquan McDonald was killed for interrupting the order of the street, Jordan Davis was killed for interrupting sonic white rule with the cultures of the Black lumpenproletariat. Michael Dunn said he asked politely for Jordan to turn his music down, and when he refused, he shot him because he feared for his life. The media would offer that there were two sides to every story, suggesting the fear of blacks must be heard out. This was the line at least until it was discovered that Michael said, "I hate that thug music" and "if more people would arm themselves and kill these fucking idiots when they're threatening you, eventually they may take the hint and change their behavior."[29] Mike Brown's murder launched a conversation about whether or not Mike Brown had his hands up, that is, assumed the proper prostrate position in arrest. If he did, then that might grant us a conversation about whether or not he was justly murdered. Darren Wilson said that he saw the devil in Mike Brown as Brown lunged at him in insolent and rebellious violence (a charge George Zimmerman also leveled at Trayvon Martin), and so he killed him and then, like Zimmerman, he cashed in his "I feared for my life" chip. Mike Brown's body was left on the ground and the flower memorial destroyed,[30] which community members said was a deliberate attempt to intimidate them. An act that calls back to the heads of rebel slaves left on spikes and signposts, and the bodies of Black people hung by mobs displayed on trees. Of course, Black people forced to plead fare no better. George Floyd and Eric Garner, surviving in the illicit economy, were strangled while pleading. Elijah McClain pleaded, offering even that he was an introvert but was killed by police, with the collusion of paramedics, after a 911 call about a suspicious person.[31] A white man called 911 to report 'hoodlums,' said that he was going to do something about it, and then shot a Black teen from behind his garage door.[32] Police shot Andre Maurice Hill while he was standing in his garage, did not provide first aid. Instead, like Slager, he required the body to roll over and put its hands up.[33] Neither these nor millions more during this half-millennia-long punitive expedition against Black people will lead even the best colonist, however successful their rebrand as an "abolitionist," to an abandonment of settler-colonial society.

Unlike white supremacist eras of the past, in which it was freely argued that the slaves were happy, a time when "anti-Tom" novels and essays were written to present police and slaveholders as victims of the ungrateful and dangerous African aggressor, for the first time in the history of the colony, settler power no longer has unquestioned control of the discursive apparatuses of the public sphere. The widespread availability of smartphone cameras, which, unlike body cams and security cameras, are for now out of the reach of immediate police manipulation, has verified the native quarter's (slave) narratives of torture. Similarly, the rise of social media, especially *Black Twitter* before its occupation by *X*, has meant that the state and capital no longer maintain total control of publication and distribution, making it possible for non-police(d) narratives to avoid stifling and banishment to the bantustans of Hip-Hop, Ethnic Studies, and formal Black radical writing. A crack in totalitarian control of discourse has led to a crisis where even the liberal instinct to both-sidesism, to search for a justification for their desire to offer the benefit of the doubt to a mob of folks still clad in the blood-spangled hand-me-downs of participants of the race riots, is exposed and shamed. After incidents like the recording of conservative students and correctional officers re-creating the scene of George Floyd's killing, it became increasingly difficult to spin the lynch mob's bloodlust as a societal problem resulting from "a lack of trust between police and the community they serve." Those who rush to the online scene of the red taped-off, filmed murder of an insolent Negro with "reasonable minds can disagree" stutter as the mob invents increasingly implausible defenses of killings. New 21-foot rules.[34] As it becomes undeniable that what is operative is the same old desire for the destruction of the disobedient "black" and not an interest in uniform obedience to the rule of law and respect, that the disarticulated lynch mob is not driven by anxieties and grievances, as MSNBC and PBS offer, each video of murder, each absurd defense, each white-voiced anger at the protests for Black life demonstrates the interest in eliminating all Black life outside of that which is prostrate. Permitting life only to that obsequious flesh that the totalitarian regiments of slavery attempted to tenderize into being. The suitably-dressed, well-behaved, housed and locatable black whose speech only confirms and assures, offers back rubs and politely disagrees. And even there, alongside their live token, the settler, in uttering the "I feared for my life" magic phrase, claims the slave owner's *patria potestas*. The master's inalienable right to kill the prostrated.

Just as the videos of killing verify the lumpen narrative of an ongoing pogrom the *Replies* sections of social media sites prove that contrary to putative belief, the lynch mob has not disappeared. There, the crowds still gather around the video-spectacle of the Black being killed to point, mock, gawk, and celebrate the deaths. It becomes difficult to say the colony has changed when comments sections, like a hidden witness's cellphone recording of lynch mob society's internal dialogue, feature accounts leaving messages that, taken collectively, spell out the same negrophobic desires of all other generations. Fantasizing greater white supremacist violence, not less, at the site of the hung. One does not need to snoop around on *8Chan or Truth Social* to know that it would read somewhere between a lynching bee's sneers and flyering after the Nuremberg rally. It is difficult to deny the lynch mob society's return to state office after the second election of Donald Trump. One cannot make out the protestations that Trumpism's victory reflects "the disgruntled frustrations of people feeling progress has left them behind" over the echoes of *Dixie*, the Confederate anthem, reverberating from Madison Square Garden's new American Nazi rallies two weeks before the election.

This celebration of Black death and torture, the ubiquity of its representation, the permanent face position of shock and performed regret from the media, the predictable immunity of the negrophobe aggressor, and the pressing of lynch mob society against our private screens have spurred a global Black lumpen revolt. A revolt responding to and mediated through the society of the white supremacist spectacle. The task of contesting the space of its counter spectacle, to quarantine the Black uprising, to bring the neo-slave revolt to heel and return it to the preferred prostrate position of peaceful, ineffective protest has fallen to the liberal media.

Chris and Kyle

On November 19, 2021, the afternoon of the "Not guilty on all counts" verdict in Kyle Rittenhouse's trial for fatally shooting two protestors during the 2020 uprising for Black lives that spread to Kenosha, Wisconsin, President Joe Biden gave a statement. He replied to a reporter's question about whether he stood by his past comments linking Kyle's actions with white supremacy with: "Look, I stand by what the jury has concluded. The jury system works, and we have to abide by it."[35] In an echo of Obama's statement after the killing of Trayvon Martin: "We are a nation of laws, and a jury has spoken," Biden, too, washed his hands of the matter. The liberal administration "regretfully" deferred to the wisdom of the colonial court, sanctioning the lynch mob's violence and instructing its victims to obey. They did this even as white supremacist power has openly defied desegregation court orders since 1954 and, even during that year, officials of the previous Trump administration were ignoring court-ordered subpoenas. The subpoenas being defied were requesting information on the former administration's refusal to abide by election rules and its attempted overthrow of the state. Thus, the "rule of law" concept was exposed again as not the state's strictures for the production of order and good conduct universally and equally applied to all citizens but a disciplining rhetorical device to keep the colonized in check. What is sanitized in liberal ideology as "our flawed legal system" and "unequal application of the law"[36] is, apartheid. It is the federalization of the *Black Codes*. Kyle's defense argued successfully that he traveled to Kenosha with an AR-15 to protect a car dealership during the "Black Lives Matter riots" and was set upon by what the mob temporarily named "Antifa" and "Black Lives Matter punks."[37] Now enriched with crowdfunding and made famous through book deals and white nationalist television interviews, Kyle went home to be carried on the shoulders of lynch mob society.

Later in the afternoon, Biden issued a statement from the White House, closing out the Obama routine. First, the declaration of sympathy: the verdict, he said, "will leave many Americans feeling angry and concerned, myself included." He followed with the updated warning to the disconsolate Blacks: "violence and destruction of property have no place in our democracy," a statement which might have been uttered by Dr. King or Kyle himself. An order for the revolt to transform into the law-abiding, civil, police-managed, respectable "demonstration." The nonviolent protest being the animation of Black supplication—the walking, marching, anti-slavery medallion. The president added that the "Federal authorities have been in contact with [Wisconsin] Governor Evers's office to prepare for any outcome in this case . . . offered support . . . to ensure public safety." Rittenhouse's patrol of the angry blacks and the killing of one in their camp would now be assisted by hundreds of federal agents deployed by the liberal administration. Finally, after centuries, some state support for the volunteer militia putting down the slave revolt. Federal occupation of the Black uprising in the alliance of settler and liberal administrative state against the enslaved's unrest.

On the day of the verdict, Chris Hayes, host of the *All In with Chris Hayes* prime time evening news program on MSNBC—the liberal counter to the white nationalist Fox News, (as it happens, Fox News is the most watched news channel in the colony)—tweeted "Honestly hope that kid takes the opportunity to turn his life around and tries to make the world a better place rather than pursuing the George Zimmerman [killer of Trayvon Martin] Life Trajectory."[38] Hayes, interestingly enough, is not otherwise given to fanciful hope. He once called "moderate Republican" Senator Susan Collins's hope that President Trump would change course after learning from his first impeachment "manifestly absurd."[39] But for the alleged white power sign flashing Kyle Rittenhouse, it seemed for Hayes, too, hope springs eternal.

Chris Hayes' hope in Kyle Rittenhouse, and white liberals' perpetual hope in the coming around of racist America is costly. And it is a price their victims are required to pay. One can hope that a man who killed people protesting in support of ending police murder of Black people might "turn his life around." One might brush aside the flashed white power sign, the riling up and emboldening of individuals on the side of killing protestors, of sitting down with giddy, congratulatory white nationalist news personalities and politicians; one might put away the girthy, hot-breathed history of white nationalist mob violence against Black people fighting for their lives and say, "I hope he understands" "he did something terrible and seeks forgiveness," because what is waged in the gamble is Black life. If you are wrong, all that is lost are more of the traditional targets of white supremacist violence—Black people, Black people especially. It is not only the killers who believe Black life is disposable. Black liberation theologian James H. Cone identified the white liberal's patience with cruelty. In 1978 anti-apartheid thinker Steve Biko put it as follows:

> First the black-white circles are almost always a creation of white liberals. As a testimony to their claim of complete identification with the blacks, they call a few "intelligent and articulate" blacks to "come around for tea at home", where all present ask each other the same old hackneyed question "how can we bring about change in South Africa?" The more such tea-parties one calls the more of a liberal he is and the freer he shall feel from the guilt that harnesses and binds his conscience. Hence he moves around his white circles—whites-only hotels, beaches, restaurants and cinemas—with a lighter load, feeling that he is not like the rest of the others. Yet at the back of his mind is a constant reminder that he is quite comfortable as things stand and therefore should not bother about change. Although he does not vote for the [National Party] (now that they are in the majority anyway), he feels quite secure under the protection offered by the Nats and subconsciously shuns the idea of a change. This is what demarcates the liberal from the black world. The liberals view the oppression of blacks as a problem that has to be solved, an eye sore spoiling an otherwise beautiful view. From time to time the liberals make themselves forget about the problem or take their eyes off the eyesore. On the other hand, in oppression the blacks are experiencing a situation from which they are unable to escape at any given moment. Theirs is a struggle to get out of the situation and not merely to solve a peripheral problem as in the case of the liberals. This is why blacks speak with a greater sense of urgency than whites".[40]

There is no scarcity of cable news hosts, stenographers of liberal sentiment, comfortable behind their news desks beside the smiling, articulate Black liberal expert guest, ready to ask in faux urgency "how can we bring about change in America?" Who do not vote for the Nationalist Populist party but are certain that the "tragedies" and "senseless violence" will be forever far removed from their door. Who could stare at the fatigue-wearing volunteer auxiliary force self-appointed to patrol the riotous blacks who killed two people and see a baby-faced kid who could turn his life around.

Of course, it makes no more sense to hope that Hayes will turn his life around either. Or that he or his producers might book radical Black activists and participants in the uprising instead of the Black liberal preachers[41] and academics[42] invited to explain them, who are prepared to minister and soothe, extinguishing the anger of the revolt with banter and in the baritone of the faithful servant. Or that Rachel Maddow will, and turn away from mourning how racial justice seems always just out of reach "for our country," nightly. No hope in MSNBC, or CNN, or the other American liberal cable news channels, or in "progressive" congresspeople. Indeed, it makes no sense to hope in those privileged enough to referee the debate on the pattern of racial violence but need not speak with any urgency. Even as the Kristallnacht of our everyday has spread out from the native quarters and now invaded the private residence of the fortune-fortified Speaker of the House,[43] even amidst declarations of intention to arrest the media, the liberal media is incapable of seeing anti-Black oppression as anything more than an eyesore spoiling the beautiful view of "our country." It is as if they are structurally incapable of understanding, despite that Baldwin quote on their screensaver warning that if they come for us in the morning they will be coming for you that night.[44]

It is a mistake to share in hope with those who can afford to be wrong. Even with those who cannot. Like that segment of still hopeful Black people trained to wait on "equality" who have been waiting for centuries, watching entire nations rise and disintegrate while they wither, hat in hand, at the door of settler-colonialism. A door leading to, as even that greatest of mustachioed baby-faced hopers suspected, a burning house. Hope, once an ally to strugglers everywhere, has been cheapened in such hands, beaten to a pulp, watered down, shopped around, and too quick to declare, if not mission accomplished, then "is this a turning point?" at every mild adjustment in colonial administrative practice. Hope within colonialism has died, and its killers masquerade in its corpse.

4. Supplication in the Spectacle 133

On May 28th, the second night of the 2020 uprising launched from Minneapolis, Minnesota after the death of George Floyd, MSNBC's Rachel Maddow of "The Rachel Maddow Show," a program immediately following Chris Hayes' *All In*, spoke directly to her audience. She informed them that "the mayor of Minneapolis, Jacob Frey, is . . . trying to hold his city together as the whole country looks at Minneapolis tonight, basically just holding our breath."[45] Of course, the "we" said to be "holding our breath" was not the colonized watching in anti-colonial hope that the society that regularized the arbitrary killing of Black people would be somewhat gutted. It is those worried about the damage the violence of a revolt in the colony might mean for property and order. This perspective is not the universal perspective. It was not the perspectives of those rising against masters' society. It is the perspective of the white liberal audience that is so easily fitted with the term "we" because the Black and suffering and radical are unspeaking animals in white liberal thought, only to be seen prostrated and not to be heard save in plea. The "we," the national we, is the settler we. The we of the imagined community reading in horror about the slave revolt in their newspapers, not the we chased down by the slave-hunt—the department store window-smashing we. No anti-colonialist was "holding their breath" for the safety of the plantation. None joined police and mayors' press conferences in tears asking "we sick?" in a state governed by Amy Klobuchar elected to Congress, like most Democrats and all conservatives, through a promise to expand and fortify some of the most discriminatory institutions in human history, that is, US law and prisons. A governor, who, like the other "Democrat moderates" like Pete Buttigieg, Kamala Harris, and Michael Bloomberg, suddenly found themselves out in the cold as the uprising made pride in the records of supporting the institutions of Black harm a liability overnight. An uprising so impactful that the intellectual space it opened up produced a brief four-year reprieve from lynch mob society's onward march to take back the state apparatus. One that Kamala Harris and Minnesota governor Tim Walz' presidential campaign spectacularly failed to extend despite its unending overtures to American Nazism and attempts to tempt attendees of the Trump campaign's pre-election race rally in Madison Square Garden away from Trumpism with promises of shared government and Dick and Liz Cheney.

As the urban cane fields of Minnesota burned, Maddow had the city's mayor on for an interview. He had apparently memorized anti-racist talking points about "institutionalized racism" and could drop points about racially restrictive covenants and 400 years of anti-Black oppression at will, using the familiar disingenuously earnest tone of the progressive's stump speech. But he did not camouflage the fact that although he intended to let the community express "righteous anger" and sadness that the looting must stop. That is, he was engaged in the management of social unrest by using the policing tactic of opening a release valve by letting the oppressed express their temper tantrum for a while, burn a few things, and then tire themselves out and "we" fall back into the regular order of unprotested police murders, or what the colony calls "peace."[46] Maddow invited the mayor to speak. Not the bowels of the colonial prison, nor the Black lumpenproletariat in the streets who are less "unheard" than they are uninvited. I expected no guest on the Rachel Maddow show who would ask why those, like MSNBC, who were putatively for social justice would be holding their breath when social justice was attempted to be taken after it had been wrongly denied. Or ask why would "we all" hold our breath at the anger brought on after a public suffocation? The relieved, excited, cautiously optimistic, pleased, vengeful who finally, after so long a time, could luxuriate in this likely brief moment of allowed exhalation, are never invited to a sit-down on colonist media. And if the colonized were, and explained that "we are all enjoying a useful response to negrophobic police sport-killing," not only would our "we" not be recognized, but we would be politely invited off-set. The colonized have never been given access to the colonial's ideological apparatus. The "representation" of Black bodies occupying the seats of capitalism's news anchors and journalists, tokens who are proscribed from departing from the colonist line, is not the same as the colonized seizing the means of ideological production. Al Sharpton has been given a television show. Mumia Abu-Jamal spent thirty years on death row. Ken Saro-Wiwa was hung,[47] *Hood Communist* was removed from *Twitter, and* journalists are murdered in heaps in Gaza. Colonist media can be no more reformed or "diversified" than the colony's constabulary.

The white abolitionist's "we" never includes the insurrectionist slave. The liberal's "we" does not include those angry at Black suffering—and those who express Black outrage must have it nullified by colonist hope and set on a path toward forgiveness, reconciliation, and the racist's peace.[48] In a podcast interview, "What the 1960s can teach us about modern-day protests," published at the outbreak of the uprising, PBS's Hari Sreenivasan conducted with Omar Wasow included the following exchange:

> OW: What I see in the 1960s is that counties that were near non-violent protests vote more in the coalition that is aligned

with Black interests ... at the same time what I also see is that counties that are close to violent protests vote more conservatively.

HS: So when we see peaceful protests we respond in a way that thinks about human rights and civil rights, but when we see violent protests, or riots, we respond in a way that wants more law and order? Is that roughly, am I summarizing it correctly?

OW: Yeah, I think that is a very good summary...[49]

Let's leave aside whether the violent protests they speak of include violence against property, and the specious conclusion that the violence in protests is what leads counties to vote conservatively. Who are the "we" who respond to the protestors? The "we" who see the protests and then want more law and order? It certainly is not the protestors. Maddow and Sreenivasan's "we" who observes is a we with a view from the voting public, the public that has historically not invited the Black lumpenproletariat to political power or to speak freely. The protestors are the objects, a part of the event that is occurring. The voters and the onlookers are the subjects. From this position, they are able to warn Black people without explicitly warning them that although people sympathize with the "horrific" video of the killing of George Floyd, their patience will run out. It is the national "we" which is deployed to discipline Black uprisings, to encourage peaceful—that is to say, non-effective—protest, and, as if an official branch of police power, to warn that the white public will only be sympathetic to rebellious Blacks for so long. The colonized is not included in the we who sees, who votes, who is the public. And yet the colonizing we, the "we" that is given political prerogative, is considered a we that is diverse. When the door of the colonist "we" is open, it is the "we" of the pleading and forgiving peaceful Blackness who are invited in, not the revolting we, which it seeks to replace. It is the we of the Black politicians somberly affirming "We know Joe [Biden].[50]" Professors and pastors who serve as the uncles or aunties, the good slave of the slaveholder's imagination, are brought onto television programs to offer comfort to liberal news anchors. Part native informants, part spinners, representing the Black anti-colonial revolt as a Civil Rights pleading, they are there to displace and remove the voice box of the Black uprising. The revolt's *We* is barred from entry from the colonist "we" even as colonialism forcibly reminds us that progress has been made in terms of representation. The colonist's we disciplines. It is the we of "we are a nation of laws" and "leaving the sidewalk during a protest is un-American." (Indeed, the Civil Rights invention of the peaceful protest being understood as American tradition is evidence enough of anti-racist Civil Rights' incorporation into the racist state.)[51] It always seems to be unintentionally revealed that they imagine "we" to include only those who look at the cotton fields from the parlor window—the Black liberal "expert guest" in the doorway, balancing the tea service set. The figure of the supplicating slave displaces the revolt. Black radical thought is occupied in public by the platforming of the radically token. The colonial world is a world in which the object of the blacks is represented, proliferates, is ubiquitous in the society of white supremacist spectacle, but the Black noncompliant, and anti-colonial thought remains uninvited. In the colony, Black humanity is not the black expected to come to dinner.

Forced to "Take a Knee"

In the heat of the night of revolt, when stores were burning and riot police were deployed to contain the uprising against pleasure killing and general white supremacist impunity on display in the recorded slow-murder of George Floyd a month earlier, Cory Booker stepped out and delivered a speech.[52] It included the lines, "It's why so many Black Americans scream out 'Do you see me? I do not have your equal justice under law. Do you see me? . . . I matter. I matter. Black lives matter. Black bodies matter. America, I love you do you see me? Do you know my experiences? Do you see the failings of our ideals?'"[53] Although not nearly as iconic and impactful as the speeches considered in the previous chapter, it is nevertheless important to reflect upon here. It is almost a too perfect representation of the liberal stamping out the slave revolt and placing in it its stead their ventriloquizing of the Supplicant Negro.

I find this speech to be horrific. To transform the memories of the dead and injured into puppets of supplication to the colonial state. Turning still-warm corpses into the "Emancipation Memorial" statue on Capitol Hill, the kneeling, naked slave being petted by the "the great Emancipator" president. To speechify on Black death and exclude so perfectly Black people from the intended audience. To perform the worst cliches of liberal race cinema to win the hearts of congresspeople so dedicated to white supremacy that they would defend its officiate no matter how ridiculous a person. The dullness of the senator's poetics is a perfect complement to the fecklessness of all proposed progressive reforms. It showcases how base and empty is the position of pleading with the political enemies of Black freedom. It is the result either of a deep callousness, interested in performing the Black spokesman for the people for political clout with no expectation of radical reform, or an earnest plea and belief that radical reform might be won after a speech testifying that the killed blacks love America. It is as if he believes the politicians in both houses, who have supported a white supremacist president and pushed laws that reduced voting and life chances of Black people, were in fact genuinely committed to ideals of liberty for all and could be moved by filmed slaughter and a heart-tugging speech into dropping racism at the door and making a change. A belief that could only come about by a deep disinterest in the history of Black life in white supremacist society and a rush to give white supremacists the benefit of the doubt. The senator channeled the Supplicant Negro figure in his speech to help neutralize the uprising and recenter the moribund campaign for equal rights and policy change for Black people in colonialism. It was a stone's throw away from Van Jones' lucrative performance—crying and comforting white people during a people's uprising for Black life—not that the senator would ever throw a stone.

I used to work in Newark, New Jersey, where Cory Booker was mayor. I was a frequent visitor to many of its most exploited "native quarters." Never once have I heard anyone crying out "America I love you do you see me," nor anything or any action that would justify such a plea sky-written over the native quarters of Newark or any other city. None of us are bound by so soiled a straitjacket. Big Sam, Uncle Tom, Nigger Jim, Prissy, and any such huggable dotards never existed, no matter how often Black liberal politicians, colonial explorers, white abolitionists, Klansmen novelists, and news anchors will them into existence. There is no mass of colonized anywhere who would elect to have their memory desecrated like this and, after being murdered by a colonial agent, would rest peacefully knowing that their corpse was made to beg colonialism to be "seen."

It does not matter if the colonized, the Black lumpenproletariat, love America or not. Fealty to the state is not the slave pass they must present on demand in order to keep their life. George Floyd does not need to be converted into a cherubim looking down on us as former House Speaker Nancy Pelosi prayed, a minstrel cherubim guiding the Democrats' reform bill. He can be a complex human being, an "informal market" hustler, a survivor of anti-Black colonial life. He must not be forced, without his consent, into a smiling, peaceable Uncle Tom figure shining down from heaven after "sacrificing [his] life for justice."[54]

The conservative attempt to push back on the swell of the uprising with the usual tar and feathering of the Black corpse, intimidated by the display of global sympathy for Black people, could not state as forcefully at the beginning as they did of Mike Brown, Trayvon Martin, and Ahmaud Arbery that they were criminal thugs who deserved their death. A softening of the language was detectable—despite no change in meaning. A phrase that began to be heard was that people should select a different martyr for their cause than George Floyd, who was a bad person and was "no angel."[55] In fear of the traction George Floyd, forced into supplicating figure, was gaining in the world, conservatives, just as pro-slavery advocates pushed anti-Tom literature to counter the traction and abolitionist threat of Stowe's novel two centuries earlier, designed an alternative image of Floyd as a petty criminal, defiant and noncompliant. A police-resistor that did not deserve canonization. But I can be "no angel." I can dress like Tom Sawyer and trespass on construction sites while Black. I can fight my stalker, I can pay with a counterfeit bill, I can be armed, I can be guilty of crimes, the colonist does not have any God-given right to kill me. I have no obligation to obey any human being, ever. I am militantly free. I am maroon free. In life, in death, in afterlife. In my body, in its conduct, its expression, my freedom is absolute. In every plane of existence. The figure of the Supplicant Negro, drawn directly from white supremacist fantasies and that bears such a likeness to Booker's description of Black people, is foreign to me. Indeed, it cannot exist. The rebels, before execution, asked that their heads be turned to face Africa—not bowed with their hands clasped in prayers for the state. The liberal should keep their hands off the body and memory of the victims of their beloved colonialism.

The most unambiguous display of Black supplication in the contemporary era is of course that of "taking a knee." In the 2016 NFL Pre-season, Colin Kaepernick, a San Francisco 49ers quarterback, began to "take a knee," kneeling during the playing of the US National Anthem. Kaepernick explained his action. "I am not going to stand up to show pride in a flag for a country that oppresses black people and people of color. To me, this is bigger than football and it would be selfish on my part to look the other way. There are bodies in the street and people getting paid leave and getting away with murder."[56] As if a live-action Wedgwood anti-slavery medallion, Kaepernick embodied the archetypal Supplicant Negro: respectful protest of the slaughter of Black people. Despite the deluge of right-wing anger claimed to be at his disrespect of the military, more members of sports teams began to take a knee during the anthem, and after the murder of George Floyd, the action seemed to be everywhere. Police were taking photo ops kneeling with protestors as were European football players in protest against far-right anti-black slur chanting and banana-throwing fans. In an act that can be seen as the culmination and the homecoming of Black supplication, Nancy Pelosi, flanked by Democrats and Black liberal politicians, was photographed "taking a knee" while wearing kente cloths in the Capitol building's Emancipation Hall. Lawmakers performing the supplication the Supplicant Negro performed for the law. A full circle of feckless performativity. The building would be overrun by a lynch mob months later.

Twenty-four-hour news, especially the proliferation of active white supremacist news channels, coupled with social media websites, especially X (formerly Twitter), have created a situation in which Black suffering, Black minstrelsy, anti-Black derision, and Black supplication are on perennial display and consumed by a colonial public (and the world) more than ever before. As dominant as the imagery of Black supplication and lowliness has been in colonies since white abolition efforts, hungry white supremacists would still have to travel to a lynching bee, purchase tickets to a minstrel show, be property-owners or overseers, or read white supremacist literature to get their fill of Black supplication and suffering. Today they can consume it from the comfort of their gaming chairs and, moreover, can like, share, lambast, mock, and otherwise interact with the figure of the prostrated Black person. In late settler-colonialism, the spectacle of Black supplication is accumulated to the point it becomes *the political*.[57]

The age of social media has brought with it #Blacklivesmatter, at once a threatening idea in a colonialism structured around the disposability of Black and Indigenous lives, and on the other hand, one of the most tangible developments in Black supplication. Black Lives Matter is an attractive phrase to several political positions. It is both a philosophical statement and can be interpreted as the force of anti-colonialism where the native asserts their right to existence despite the colonial order built on their disposability. It can also be read as a plea. Like Colin Kaepernick's "taking a knee," it stares in the face of colonial atrocity and replies, meekly, vulnerably, and unarmed, that it is in fact "a man and a brother" and should be treated fairly. Just as the narrative of the Civil Rights Movement misnames, appropriates, and blurs the centuries-long Black uprising against racial totalitarianism, the anti-colonial uprising of 2020 after the murder of George Floyd blurs with this BLM "movement" and precisely because of the ambiguity of interpretations has brought liberals and radicals at moments in proximity to one another, if not together. Together against "police brutality"[58] for the former and together against the police-state for the latter. As I've written elsewhere[59] due to liberal political dominance and privilege in the space of formalized (i.e., State Ideological Apparatus adjacent)[60] Black thought Black liberalism has been equipped to shout over the uprising and has, with limited success, tried to lasso the anger of the native quarter into the peaceful protest tradition of Civil Rights. Of course, both the Black philosophical statement and plea have been hated by settler supremacist power. The Black speaker is hated whether kneeling or standing—whether shrieking threats of Black freedom or politely "demanding" the plea for rights be heard. In the colony, which has always been a lynch mob society, any protest against the murder of Black people is terroristic and impertinent no matter how meekly stated.

The Masters' Fiddler

Colonist media, where it is not "right-wing" and in giddy celebration of white supremacist murder, rushing to the racists' side with any veneer of plausible deniability it can muster, has as its first function providing white supremacy with the benefit of the doubt. Whether this is due to the nefarious plotting and conspiracy by individual media bosses or an effect of the exigencies of racial capitalism is immaterial. Be it the police order, prisons, the leader of a white nationalist movement become president, or the state, the media—often through an appeal to patriotism and good order—plays second fiddle to the institutions responsible for anti-Black atrocity the world over. Colonist media is not only a central artery for the dissemination of the figure of the Black supplicant but the sentinel of masters' society and protector of the idea of the racists' essential humanity.

Instead of interpreting colonial society as a lynch mob that has taken pleasure in multiple clearing grounds of Black suffering, always seeking to expand them, colonist media generates myths about an empathetic human nature as the essence of all of the colony's citizens. Lynch mob society becomes a country that has "unfortunately" and "tragically" not yet found the wisdom and strength within itself to rid its body of "racial discrimination." It is presumed that "All Americans" deep down want the best for their fellow citizens. A presumption that would imply that those hunting and disenfranchising the "n*gger" through the centuries were not aware of Black people's citizenship status. As if the forcible deportation plans of Lincoln and the

4. Supplication in the Spectacle 141

American Colonization Society, the Dred Scott decision, the anger at the Fourteenth Amendment, or contemporary white supremacists' (rebranding once again as the far-right, Christian nationalism, or Trumpism) focus on Black "ersatz" blood are but aberrations in the general, inclusive, and well-intentioned colonial culture. The inevitably white supremacist nature of settler-colonialism being impossible to admit, colonist media's task (ably supported by the rest of those institutions and ideological apparatuses tasked with producing information, including academia) is to explain anti-Blackness and the hostile attitudes against the colonized—which is typical in all settler-colonies—as a failure of empathy brought on by ignorance. An ignorance, as it turns out, not of Black thought but ignorance of the worthiness of Black people; that they do not deserve being hit, as is proven by their supplication. The organizing logic of invasion, compiled discourses, and justificatory strategies of apartheid, in media becomes "racism." A character flaw of certain sheltered individuals who, through no or little fault of their own, happen to not have been confronted with evidence of Black humanity and the depths of suffering of Black people. The racist is simply one who has not been made aware of or persuaded by the Wedgwood anti-slavery medallion. This ignorance, once remedied by extended "dialogue" and "starting the conversation," will, they say, hopefully procure a better, more just polity fulfilling the dreams, however imperfectly, of everyone from Dr. King to the Founders, to the captured seventeenth-century African who would never see freedom but nevertheless had the glint of the American promise in her eye.

This liberal colonial hope works in tandem with overt white supremacist action that seeks to retain the lash by other means and redeem enslavement culture. The first mechanism keeps the revolt from gathering, derailing its would-be ranks through an appeal to the concept of hope in a state they have been trained to believe is theirs and their friend, while the latter continues disciplinary atrocity. The missionary and anthropologist are accompanied by the King's African Rifles and the volunteer settler auxiliary force. The newsroom's talking head keeps step with the police; knowledge arrives with power. The tag-teaming of colonists, both the ideological and repressive apparatuses, joined to ensure the colonial situation is obfuscated by appeals to an ever-progressing "country."

It is, of course, absurd to give white supremacy the benefit of the doubt post-twentieth-century colonialism and the Holocaust. The direction to open dialogue with those who have not had the common courtesy to tuck their sjamboks and swastikas into their trad-man pantaloons is offensive. The charred remains of most of the world would be enough, in another coming world order, to have anyone caught with the paraphernalia of white supremacy from craniometrers or slave masters' countries excommunicated. But it is not absurd for colonists. Colonialism, for all its progress into the "enlightened, perfecting democracy," has not found it as easy to quit racial science and genocidal ideation as it has the theory of a flat earth or fossil fuels. For the colonist, the aspiring slave master is a countryman. For the white abolitionist that is, liberal colonist, the members of the lynch mob are always a book or Black History Month display away from redemption. The problem is ignorance, which breeds separate "echo chambers," which breeds mistrust, racial resentment, and grievance, preventing the move forward together—as Americans. Despite the smoke billowing from the slums, the settler cry to put down the criminal and/or communist natives, the moderate Republicans bullied into denying they pulled down the flags of slavery after a massacre in a Black church, America, it is said, is not French Algeria. It is not Apartheid South Africa, Kenya Colony, Rhodesia, or Israel. America is exceptional. There is no lynching bee cowering over a dehumanized native quarter here. Only disagreeing friends.

The belief in the superability of racists to be redeemed into antiracism during their racism, and that those they make suffer should await the racists' enlightenment while suffering and dying, is white supremacist. Knowledge of a subject people's suffering has never in the history of the settler-colony created the promised watershed moment of empathetic change, to underline Assata.[61] Whatever Civil Rights and liberal nationalist myths are promoted, be they the change after "Emancipation" and the sympathetic Lincoln, the change after *Brown v. Board* after the sympathetic Eisenhower, or the change after the post-2020 George Floyd protest "racial reckoning" after a sympathetic Trump, Black liberation has never come about by a move in white sympathy and is only thinkable at all at the permanent incapacitation of colonial power.

It is no more reasonable to think colonist media can be reformed than it is to believe in police or legal reform. Like the latter, the "fourth estate" is inseparable from colonial power and interests, but emerges from and is conditioned by it. The Supplicant Negro will be mic'ed up; the anti-colonist will be muted. Permissible discourse, that which can be mainstreamed, cannot be allowed to threaten colonialism. All anti-colonial thought is impermissible and made illegal as soon as it threatens reaching striking distance of liberation. Neither the runaway nor the anti-colonialist can speak freely. For the enslaved, it has always been "I think therefore I am criminal." Liberal colonist "book bans" have been much more thorough and complete than the symbolic banning of books by activist white supremacist political officers and have created a veritable silencing, or the exiling of dangerous thinking to the new hush arbors of blogospheres, poetry, and gritty basements of Africana Studies programs, where often the single anti-colonial thinker is piled over and smothered by Civil Rights academics now busy "decolonizing their syllabi." Colonial media produces and permits only those with an interest in reproducing colonialism, and that requires the production of Black supplication, the always forgiving black and the always redeemable klansman. Black forgiveness and white supremacist impunity are two sides of the same Confederate coin.

Giving white supremacy the benefit of the doubt

> "I think God intended the niggers to be slaves. Now since man has deranged God's plan, I think the best we can do is keep 'em as near to a state of bondage as possible. . . . My theory is, feed 'em well, clothe 'em well, and then, if they don't work . . . whip 'em well."
>
> Yazoo Delta planter, 1866[62]

In the province of settler-colonialism known by its apologists as the United States, the Confederacy, if it is to be said that it has been dissolved, has nonetheless been allowed to continue the pursuit of its business by other means with the proviso that they call themselves conservatives. In the nineteenth century, slave revolts made slaveholding unsafe business. There was an ever-present risk of the followers of Flore Bois Gaillard, Queen Leonor of Cartagena, Queen Nanny of the Maroons, Boukman and Cécile Fatiman invading the occupied shores of the colony and bringing a counter-freedom to the land of the slaveholding free. After the failure of the slaveholders' insurrection, in 1865 when Americans' fight to keep outdoor slavery all but ended, it became necessary to invite the compatriot belligerents back into the fold of the nation to further the colonial project. The Confederacy, said to be no more, meant its supporters could no longer be enemies of the state. In the interests of settlers' peace, they were not hanged or tried for treason but converted into the misguided, anachronistic, ignorant brother of the North. The other side to the debate about whether Black people should have their children sold. The devil's advocate. The spoils of Confederate interests were distributed into invented categories of conservatism or racism, the former being the politics liberal white supremacy could absorb and thereby deem legitimate, and the latter that which it could not, the categories shifting according to the exigencies of colonialism. But the war did not dissolve the Confederacy nor its aims. This is obvious, if denied. It is seen in the continuation in the Confederate battle flag to represent "Southern heritage," monuments to slaveholders and Confederate generals, sentiments such as "the South will Rise again," and, most importantly, the hatred of the freed enslaved. The "South" and the "Confederacy" refer neither to geography nor political institution but to the core of settler white supremacist violence constantly in rebellion against the dominant liberal white supremacy[63] with a view to taking the state. It considers liberal white supremacy effete, colonial governance under liberal administration too "coddling of the negro," or in contemporary racist language, "too woke." Until state capture[64] the slaveholder's interest, like the Yazoo Delta planter's, has to be pursued by other means and branded differently. US Conservatism is the slaveholder's war of position; it is legislative and legitimated anti-Black violence. The continuation of slavery by other means.

For reasons of state, the stability and unity of the colony, the liberal has had to deny the persistence of the Confederacy and the pursuit of slavery even when conservative interests are identical to the announced interests of former slave masters. They have had to pretend not to be able to decode the hieroglyphics of the raised Confederate flag and the misspeaking that always seems to err in the direction of the N-word. Repressive violence, imprisonment, dehumanizing rhetoric, the priming of populations for their exploitation, and other techniques used to continue colonialism's dispossessing Black people of life, land, liberty, and property do not reveal a continuation of slaveholding interests, but "our politically differing worldviews." Every foray of slaveholder culture is rebranded as racism, ignorance, tragedy, or injustice. Anything to keep their compatriot. The war aims of the slaveholding class, including those who in Frederick Douglass's words are slaveholders at heart,[65] are individualized and localized, rendering invisible the structured whole of the Confederacy and presenting their pro-slavery efforts as stubborn "legacies"[66] and character flaws. This arrangement with slaveholding interests has given both white liberals and conservatives plausible deniability. In the face of clear, systemic patterns of anti-Blackness, evidence of the master's interests enduring, media, scholarship, families, the colony's ideological apparatuses work to ensure that the Confederacy is denied, and the ignorant appear in its stead. Dead Black bodies on the side of the road lying in the same position whether after genocides in Virginia in the nineteenth century, Tulsa in the twentieth, a grocery store in Buffalo or Jacksonville, or a church in Charleston in the twenty-first are converted into passing tragedies instead of the continued colonial same. In the liberals' bargain, the "racists" can continue Confederate attacks against non-white people and the ongoing colonialism branded "America" can remain fundamentally "the Good."

Still, settler white supremacists, those aggrieved of their loss of Black chattel and those whose families never owned property but still found themselves identifying with those with "property in man," have not been sated, and denial has not meant their disappearance. There is a significant part of the US population who believe, quite literally, that Black lives do not matter. They carry the torch for the advocates of that peculiar institution based on the fact that Black lives did not matter. These temporally embarrassed slave masters still wish it to be known that they will never relinquish control of Black backs—a source of constant frustration for colonialism's white abolitionist apologists who must constantly reframe every body left on the side of the road and spin every welt left with improved technology as un-American. In Americanism, the enslaver has put on a hat reading "conservative" and disappeared.[67] The lynch mob, once stood mocking the bleeding attacked Black victim, is now sat in the clearing of social media comments and mentions that they are merely "trolling." And just like that the klansman vanishes from liberal sight. The Southern field culture of laughing at our lynched bodies is now represented as merely the insensitivity of bullies. The same crowd surrounding and spitting at the corpse are now just "trolls" and "edgelords." The liberal media lacks object permanence. When the *White Citizens' Councils* put on the cloak of the *Conservative Citizens' Council*, they did not need a dressing room or telephone booth. Not even a slur-shouting, Black-chasing mob is named for what it is—even though they brought nooses. They are not even required to deny that they are pursuing the interests of the Confederacy, as their dressing in the Confederate flag would seem to indicate. The media offers the activist white supremacist a usable imprecision of analysis on the house.

The instinct of contemporary liberalism is to give white supremacists the benefit of the doubt. Despite the conservative penchant for the Confederacy, the fight to retain the Confederate battle flag and monuments to slave owners, or the push to ban Black writing and have the only recollection of slavery allowed be books that present slavery as a complicated romance, the interest in enslavement is said to be of yesterday. It is taken as fact that there is no continuation of the will to enslave in the present. Any recalling of the burnings and any tracing of the still live embers of negrophobia from the smelting of Africans in the field are actually evidence of anti-white racism. "Slavery, colonialism, can't be blamed for everything. And maybe it didn't even happen. Perhaps we should burn all the books that say it did."

The new era, media tells us, is of a "politically divided country," two separate but equal stories of one America. They say this despite the fact that "left-wing" and "right-wing" identity in the colony says less about where one stands on the question of government spending or on funding Ukraine than it does about how one feels about a knee on a Black person's neck. Yet despite the Confederacy and the lynch mob being confined to America's tragic past, there seems to be a significant portion of the population on a mission to re-envision slavery and defend lynching. There seems to be a significant element of the population doing exactly what a slave master would be expected to do in the environment where chattel slavery is no longer permissable: fight for the harm and political disenfranchisement of Black people, reduce the power to resist the violence of authority, separate families, and support the human caging business. The mission to keep them as close to bondage as possible and to whip them well. The class of slave masters has disappeared under hats, and the liberal media is supposedly constantly aghast at why Black people are hunted down in pickup trucks or sold to prisons or a political movement to make America great again, that excites known white supremacists and conservatives despite eschewing political and personal civility, has "defied all political logic," and won. Twice. It is not at all considered that logic and reason have been put on the pyre to save the colony and appease the lynch mob detectorists looking for traces of lizard-men in their luxurious backyards. For subscribers to the belief that colonial racism is a fading legacy, all reality cannot but be befuddling.

Things are, despite nationalist and media narrative, however, as open as they have always been in any other era. There are no "dog-whistles," nor "misspeaking." No "saying the quiet part out loud." There are no quiet parts. The media comes to anti-Blackness with thin veils, casts it over it and ordains it "thinly-veiled racism." It is obvious that the Trump movement is a white supremacist movement. That it is the tomb of the Confederacy, resurrected and infused with modern European Nazism. But due to the cessation of hostilities between the North and the South, white state abolition and settler lynch mob power, the media has agreed to present every evidence of typical white supremacist colonial desire as an aberration. Centuries of appeasement of slave owners and lynching bees, the constant offer of the benefit of the doubt to white supremacy and white supremacists, fashioned in abolitionist discourse as (colonial) "hope," have facilitated the lynch mob's, stuttered, capture of the state apparatus. The "conservatives" do a thing entirely expected of the Confederacy, for example, strip Black communities of voting rights, defend white nationalism in the US military, rip Black books from school shelves, threaten the military occupation of Black neighborhoods, have their spokespeople float returning hanging from trees as criminal punishment, fight slavery reparations on the grounds of Black criminality, and so on, and the liberal press asks whether this is "racially-charged" or condemns the "dangerous rhetoric." It takes them at their word when racists say they "just want more Black fathers in the home," as if the conservative requiring Black fathers in the home is requiring anything other than the presence of the police. The surveilled slave quarter. They are not imagining a Black father who raises his children up in the idea that they should not be mistreated by the state or people. They do not want the father that imparts life lessons that Black Lives Matter but one to impart that it is important to obey authority. That Black orderliness and behavior that doesn't upset the prevailing power matters. That Black subservience matters—more than that, it is essential. US Conservatives, of course, have always been the most radical advocates for big government.[68] That this is not immediately clear is testament to a logic of Black disposability—in which people are not counted. Big government, yes, but for "the blacks." The politics associated with "pull up your pants," "no spitting, no profanity, reckless eyeballing," have no children out of wedlock, squat, cough, buzz cuts only, dress your gender, expand prisons, don't let me catch you here after sundown, and show respect to the police is a most perfect expression of totalitarian governmental authority.[69] The lynch mob makes its interest in returning the order of the absolute slave master's impunity and the white supremacist anti-Blackness of the antebellum period as clear as is feasible, and the colony's ideological institutions respond by turning their faces away from the clear messaging and choosing to presume they mean well but they, like the rest of the country, still have a long way to go to rectify the racist legacies of the past. The US white supremacist movement has played a game of *Red Light, Green Light* with the liberal press for the prize of state capture, and the contemporary era has seen the MAGA movement emerge, despite once-guffawed at incompetence and fundraising issues, victorious. The era is the era of Trump's discovery, where the white supremacist movement has discovered that liberal dominance in the colony was a paper tiger and that there is no limit to how far the capitalist press's back won't bend to avoid explaining who they are. That they will call the lynch mob "our fellow citizens" even, and especially when they return that love letter with nooses for the "Lügenpresse." Colonial hope is an armament program for white activist white supremacists. In the time they have been granted by liberals to turn around and recognize that we are all Americans and countrymen, they have "prepped" for a race war, "infiltrated" the West's militaries, and won in "shock" elections. The "painfully slow progress" society has made in "race relations" has ended up in the current moment where over half of the electorate cheers on a Nazi presidential candidate. Democracy is slow, we are told amidst the lightning victories of fascists in the parliaments of Europe and the offices of the US. The question "if democracy is slow but genocidal white supremacy is fast why it is that democracy is what is required here?" is never answered.

The Venus flytrap that is colonial hope must be avoided. It should not be doubted that the moment a critical mass of power is gained, they will not do exactly what is done to marginalized people in settler-colonies everywhere. It should not be fantasized that the battle between liberal white supremacy and the stable state administration required for capitalist reproduction on the one hand, and the lynch mob on the other, occurring at all times in settler-colonial space, will not result in what it has elsewhere at the moment of settler mob state capture. Nor should it be dreamed that colonist media will one day refuse to give the white supremacist the benefit of the doubt. The police who raped a Black man for being found in a white woman's house on the wrong side of town was "abused as a child." The perpetrator of a massacre of Black people suffers from mental health issues, violence in gaming, divisive rhetoric, and the availability of guns. These are contemporary problems that plague modern American youth, despite their aftermath—with Black corpses strewn about—being identical to scenes in every one of the last 500 years. The mob assembles out of "resentment" and is tricked by a demagogue, we are told. Moderate conservatives hold their noses and vote. Disenchanted youths like Dylann Roof champion the Great Replacement theory because of fears of demographic change and immigration policy. It is not that all settler-colonies from inception have militated against the "demographic bomb" of the subject races. It is that the silent majority fears being left behind in the new economy, and economic anxiety has left them prone to white supremacist conspiracies. It is not that the great replacement of the native with the conservative body, language, and state is synonymous with the settler-colonial project, and settler anxiety is about the same old feared anti-colonial reckoning. The terror that there is something not servile in ol' handkerchief-headed auntie's eye. In colonist liberalism, the white supremacist is given the benefit of the doubt because liberal white supremacism is the compatriot of conservative white supremacism. That is what settler-colonialism is.

On July 16, 2020, Rachel Maddow asked Donald Trump's niece, Mary Trump if she heard the ex-president use the N-word, to which Mary Trump affirmed that she had. It is unclear if Maddow expected the news to be a bombshell, but it seemed to fall flat. There was no fallout. Trump did not have to give a press conference forcefully denying her claims, nor did he seem to lose droves of supporters who were left bewildered that their champion of fiscal responsibility turned out to be nothing but a common racist. It was not a bombshell because it is known by all that the "Trump movement" is a white supremacist movement, led by a white supremacist who has managed not to be recorded saying the N-word but stays within the borders of what the media accepts as plausibly deniable. Trump saying he loves his beautiful white skin, that Haitians steal and eat pets, and that he wants an effective migration system that prioritizes migrants from Norway and not shithole countries like Haiti and Nigeria should not be read into, or else it is a playful racism. With this implausible deniability—pretended as plausible by the media that offers an excuse to any traditional white supremacist speech that does not contain a slur—Trumpism keeps its end of the unspoken bargain between the American Nazi movement and the white supremacist-coddling liberal press. But the emperor has never had any clothes; the Klansman is in full display, de-robed. Everyone knows what is going on. The "ultimate logic of racism is genocide." Americanism has always been arriving at contemporary America. The slowness of its progress is due to the hindrance that is Black survival. Every indicator of what "America" is, is presented by the American liberal press not as evidence, but a dangerous indicator of what is to come. Colonist discourse which at its heart cannot conceive of Black lives counting is forever cautioning the eventual "descent into fascism" or about "the worst instincts of the base" in a country of our charred remains. The state invented by Black-children-seizing-tyrants is in danger of falling to dictatorship. Mary Trump's accusation that Trump uses the N-word fell flat precisely because everyone knows what Trump symbolizes, and all but the most callous to the history of Black lives in colonialism are aware of what an N-word shouting mob with nooses targeting the Capitol building means. There is no real shock, no "defying political logic," and no brainwashing the economically depressed and "racially resentful" overlooked part of the population. The liberal media sets up to wait for a watershed moment when the Nazism of the contemporary conservatism is exposed, when it is totally without a doubt that the American Trump movement is racist, when Trump says the N-word. It presents things as if we are always descending to that irrevocable proof. But things are not "getting fascist and dangerous." We have already been attacked, plans for concentration camps are drawn up, you cannot see it because what happens to the Black people in the field does not count. We do not have lives. What happens to our bodies now are unfortunate legacies. Our bleeding is saintly sacrifices urging the need for staged conversations about colonial reform. The media is constantly warning that the lamb is being led to the slaughter, careful not to show that it holds the reins and the lamb has protested and fights to escape. It obfuscates the reality of colonial violence into a present continuous danger that if we don't do something soon, will lead to colonial violence. But it was enough that there were shootings in black churches and synagogues burned. Enough that children were chased down by drivers in pickup trucks shouting "nigger" and shotgunned. We're not waiting for anyone's eureka moment.

In the settler-colony, the pendulum of progress swings only between two poles. In early 1900s Kenya, it was between the settlers who wanted to overthrow the colonial administration for interfering with their right to flog the natives at will and that liberal white supremacist administration who took Indigenous land and considered progress limiting the flogging of the Africans to fifty lashes. In 1940s South Africa, it was the United Party, a party of mass incarceration, less-codified racial discrimination, pro-police and imperialist violence, and the Nats, who history judges to be the racists, who thought colonialism was not violent enough and instituted Apartheid and Soweto raids and Sharpeville Massacres. In 2020s "America," it is between Democrats, the staunch ally of police and Israel's colonial war, and the GOP, who have supported a move to take the Capitol by force and instituted a more draconian white supremacy with its ideologues calling for the (expanded) military occupation of Black communities. Two poles. The administration of Black repression for the effective accumulation of capital or the pleasure of the clearing and the spectacle of anti-Black violence. The electoral left desires the efficient management of anti-Black institutions for economic growth. The settler mob desires to watch France invade the Algerian native quarters, the casspirs occupying Soweto, the IDF invading Gaza, mobilizing the instruments of the state to deploy against the colonized in defiance of the capitalist state they feel "coddles the native" too much.

But the practice of the runaway is to consider the surrounding horizons of liberal white supremacy and conservative white supremacy as the paper tiger. For the maroon, there is more to life than being pinged back and forth between these two arbitrarily placed poles. Between the liberal white supremacist who says the native should be whipped no more than fifty times and the "racist" who wants no limits and shouts down this "government overreach." There is more to life than to cower[70] with crossed fingers every time the mob regains the reins of the state— as inevitably they do—in prayer that they will not have enough time to do what they intend or that the red tape will be wound tightly enough to prevent them. And that we can be shuffled back to the more equitable, liberal prison, awaiting their next foray. If the pendulum can only swing between liberal white power and conservative white power, then it is better to stop the time.

CONCLUSION
THE BRAVE RUN

I have been locked by the lawless.
Handcuffed by the haters.
Gagged by the greedy.
And, if i know any thing at all,
it's that a wall is just a wall
and nothing more at all.
It can be broken down . . .

And i believe that a lost ship,
steered by tired, seasick sailors,
can still be guided home
to port.[1]

Come, then, comrades . . . We must leave our dreams and abandon our old beliefs and friendships of the time before life began. Let us waste no time in sterile litanies and nauseating mimicry. Leave this Europe where they are never done talking of Man, yet murder men everywhere they find them, at the corner of every one of their own streets, in all the corners of the globe. For centuries they have stifled almost the whole of humanity in the name of a so-called spiritual experience. Look at them today swaying between atomic and spiritual disintegration.[2]

Come, then, comrades, leave this America where they are never done talking of racial progress, yet leave Black lives destroyed on every street corner and require of us hope—declarations of faith in the institutions of the men that murdered and hunted us and scalped our comrades. Come up off the cross, up from supplication, stride away from them without even spitting back in their direction as they shout we are poisoned with pessimism and lofty ideas in our losing hope that the back-flailers and merchants of children and human wombs would come around. Get up from supplication, reject further interlocution and companionship with those who still cherish the political institutions of men with our blood on their breath. Leave the plantation, the patriots and the patriotism to cotton field occupation of Indigenous land they shoved at us with the butt of a gun. Our existence is not put to the service of a better colonialism. We do not exist merely to be forever pulling the colony from the brink. Our creative energies can be put to things other than encouraging colonialism to "do right by us." Such as the development of modes to undo and escape the colonial project and to building worlds post-America. Not preachers, and leaders and writers for white audiences, but runners and plantation arsonists and the never heard from again. Now that they sway between accelerating climate ruin and the humanization of the Nazi position, leave this America. Rub onions and pine on your boots and "divert the scent of the dogs."[3]

The question from marronage, as urgent as it is unasked, is "who are these people to you?" Why is staying in their company of so much importance? What obliges you to them, those who hold you by the ankle and nail it to their state? They are not beguiled by you, despite their advertising campaigns of "Black Girl Magic" or inviting you on set during February to explain to the audience at home why Black history is important to know and celebrate. They sit and compromise with the men who inherited souvenirs of lynching from their grandfathers. Who are these people to you? You do not need them. Neither the hooded horseman nor the friend that invites him to the table.

The racist cannot improve. Or if they can be improved, it will not happen in a satisfactorily timely manner. In any case, the negrophobe does not deserve our forgiveness. Certainly not our constant urging to change, nor our patience. But neither does the liberal colonist. It is not clear to them that those who fly the flag of holocausts do not deserve our anti-racist tutelage. That the nearness of a white supremacist is not enough to make them retch is enough reason to lock the doors when they arrive with the stench of Nazi-forgiveness on their skin. The runaways did not give the masters unlimited time to learn to oppose the selling and killing of their children—any hesitation was enough. The liberal colonist will forever supplicate before their masters, appeasing and attempting to understand them, as if their genocidal slogans are layered and in need of deciphering. They will forever keep inviting the racist into the human community, knowing full well it is the only being on earth that throws bananas at people at sporting events and parliament. The racist has met their evolutionary ceiling. Nothing new comes from them. There is no sentiment, no argument they possess that cannot be found in writings of some nineteenth-century planter. Every debate with them is a backpedaling. Every plea, every shaking of their shoulder reveals a scarecrow. On a plantation, the brave run. They take the Amistad to the outer ocean with or without a compass.

Settler-colonialism does not deserve Black patience, nor audacious Black hope. Hope is their armament program. The race riot—well-preserved in Neo-Nuremberg rallies, that carry the murderers of protestors on their shoulders just as they carried the hangmen of accused Black teenagers in the last centuries, or the slave catchers the century before—do not deserve time to see the light. No more centuries of waiting, no more hope from bended knee, no ceding settler futurity. The racist and its racism are not adapted for the future but will go the way of the pager and the cotton gin, shrieking climate crisis denial, gender immutability, and "Rhodesia will rise again" only to be drowned out by Amapiano mixed with trap RnB.

The future is a fugitive who was never on the path of the West's trajectory despite what the massive shifting gears of dominant thought may represent. It is wrapped in a baby's cloth and carried on a back fleeing through the shadows and the swamps that will not countenance, not even stomach any more lights of a colonial city. Or it swaggers about in the town as the masters demand it to return to work for them. Stop all conversations with the mediocre men who throw themselves at the racists, grabbing hold of the ankles thinking them indispensable. Stop taking whippings and promises, believing that one day they will credit your contributions to colonialism. Come up off the cross and your knees; you are not being worshiped, you are being bled. The anti-humanism at the heart of white supremacy is degenerate—it is of a culture that cannot learn and is self-condemned to stagnation. It begins with the non-science of racist science. It is stuck in Linnaeus' sketches. The parasite of a salvageable human future declares, despite the denials of the liberals, that it seeks the elimination of its host. Cure yourself, wash your hands and your clothes, and leave the past where they belong.

It is time to build a world without asking. Atop imperialism and powdered-wig institutions and texts until colonialism sinks into the ground like the villages it rounded up and death-marched there. To build it audaciously, without permission, on their heads, with the same ferociousness with which they built their shrines to capitalism above our stolen labor and land. We are not Man's men and we are not their brothers. Nor are we confused about their ragtag auxiliary army of negrophobes of color who, uncultured, wait with hat in hand because of their phenotypical proximity to the Grand House. Expecting to be let in, shouting with more forceful bark at the blacks of the field. They can go to. Along with any Marxist who is still waiting for the errand boys of the masters to develop class consciousness and requires our patience with racist class "allies" or devises some way to put Black struggle at the back of the red bus. Who peered into the QAnon Shaman or J.D. Vance until they believed they could see a comrade and got played. Who are either unwilling or unable to learn from the Rand Rebellion and German Nazism that it is *they*, not the white working overseer class, that is disillusioned. It is *they* who must develop class consciousness. Who must hitch the wagon to the brigands, not lead them. And if they're adamant that the rowdy mob who joins the masters as second dogs on the excitement of the negro hunt are one book away from class solidarity, abandon them. Leave that Europe too. And if all this leaving leaves us isolated and alone, so be it. The runaway slave left in more dire circumstances and could rely on even less support. It's better to climb the summit of the southernmost hill and wait on reinforcements from Maroon-revolt Ayiti that will never arrive than wait for friends or justice here. "If we must die, let it not be like hogs"[4] pleading for a change of heart in the abattoir. Run. Leave. There is not one faintly possible anti-colonial future that is not worth the risk of losing the settlers' day. Not one undiscovered, unthought time that is lesser than the promised Jetsons flying cars which have turned out, unsurprisingly, to be drones harassing homeless people for views in a "country" where half the population is ambiguous on whether fascism is to be avoided.

Settler-colonialism, everywhere, and its metropoles, are bounding toward the genocidal. The expelling, reducing, and extermination of its "surplus populations," whose upkeep is deemed more expensive than their productive capacity. Forced repatriation of those of "ersatz blood" was on the tongue of settler presidents and paupers from the first moment Black Emancipation was considered. It is echoed in those who pray for stronger prisons and support governors who trap migrants in the levees, or political parties who order coast guards to shoot at dinghies. It was always unavoidable. From Canada's Hitler-revisioning truckers' revolt to Australia's "Nigger Creek," to Wilmington, North Carolina's "Nigger Head Point Road," the promise of de-racialized multiculturalism has devolved into societies meekly fighting to push back against the romanticization of Adolf Hitler and which elect "Jacksonian" presidents. It is time to accept that settler societies lack the ingredients necessary for Black and Indigenous freedom. That the sustained oppression of the native and slave everywhere is no tragic coincidence. In their courts, it will always be the case that it will be more difficult to charge a white supremacist for openly trying to overthrow colonial democracy than it is to convict a Black youth for nothing. That white women tenants get paid more than Black women tenants in victories against landlords.[5] In their economies, it will always be the case that the price drops if a Black person is found to have lived in the house rather than a white person. Reparations cannot repair colonial market logic. This is colonialism's world order. In their media, they will remain shocked, and every scene of the pogrom will be merely a warning of a descent into fascism. Kristallnacht never happens. All is spectacle, premonition. The genius of the trap is that it teaches us that it is not that the pieces of the puzzle are inadequate, but that it is our fault for not working hard enough to arrange them correctly, and then shames us for deciding that the pieces are wrong. But they are wrong. It is time now to admit that whatever we were sold about the utopian possibilities of America of the future, it is not worth staying at the flogging tree. Whatever the master promised us America could be, he has taken too long to fulfill. Whatever else America can be, it must be admitted now that it is also an occasion when the greatest accumulation of power in human history has been handed off to a mob nostalgic for the clearing in the woods.

The violence against Black people is unprovoked. It has always been unprovoked. There is nothing one can trade with them to stop it. No stolen item to return, no wrong to undo. Not your hope, not your forgiving heart, not your pleading. The Black colonist liberal will disagree; they will say you are too quick to judge what is wrong with America and forget what is good with America. The colonized intellectual, fed by the colonist regime, says the same to the anti-colonial revolt in Colonial Algeria and Kenya Colony. The Civil Rightser says it to Malcolm X. The informer to the slave revolt plotter. The house negro says, "we sick," the field negro prays for a stronger breeze. Just as there is a conflict between settler power and administrative power over the reins of government, there is one between the colonized intellectual, the Supplicant Negro, and the runaway. It is the fires over the Target in 2020 and the attempt to put it out by Killer Mike and other policymakers. Despite who MSNBC and the like decide to invite to be the spokespeople for Black pain who say nothing but some version of "Am I Not a Man and a Brother?" it is the Black colonized lumpenproletariat that holds their truth in their very being. In the colony, the colonized lumpenproletariat is the only revolutionary class. They are the ones who have taken the baton from the freedoms of escape in the swamps and returned, like Adam, to saunter "saucily" in the city. Those of the slum, pushed out of schools and labor markets and so uneducated into supplication. The Black revolt in the shacks of both hemispheres, inscrutable, unmic'd, like the swamps surrounding the plantation, brought to their knees in false supplication only by napalm and rifle butts. The slave revolt has not ended. The runaway returns as Adam. The maroon in town.

> the colonized swarm into the forbidden cities. To blow the colonial world to smithereens is henceforth a clear image within the grasp and imagination of every colonized subject To dislocate the colonial world does not mean that once the borders have been eliminated there will be a right of way between the two sectors. To destroy the colonial world means nothing less than demolishing the colonist's sector, burying it deep within the earth or banishing it from the territory.[6]

No "decolonizing syllabi." No singing, only swinging. And if singing it is not Sam Cooke's "I was born by the river . . . Change Gon Come" it is Sexyy Redd's "I was born by the river I was getting them stacks." The new, new negro is the old fugitive of the plantation, in shiesty mask, standing atop the ruins of white power asking them to "come get it back in blood."[7]

NOTES

Introduction

1. National Park Service, "Emancipation Memorial," Accessed April 2, 2024, https://www.nps.gov/places/000/emancipation-memorial.htm.
2. "John Wilkes Booth Shoots Abraham Lincoln," History, Accessed April 2, 2024, https://www.history.com/this-day-in-history/john-wilkes-booth-shoots-abraham-lincoln.
3. See Taylor Simone Thomas, "Reclaiming Images of Black Women: An Investigation of Black Womanhood in Visual Communication," (2020), Accessed April 2, 2024, https://ir.library.louisville.edu/.
4. Maria St. John suggests the bigness and blackness of mammy is tied "to the materiality of maternity in contrast to her white counterpart [Scarlett O'Hara]." This bigness and maternity are part of the dominant fantasy of mammy, a Black woman with "a dark breast . . . perennially available and inexhaustible." Maria St. John, "'It Ain't Fittin': Cinematic and Fantasmatic Contours of Mammy in Gone with the Wind and Beyond," *Qui Parle* 11, no. 2 (1999): 132–3.
5. In the early 1700s, an Indigenous Man "Sam" and a "Negro Woman" together murdered the family who considered themselves to be their masters—William Hallet Jr., his wife, and three children. The Indigenous man was hung; the Black woman, referred to as "the negro fiend" was burned alive at the stake. Rebecca Hall, *Wake: The Hidden History of Women-Led Slave Revolts* (New York: Simon & Schuster), 84–5.
6. The gendering of Blackness as male being a collusion between patriarchal society and some Black male-led liberation organizations' historical disinterest in examining "the implications of sexual politics in Black women's lives." See Gloria T. Hull, Patricia Bell Scott, and Barbara Smith, *All the Women Are White, All the Blacks Are Men, But Some of Us Are Brave: Black Women's Studies* (The Feminist Press at CUNY, 1982), xxi. Saidiya Hartman argues that effacing women from the discourses of freedom was an essential part of conservative Black racial uplift movements which conflated the capacity to make things, understood to be men's work, with the remaking of the self. Saidiya Hartman, *Scenes of Subjection: Terror, Slavery, and Self-Making in Nineteenth-Century America* (New York and Oxford: Oxford University Press, 1997), 152.
7. Although I try to remain attentive to the danger that the felling of monuments can have the unintended effect of obscuring the nature of colony and providing the optical illusion of (a possible) colonial progress.

8. Colonial Society of Massachusetts, "Volume 1: Transactions 1892-1894: March Meeting, 1893," Accessed April 2, 2024, https://www.colonialsociety.org/node/51.
9. I borrow the term from Guy Debord. See Guy Debord, *The Society of the Spectacle*, trans. Donald Nicholson-Smith (New York: Zone Books, 2006).
10. Yannick Giovanni Marshall, "Black Liberal, Your Time is up," *Al Jazeera*, June 1, 2020, Accessed April 2, 2024, https://www.aljazeera.com/opinions/2020/6/1/black-liberal-your-time-is-up.
11. Adam Forrest, "Boris Johnson says Describing Black People as Having 'Watermelon Smiles' was 'Wholly Satirical,'" *The Independent*, June 22, 2019, Accessed April 2, 2024, https://www.independent.co.uk/news/uk/politics/boris-johnson-conservative-leadership-latest-racism-watermelon-smiles-satirical-a8981166.html.
12. Tom Kington, "Italy's First Black Minister: I had Bananas Thrown at me but I'm here to Stay," *The Guardian*, September 7, 2013, Accessed April 2, 2024, https://www.theguardian.com/world/2013/sep/08/cecile-kyenge-quest-for-tolerance.
13. See Yannick Giovanni Marshall, "The Coming Battle for the Racist Vote in America," *Al Jazeera*, December 28, 2022, Accessed April 2, 2024, https://www.aljazeera.com/opinions/2022/12/28/the-coming-battle-for-the-racist-vote-in-america.
14. "Among the Klan's favorite targets were Northern white teachers who had traveled south to instruct black children about the rights and responsibilities of freedom. Local white opinion of these teachers was very harsh. The historian of Oktibbeha County described them as 'obnoxious agitators' who 'incited the darkeys against their old friends, the Southern whites.' How? By teaching blacks that freedom meant thinking for themselves." David M. Oshinsky, *Worse Than Slavery: Parchman Farm and the Ordeal of Jim Crow Justice* (New York: Free Press, 1996), 28.
15. Hall, *Wake*, 33.
16. See Fred Moten and Robin D. G. Kelley, "Do Black Lives Matter," Vimeo video, Accessed April 2, 2023, https://vimeo.com/116111740.
17. Fanon says the colonized intellectual is "violent in their words and reformist in the attitudes." Frantz Fanon, *The Wretched of the Earth* (New York: Grove, 2004), 22.
18. Audre Lorde, *Sister Outsider: Essays and Speeches*. (Berkeley: Crossing Press, 2007), 38–9.
19. Hartman, *Scenes*, 47.

Chapter 1

1. Judge Nash of the North Carolina Supreme Court, June 1852, quoted in Herbert Aptheker, *American Negro Slave Revolts* (New York: Columbia University Press, 1943), 55.

2 Colonial, "Meeting."
3 The first name of "slave owners" is used to refer to them as a gesture of balance between the enslaved and the enslaver as well as to set up some distance between myself and the archivists and historians who refer to the enslaved "Adam" as Adam, but the slave owner John Saffin and slave driver Thomas Shepherd as "Saffin" and "Shepherd" respectively.
4 Colonial, "Meeting."
5 Colonial, "Meeting."
6 Samuel Sewall, *Diary of Sam Sewall 1674-1729 v. 1* (Boston: Massachusetts Historical Society 1878), 41, https://archive.org/details/samuel06sewa/page/41/mode/2up.
7 Italics mine. Colonial, "Meeting."
8 Colonial, "Meeting."
9 Gerald Horne, *The Counter-Revolution of 1776: Slave Resistance and the Origins of the United States of America* (New York: New York University Press, 2014), chap 1, Google Books, Accessed April 2, 2024, https://books.google.com/books?id=jC45AgAAQBAJ.
10 Slave Voyages. "Intra-American Slave Trade," *Slave Voyages*, 2018, Accessed April 2, 2024, https://www.slavevoyages.org/american/about#methodology/0/classification/2/en/.
11 Colonial, "Meeting."
12 See Horne, *Counter-Revolution*, chap 1.
13 Colonial, "Meeting."
14 The ideological dimensions of trading the enslaved from private to public, that is to say, from settler hands to the settlers' state, are taken up in the following chapters. But the literal transfers, for example, convict leasing, are of no less importance. See Oshinsky, *Worse*. And Michelle Alexander, *The New Jim Crow: Mass Incarceration in the Age of Colorblindness* (New York: The New Press, 2012).
15 Fanon, *Wretched*, 6.
16 It was not, however, the first. For example, an earlier text (1686) entitled "Friendly Advice to the Gentlemen-Planters of the East and West Indies in Three Parts" asked whether it was right that "a man be made a slave forever merely because his beard is Red or his Eyebrows Black?" Horne, *Counter-Revolution*, chap. 1.
17 See, Chapter 2.
18 Louis Althusser, "Ideology and Ideological State Apparatuses (Notes Towards an Investigation)," in *The Anthropology of the State: A Reader*, ed. Aradhana Sharma and Akhil Gupta (Malden: Blackwell Publishing, 2006), 86–112.
19 Fanon makes the distinction between "capitalist countries" and "colonized countries" experiencing two forms of police control. The former experiencing ideological power, that is, sermonizers and counselors; the latter the repressive apparatus of, that is, police force. In the settler-

colonies of North America, however, especially in the spaces of chattel slavery, both forms of control are wielded in concentrated forms so as to make the distinction unhelpful. Fanon, *Wretched*, 4.
20 Fanon, *Wretched*, 4.
21 Fanon, *Wretched*, 2.
22 Fanon notes that in colonial white supremacist society, the Black person's experience of their body is as if in the third person. Frantz Fanon, *Black Skin, White Masks*, trans. Richard Philcox (New York: Grove Press, 2007), 90.
23 Hartman, *Scenes*, 43.
24 Fanon, *Wretched*, 46.
25 Steve Biko, *I Write What I Like: Selected Writings* (Chicago: University of Chicago Press, 2002), 68.
26 See, for instance, an incident in McKinney, Texas in 2015 when Dajerria Becton—who the mayor called "a verbally abusive disobedient girl"—was thrown to the ground by a police officer. Andrea J. Ritchie. "Dajerria Becton's Arrest at a Pool Party in Texas Went Viral: Where Is She Now?" Teen Vogue, Condé Nast, June 19, 2018, https://www.teenvogue.com/story/dajerria-becton-arrest-pool-party-viral.
27 Sarah Haley, *No Mercy Here: Gender, Punishment, and the Making of Jim Crow Modernity* (Chapel Hill: University of North Carolina Press, 2016), 195–6.
28 Harriet Beecher Stowe, *Uncle Tom's Cabin or, Life Among the Lowly* (London: Penguin Books, 1986), 512.
29 Robert A. Williams Jr. has argued that colonial law was the "West's most vital and effective instrument of empire during its genocidal conquest and colonization of the non-Western peoples of the New World, the American Indian." Robert A. Williams Jr., *The American Indian in Western Legal Thought: The Discourses of Conquest* (Oxford: Oxford University Press, 1992), 6.
30 Ida B. Wells-Barnett, *Southern Horrors: Lynch Law in All Its Phases* (1892), Accessed April 3, 2024, https://ia800206.us.archive.org/6/items/southernhorrors14975gut/14975-h/14975-h.htm.
31 A Black, "native" police officer.
32 Brett Lindsay Shadle, *The Souls of White Folk: White Settlers in Kenya, 1900s-1920s* (Manchester: Manchester University Press, 2015), 187–8.
33 In settler-colonialism, the term vigilante is misleading when referring to white supremacists. It sets up a binary space of legitimate and illegitimate law enforcement based on the fiction of the legitimacy of settler-colonial law. In reality, white supremacist vigilantes and officers recruit from each other, often support one another and in older colonies especially were often explicitly appointed as the colonial auxiliary volunteer force, that is, officially part of the colonial police structure.

34 "Klan Is Blamed for Night Raid on Center at Delaware U. Campus," *The New York Times*, December 15, 1970, Accessed April 3, 2024, https://www.nytimes.com/1970/12/15/archives/klan-is-blamed-for-night-raid-on-center-at-delaware-u-campus.html#:~:text=The%20raid%2C%20which%20Police%20Chief,Maryland%20and%20Penn%20sylvania%20meet.
35 See Chap. 3.
36 Walter Fleming, *Documents Relating to Reconstruction* (Morgantown: Morgantown, 1905).
37 See Russ Bynum, "Judge Rejects Effort to Dismiss Case Against Former DA Charged in Ahmaud Arbery Killing's Aftermath," *AP News*, November 28, 2023, Accessed April 2, 2024, https://apnews.com/article/ahmaud-arbery-district-attorney-jackie-johnson-a3018236a409178d81c0048b52e24f1c.
38 The racist is often aware that the police are known to be in the pocket of the settler, and this is often expressed openly by lynch mobs. Fifty years after the Delaware incident, on January 6th, 2021, a noose-carrying, Confederate flag-waving lynch mob, usefully misnamed rioters (perhaps to draw false equivalences with the uprising for Black lives which notably did not have nooses nor did it emerge from the culture of lynching), were heard to say, "we love the police" even as they beat them. They were angry that the state was "woke," that is to say, not racist enough.
39 Walter Benjamin, "Critique of Violence," in *Selected Writings Volume 1: 1913-1926*, ed. Michael W. Jennings (Cambridge, MA: Harvard University Press, 1996), 242.
40 See "Introduction" in Yannick Marshall, "The Bleaching Carceral: Police, Native and Location in Nairobi, 1844-1906" (PhD diss., Columbia University, 2017), Accessed April 2, 2024, https://academiccommons.columbia.edu/doi/10.7916/D8W09JGD.
41 Etienne Balibar diagnoses the fiction of national formation, or "the country" in which the people are constructed by the state institutions. I add here that these "institutions" are the originary violence and persistent aftermath of settler invasion—and the colonists are made to think of themselves as a "people" and "nation" independent of that violence. "In the case of national formations, the imaginary which inscribes itself in the real in this way is that of the 'people'. It is that of a community which recognizes itself in advance in the institution of the state, which recognizes that state as 'its own' in opposition to other states and, in particular, inscribes its political struggles within the horizon of that state—by, for example, formulating its aspirations for reform and social revolution as projects for the transformation of 'its national state'. But such a people does not exist naturally, and even when it is tendentially constituted, it does not exist for all time. No modern nation possesses a given 'ethnic' basis, even when it arises out of a national independence struggle. And, moreover, no modern nation, however 'egalitarian' it may be, corresponds

to the extinction of class conflicts. The fundamental problem is therefore to produce the people. More exactly, it is to make the people produce itself continually as national community. Or again, it is to produce the effect of unity by virtue of which the people will appear, in everyone's eyes, 'as a people', that is, as the basis and origin of political power." Étienne Balibar and Immanuel Wallerstein, *Race, Nation, Class: Ambiguous Identities* (London: Verso, 1991), 93–4.

42 Here, I re-contextualize Timothy Mitchell's notion of the state being an effect, performatively constituted through the rituals of administration or "techniques that enable mundane material practices to take on the appearance of an abstract, nonmaterial form" in the settler-colonial context. Abandoning the notion of the state as a material reality as well as nationalist fictions of national space in which events occur, may more sharply reveal the lynch mob as an agent (and space) and its practice of colonialism, which produces the colony-effect, rather than the dominant view of the colony or country being marred by the historical event of colonialism. Timothy Mitchell, "Society, Economy, and the State Effect," in *The Anthropology of the State: A Reader*, ed. Aradhana Sharma and Akhil Gupta (John Wiley & Sons, 2009), 169–86. For an examination of the process in the "postcolonial state," see Joseph Massad, *Colonial Effects: The Making of National Identity in Jordan* (New York: Columbia University Press, 2001).

43 I use "Americanism" to refer to the settler-colonial ideology that produces a part of the space of the "Western Hemisphere" under settler occupation as the United States of America.

44 *Dred Scott v. Sandford*, 60 U.S. (19 How.) 393 (1857).

45 See also the case of "Citi Bank Karen," a white woman attempting to steal a bike from a Black person, screaming for help and accusing them of hurting her fetus. Angelina Velasquez, "White Woman Caught on Video Allegedly Trying to Steal Black Youth's Bike in New York City," *Revolt*, May 14, 2023, Accessed April 2, 2024, https://www.revolt.tv/article/2023-05-14/302175/karen-tries-to-steal-black-mans-bike-in-new-york-city.

46 Virginia's "An act about the casual killing of slaves" reads: An act about the casuall killing of slaves. "WHEREAS the only law in force for the punishment of refreactory servants (a) resisting their master, mistris or overseer cannot be inflicted upon negroes, nor the obstinacy of many of them by other than violent meanes suppress, Be it enacted and declared by this grand assembly, if any slave resist his master (or other by his master's order correcting him) and by the extremity of the correction should chance to die, that his death shall not be accompted ffelony, but the master (or that other person appointed by the master to punish him) be acquit from molestation, since it cannot be presumed that prepensed malice (which alone makes murther ffelony) should induce any man to destroy his owne estate." William Waller Hening, ed., *The Statutes at Large; Being a Collection of All the Laws of Virginia, from the First Session*

of the Legislature, in the Year 1619 (Richmond: Printed by and for Samuel Pleasants, junior, printer to the commonwealth, 1809), 270, https://archive.org/details/statutesatlargeb02virg/page/270/mode/2up?q=negroes. Contemporary conservative arguments in defense of slavery often echo this law. Torture and murder did not often happen, the argument goes, because the masters would have no interest in destroying their property.

47 Malcolm X, Speech at Cory Methodist Church, Cleveland, Ohio, April 3, 1964. For an example of the continuing same, see Sydney Trent, "Trump's Warning that 'Vicious Dogs' would Attack Protesters Conjured Centuries of Racial Terror," *The Washington Post*, June 1, 2020, https://www.washingtonpost.com/history/2020/06/01/trump-vicious-dogs-protesters-civil-rights-slavery/.

48 Jerry Mitchell, "On This Day in 1955: All-White Jury Acquits Emmett Till Killers," *Mississippi Today*, September 23, 2023, Accessed April 3, 2024, https://mississippitoday.org/2023/09/23/on-this-day-in-1955-all-white-jury-acquits-emmett-till-killers/.

49 See Pierre Bourdieu on the necessary ceremony and juridical theatricalization of state power. Pierre Bourdieu, *On the State: Lectures at the Collège de France, 1989-1992* (Cambridge: Polity Press, 2018), 63–4.

50 An Englishman passing by a field near Richmond, Virginia in 1804 interviewed an unnamed man accused of being part of a revolt. The man did not have faith in the colonial court. "I passed by a field [near Richmond] in which several poor slaves had lately been executed, on the charge of having an intention to rise against their masters. A lawyer who was present at their trials at Richmond, informed me that on one of them being asked, what he had to say to the court in his defence, he replied, in a manly tone of voice: 'I have nothing more to offer than what General Washington would have had to offer, had he been taken by the British and put to trial by them. I have adventured my life in endeavoring to obtain the liberty of my countrymen, and am a willing sacrifice to their cause: and I beg, as a favour, that I may be immediately led to execution. I know that you have pre-determined to shed my blood, why then all this mockery of a trial?'" Aptheker, *Revolts*, 223–4. The excerpt also reveals a white origin or influence of the gendering of the Black revolt male. A strategic mistake for slave traders who were caught off guard, believing they needed only to secure the male slaves in the ship. The unsecured African women then killed them or passed weapons to the enslaved men. "For your safety as well as mine. . . You'll have the needful guard over your Slaves, and put not too much Confidence in the Women nor Children lest they happen to be instrumental to your being surprised which may be fatal." 1776 Dr. John Bell surgeon of the Thames ship quoted in Hall, *Wake*, 153.

51 Diana Paton, "Punishment, Crime, and the Bodies of Slaves in Eighteenth-Century Jamaica," *Journal of Social History* , no. 4 (2001): 97, http://www.jstor.org/stable/3789424.

52 Settlers influenced the law to forbid Indigenous Africans from owning livestock, with laws increasingly more draconian in order to force them into laboring for them, culminating in *kifagio*. The "broom" sweeping away Black positions. Tabitha Kanogo, *Squatters and the Roots of Mau Mau, 1905-63* (London: James Currey, 1987), 35–47.
53 A Louisiana judge was caught shouting the N-word at home. "Louisiana Judge Pressed to Resign After Racist Remarks," *Equal Justice Initiative*, Accessed April 3, 2024, https://eji.org/news/louisiana-judge-pressed-to-resign-after-racist-remarks/.
54 See Michel Foucault, *Security, Territory, Population: Lectures at the Collège de France 1977-1978* (New York: Picador, 2007), 248.
55 Often explicitly. The performance of Blues produced by incarcerated Black Southern women named and attacked rape and other prison conditions in a system that thrived on silent torture. Haley, *Mercy*, 236.
56 See Patrick Wolfe, "Settler Colonialism and the Elimination of the Native," *Journal of Genocide Research* 8, no. 4 (2006): 388.
57 Prison could not hold the rebel, however. The jail failed to rehabilitate, that is, reproduce in Adam's personality the docile slave and the obsequious slave John and the others desired. According to John in the jail, "the said Negro hath often times Threatned to kill your petitioner and lately told Mr. Willard the keeper of the Prison that if he had Oppertunity he would make no more to Twist or wring off the Neck of your Petition then he would of a Snake all which is upon Oath and more to the same Effect." Colonial, "Meeting."
58 Samantha Michaels, "Minneapolis Police Union President Allegedly Wore a "White Power Patch" and Made Racist Remarks," *Mother Jones*, May 30, 2020, Accessed April 2, 2024, https://www.motherjones.com/criminal-justice/2020/05/minneapolis-police-union-president-kroll-george-floyd-racism/.
59 Colonial, "Meeting."
60 An Oklahoma district commissioner, Mark Jennings was recorded in a conversation with a senator mourning the lynching past. "Take [a Black guy] down to Mud Creek and hang them up with a damned rope. But you can't do that no more. They got more rights than we got." Josh Dulaney, "Oklahoma Sheriff and Commissioner Accused of Racism and Threats," *The Oklahoman*, April 16, 2023, https://www.oklahoman.com/story/news/2023/04/16/oklahoma-sheriff-and-commissioner-accused-of-racism-and-threats/70119918007/.
61 See John Hope Franklin and Loren Schweninger, *Runaway Slaves: Rebels on the Plantation* (Oxford: Oxford University Press, 2000), 160–2.
62 There is a remarkable continuity between colonial forms of torture in captivity. C. L. R James describes pre-revolt Haiti as follows: "[The masters] buried [the enslaved] up to the neck and smeared their heads with sugar so that the flies might devour them; fastened them near to

nests of ants or wasps; made them eat their excrement, drink their urine, and lick the saliva of other slaves. One colonist was known in moments of anger to throw himself on his slaves and stick his teeth into their flesh." C.L.R. James, *The Black Jacobins: Toussaint L'Ouverture and the San Domingo Revolution* (New York: Vintage Books, 1963), 12–13. Compare this to contemporary incidents where in Georgia, a Black man was eaten alive by insects in prison. Julia Marnin, "New Details in Death of Man 'Eaten Alive' by Insects at Georgia Jail Released by Family," *Miami Herald*, May 23, 2023, Accessed April 4, 2024, https://www.miamiherald.com/news/nation-world/national/article275662221.html. And a strike in Alabama prisons against detainment and death during a pandemic. Sam McCann, "What You Need to Know About the Alabama Prison Strike," *Vera.org*, published October 27, 2022, Accessed April 4, 2024, https://www.vera.org/news/what-you-need-to-know-about-the-alabama-prison-strike.

63 Lily Rothman, "Bill O'Reilly's Comment on Slaves Who Built White House Has a Long History," *Times Magazine*, July 27, 2016, Accessed April 4, 2024. Compare American historical revisionism with Frederick Douglass' recording of his experience. "We were therefore reduced to the wretched necessity of living at the expense of our neighbors. This we did by begging and stealing, whichever came handy in the time of need, the one being considered as legitimate as the other. A great many times have we poor creatures been nearly perishing with hunger, when food in abundance lay mouldering in the safe and smoke-house, and our pious mistress was aware of the fact; and yet that mistress and her husband would kneel every morning, and pray that God would bless them in basket and store!" Frederick Douglass, *Narrative of the Life of Frederick Douglass, an American Slave* (Written by Himself: Electronic Edition. 1818-1895), 52, Accessed April 2, 2024, https://docsouth.unc.edu/neh/douglass/douglass.html.

64 Wall Street Journal, "Ariel Castro's Full Courtroom Statement," video, *Wall Street Journal*, August 1, 2013, Accessed April 2, 2024, https://youtu.be/JIFckzMl0iU.

65 In one of the most famous scenes in Stanley Kubrick's 1987 film *Full Metal Jacket* a US soldier forces a Vietnamese man to dance at pistol point, demonstrating how war drives the dehumanization of both imperialist and colonized. This is the Black experience under colonization not only on slave ships but in Jim Crow as Robert Williams recalls "they caught a colored woman on an isolated street corner and made her dance at pistol point." Robert Franklin Williams, *Negroes with Guns* (Eastford: Martino Publishing, 2013), 17.

66 Aimé Césaire noticed this difficulty with the re-direction of colonialism as well. "[Europe] cannot forgive Hitler for is not *the crime* in itself, *the crime against man*, it is not *the humiliation of man as such*, it is the crime against the white man, the humiliation of the white man, and the fact that

he applied to Europe colonialist procedures which until then had been reserved exclusively for the Arabs of Algeria, the "coolies" of India, and the "niggers" of Africa." Aimé Césaire, *Discourse on Colonialism* (New York: New York University Press, 2000).

67 At the end of the seventeenth century, settlers began to refer to the enslaved as "'Intestine enemies,' a deadly threat that could not be easily expelled or digested." Horne, *Counter-Revolution*, chap. 1.

68 In his 1857 work *Cannibals All! Or, Slaves without Masters*, pro-slavery advocate George Fitzhugh argued the case that man has property in man. His defense of the "peculiar institution" invoked the higher law of God as expressed in the natural world where animals have slaves of their own species and in marriage where man has "property in his wife." One hundred and fifty years earlier than Fitzhugh, John Saffin made similar defenses of slavery, referencing the higher law as expressed in biblical stories. In his *Reply* to Sam Sewall, he asks how slavery could not be God-ordained as it is expressed everywhere from the subordination of man to God to the different stations of life set up by divine wisdom, from the princes and the low and the despicable. One hundred and fifty years after Fitzhugh, similar circular arguments are made, reading the hierarchy that power creates as evidence of the providence of that power and the unnaturalness of every break away from it. The United States is powerful because it is blessed by God. Black people test low on standardized tests, and are violent and poor because of their inherent God-given or cultural characteristics or lack thereof. Every instance of violence and conquest, in white supremacy, affirms white supremacist theory and evidence of the natural law of Black subjugation. George Fitzhugh, Fitzhugh, George. "Cannibals All! Or, Slaves Without Masters." Documenting the American South. University of North Carolina at Chapel Hill Library, Accessed April 6, 2024, https://docsouth.unc.edu/southlit/fitzhughcan/fitzcan.html.

69 Vlad TV, "G-Dep Explains Confessing to Murder: 'I Didn't Feel Free and Clear,'" video, *Vlad TV*, January 11, 2016, https://youtu.be/vNf886x-EAM.

70 Los Angeles Times, "Chris Rock Releases Video on How to Behave During Traffic Stop," Accessed April 2, 2024, https://www.latimes.com/entertainment/tv/la-et-st-chris-rock-video-sterling-20160707-snap-htmlstory.html.

71 Douglass, *Narrative of the Life of Frederick Douglass, an American Slave*, 71.

72 Colonial, "Meeting."

Chapter 2

1 Horne, *Counter-Revolution*, chap. 1.

2 The passage above is taken from *Uncle Tom's Cabin*, "the first novel to criticize the institution of American slavery," as American Studies scholar

Ann Douglas presented it in her biographical note preceding the text. The slave "trader" and Uncle Tom's future "good master" Augustine St. Clare are haggling over Tom's price. The trader in his amateur craniometry points to his forehead saying intelligence is useful in a slave. The good master saying it is a liability because the intelligent run off and raise the devil. Stowe, *Uncle*, 235.

3 The first settlement within the borders of what, in colonist language, is referred to as the contemporary United States was a Spanish settlement in South Carolina numbering five hundred Spaniards and a hundred Africans. The Africans rebelled and joined the Indigenous. The Spanish eventually returned to Haiti, leaving only the Africans and Indigenous in the colony. Aptheker, *Revolts*, 163.

4 Daryl Cumber Dance notes that in the Black folk lexicon, no idea has more words to express it than the idea of leaving, escaping, and running away. As Celeste Winston argues, marronage is a technology of survival, of placemaking, a transatlantic Black literary and cultural preoccupation (from Brer Rabbit to Eshu), and a movement against plantations, prisons, and patriotism. See Celeste Winston, *How to Lose the Hounds* (Durham: Duke University Press, 2023), 22–30.

5 News 19 WLTX, "Buster Murdaugh Testifies in the Trial of Alex Murdaugh: Full video," video, *News 19 WLTX*, February 21, 2023, https://youtu.be/vNf886x-EAM?si=JKR3QUw4FDR26Ws4

6 Aptheker, *Revolts*, 198.

7 The Wilmington Chronicle worried about the threat: "number of runaway Negroes, who in the daytime secrete themselves in the swamps and woods, at night committed various depredations on the neighboring plantations." Aptheker, *Revolts*, 217.

8 Simultaneously, the governor of South Carolina received information that "107 Negroes had left their Plantations. . . and joined a large number of Runaways in Colleton County." With the prospect of a full-scale slave rebellion a real possibility, the Governor not only ordered out the militia, he also brought down nearly fifty Catawba Indians to hunt out the runaways, since "Indians strike terrour into the Negroes, and the Indians manner of hunting render them more sagacious in tracking and expert in finding out the hidden recesses, where the Runaways conceal themselves from the usual searches of the English." While a slave rebellion was averted, the Governor was forced to admit that "there are several large Parties of Runaways still concealed in large Swamps" (8). https://archives.history.ac.uk/history-in-focus/Slavery/articles/lockley.html#8.

9 White supremacist occupation of Indigenous land has always provided opportunities for Indigenous people and Black people who would cooperate with the state against Black freedom to turn an easy profit. There were Indigenous and Black slaveholders as well as Indigenous

people "friendly with the whites" brought in to torture the enslaved and fend off uprisings. Aptheker, *Revolts*, 198.
10 Franklin and Schweninger, *Runaway*, 27.
11 Franklin and Schweninger, *Runaway*, 88.
12 Sylviane A. Diouf, *Slavery's Exiles: The Story of the American Maroons* (New York: New York University Press, 2014), chap. 1, Google Books.
13 In the early seventeenth century, escape into the obscure places was often a multicultural class revolt. Horne, *Counter-Revolution*, chap. 1.
14 Herbert Aptheker defines the slave revolt as involving a minimum of ten enslaved people who strike out violently and collectively in the cause for their freedom. He counts at least 250 such revolts or conspiracies to revolt in the "United States" during chattel slavery. Aptheker, *Revolts*, 162.
15 Diouf, *Exiles*, chap 1.
16 It would be centuries before this achievement of colonialism would be obtained. See the following chapters.
17 The imperialist must know the Other in order to have power over them. It is the "great imperial obligation," as Lord Curzon put it. Quoted in Edward Said, *Orientalism* (New York: Vintage, 1994), 214.
18 In 1767, as part of a rebellion in Alexandria, Virginia, several enslaved Africans poisoned several overseers. Aptheker, *Revolts*, 198.
19 This should not lead to a romanticization of maroons. It should also be remembered that Jamaican maroons agreed to return runaways to plantations as a peace treaty with the British. The very existence of black rebellious freedom inspired other revolts. Mr. Randolf of Richmond, Virginia, overheard the men plotting a revolt when one added, "you see how the blacks has killed the whites in the French Island and took it a while ago." Aptheker, *Revolts*, 214.
20 In 1711, after his Indigenous comrade Salvadore and African Scipio were caught for being about that "stick talk" and executed with their heads and other body parts were placed "in the most publick place," a certain Negro Will nevertheless continued his work and was accused of "levying war in this colony." Horne, *Counter-Revolution*, chap. 2.
21 Horne, *Counter-Revolution*, chap. 1.
22 Horne, *Counter-Revolution*, chap. 1.
23 The ruling has often been seen to have established African slavery as a distinct form of indentured servitude. Diouf, *Exiles*, chap 1.
24 Horne, *Counter-Revolution*, chap. 1.
25 Diouf, *Exiles*, chap 1.
26 Horne, *Counter-Revolution*, chap. 2. After a plot in 1732 Louisiana, one enslaved woman was killed and "four men broken on the wheel. Their heads were then stuck on poles at the upper and lower ends of New Orleans as grim and stark inducements to docility." Aptheker, *Revolts*, 189.
27 Diouf, *Exiles*, chap 1.

28 An Austin Steward noted that a house slave "will for the sake of his master and mistress, frequently betray his fellow-slave . . . he is often rewarded by his master who knows it is for his interest to keep such ones about him . . . hence it is that insurrections and stampedes are so generally detected. Such slaves are always treated with more affability than others, for the slaveholder is well aware that he stands over a volcano." Aptheker, *Revolts*, 63.

29 For this reason, maroon and Black anti-colonial societies used oathing and other security measures to ensure their security. See the depiction in Hall, *Wake*, 55–7. Blackness, it was recognized, was not enough, and "skin folk were not necessarily kinfolk." Most famously, the Kenyan Land and Freedom Army (Mau Mau) used oathing to ensure that Africans in their circle were committed to anti-colonialism. The Mau Mau war, or as the colonists called it, The Emergency is perhaps one of the most violent expansive wars of the modern period between settlers and loyalists on one side and anti-colonialists on the other.

30 Following Bell's critique of anti-feminist Black women as "pick-me's," I refer here to "influencer" Black conservatives who perform particularly outlandish and vocal negrophobia as invitations to white white supremacists to join in allyship in return for money, celebrity, love, or noogies. For example, Kanye West's declaration that slavery was its victims' fault or wearing the white supremacist slogan "white lives matter" on a shirt, offering his celebrity in the service of white supremacists Donald Trump and Nick Fuentes. See D. Procope Bell, "'Pick-Me' Black Women: Tactical Patriarchal Femininity in the Black Manosphere," *Feminist Media Studies* (2023): 1–19, https://doi.org/10.1080/14680777.2023.2262163.

31 An enslaved person's letter quoted in George Goodly to Governor Monroe, C.V.S.P., IX p. 305, quoted in Aptheker, *Revolts*, 229–30.

32 Malcolm X, "Malcolm Describes the Difference Between the 'House Negro' and the 'Field Negro.' Michigan State University, East Lansing, Michigan. 23 January 1963," *Columbia Center of Teaching and Learning*, Accessed April 2, 2024, https://ccnmtl.columbia.edu/projects/mmt/mxp/speeches/mxt17.html.

33 Daniel Horsmanden, *A Journal of the Proceedings in the Detection of the Conspiracy Formed by Some White People, in Conjunction with Negro and Other Slaves, for Burning the City of New-York in America, and Murdering the Inhabitants* (New York: James Parker, 1744), 7, Accessed April 2, 2024, https://quod.lib.umich.edu/cgi/t/text/text-idx?c=evans;cc=evans;rgn=main;view=text;idno=N04378.0001.001.

34 C. R. Foy, "Eighteenth Century 'Prize Negroes': From Britain to America," *Slavery and Abolition* 31, no. 3 (2010): 379–93, doi:10.1080/0144039X.2010.504532.

35 Horsmanden, *Conspiracy*.

36 Horsmanden, *Conspiracy*.
37 In the *Journal*, the name is spelled Quack or Quaco, a likely Anglicization of Kwaku.
38 This "playing fool to catch wise" technique of flattering power to secure release continues in contemporary prisons. Sarah Haley recounts the case of the imprisoned Emma Wimms, who in 1921 wrote to the governor asking to be released on humanitarian grounds so that she could spend the rest of her life as a True Woman. A "grave mistake" as humanity and womanhood were not attributes of the "negress." Emma Wimms then joined wiser inmates who appealed for freedom so that they could be good servants, performed infantilism, were silent about abuse in custody, and praised guards and wardens. In espousing that self-caricature in her letter, Wimms was released. Haley, *Mercy*, 207–8.
39 Quack, whose "Insolence and Ingratitude towards his Master, were very remarkable," would eventually be burned at the stake after his forced confession. Horsmanden, *Conspiracy*.
40 Haley, *Mercy*, 200.
41 Haley, *Mercy*.
42 In slavery, just as in policing, it could be pretended that the pleasure of torturing Black people did not exist. Frederick Douglass describes a master, Mr. Hopkins who replaced the cruel overseer. "Mr. Severe's place was filled by a Mr. Hopkins. He was a very different man. He was less cruel, less profane, and made less noise than Mr. Severe. His course was characterized by no extraordinary demonstrations of cruelty. He whipped, but seemed to take no pleasure in it. He was called by the slaves a good overseer." Mr. Severe and Mr. Hopkins, the latter with his dispassionate, mechanical dispensing of torture and punishment, foreshadow contemporary debates between good and bad apples in policing in colonialism. The liberal settler arguing for a time of policing that resembled Mr. Hopkins and conservatives mocking George Floyd's death by defending Mr. Severe.
43 Douglass, *Narrative of the Life of Frederick Douglass, an American Slave*, 7.
44 Douglass, *Narrative of the Life of Frederick Douglass, an American Slave*, 11.
45 Horsmanden, *Conspiracy*.
46 See Jennifer L. Morgan, *Reckoning with Slavery: Gender, Kinship, and Capitalism in the Early Black Atlantic* (Durham: Duke University Press, 2021), 223–5.
47 Morgan, *Reckoning with Slavery*.
48 Morgan, *Reckoning with Slavery*.
49 Lumpen leisure spaces as spaces of relative freedom, opacity, and fertile ground for anti-racist organizing, theory, and praxis continued into the twentieth century. Lashawn Harris, in her story of early twentieth-

century Harlem Numbers runner Madame St. Clair, describes the illicit gambling houses as spaces free from white control, where women could face relatively fewer gender and racial barriers and, in St. Clair's case, could generate from it enough personal power for anti-racist work. Lashawn Harris, *Sex Workers, Psychics, and Numbers Runners: Black Women in New York City's Underground Economy* (Urbana: University of Illinois Press, 2016), 54–6. I would argue that this persists in what might be called Digital "hush harbors" in Black social media space, especially "Black Twitter."
50 Harris, *Sex Workers, Psychics, and Numbers Runners*.
51 Enslaved people in New York the same year, for example, were thought to have planned to poison the water supply of the city, leading white New Yorkers to buy spring water from vendors out of precaution. Aptheker, *Revolts*, 192.
52 Aptheker, *Revolts*, 190.
53 It is sometimes mistakenly believed that there were burnings of women in Salem, Massachusetts, during the Salem Witch Trials 1692–1693. The stake, however, was reserved for other groups. Enslaved people were often burned alive after being suspected or accused of arson, poisoning masters and plotting revolts. The immolation "punishment" continued into the post-1863 Emancipation Proclamation era as several lynchings involved burning victims alive at the stake. In 1916, Jesse Washington, a man thought to be disabled, was paraded through Waco, Texas, while being stabbed and burned. After the Salem Witch Trials, representing for so many the epitome of barbarity and the last days of American justice's unenlightened past, immolation and show trials continued against the lives not counted. The last witch to be executed in Britain was Jenny Horne, burned at the stake in Dornoch, Scotland, in the 1720s. Runaways, enslaved rebels, and accused Black criminals continued to be burned long after this date in the colonies, continuing, arguably, to the penal witch burnings, that is, the present-day use of the electric chair in several (former) slave states of the South.
54 Aptheker, *Revolts*, 191.
55 See Afua Cooper, *The Hanging of Angelique: The Untold Story of Canadian Slavery and the Burning of Old Montreal* (New York: HarperCollins Publishers, 2006).
56 Stono, South Carolina enslaved people's rebellion of 1739 was one of the largest and most successful in the colony's history. Rebels killed the guards of an arms facility and shot at everyone, sparing only a "good master." Other enslaved joined them and burned buildings. Aptheker, *Revolts*, 187–8.
57 For a close reading of the ghetto as native quarter, see Saidiya Hartman, *Wayward Lives, Beautiful Experiments: Intimate Histories of Social Upheaval* (New York: W.W. Norton & Company, 2019).
58 Haley, *Mercy*, 236–46.

59 "The 1860 Henderson Fire," *Waymarking.com*, Accessed April 4, 2024, https://www.waymarking.com/gallery/image.aspx?f=1&guid=314c81dc-6d91-4b3f-8977-60cac73bf3c7.
60 Malcolm X, "Malcolm X tells the Parable of the 'House Negro' King Solomon Baptist Church, Detroit. 10 November 1943." *Columbia Center of Teaching and Learning*, Accessed April 2, 2024, https://ccnmtl.columbia.edu/projects/mmt/mxp/speeches/mxa29.html.
61 Horsmanden, *Conspiracy*.
62 See Chap. 3.
63 Stowe, *Uncle*, 560–2.
64 "[The Indian Sam] and the Negro Fiend are done being enslaved." Hall, *Wake*, 87.
65 Bernard Wolfe on the Black grin: "We like to depict the black man grinning at us with all his teeth. And his grin—such as we see it—such as we create it—always signifies a gift... An endless gift stretching along posters, movie screens and product labels... The blacks... are kept in their obsequious attitude by the extreme penalties of fear and force, and this is common knowledge to both the whites and blacks. Nevertheless the whites demand that the blacks be smiling, attentive and friendly in all their relationships with them." Cited in Fanon, *Black*, 32.
66 A death forced onto *Erik Killmonger*, the supervillain and anti-colonialist stand-in the 2018 film *Black Panther*.
67 See James Early, "Re-communalization of a Jamaican Kumina Drum," *Smithsonian Folklife*, August 15, 2014, Accessed April 4, 2024, https://folklife.si.edu/talkstory/2014/re-communalization-of-a-jamaican-kumina-drum.
68 See J. T. Roane's, *Dark Agoras: Insurgent Black Social Life And the Politics of Place* (New York: New York University Press, 2023), 209–42 for more on MOVE developing a "Black Commons" within the colony.
69 By which I mean the subaltern Pan-Africanisms not of conferences, organizations, states, and theses but the non-academic Pan-Africanisms of the everyday. The cross-pollination of musical and artistic ideas, Afro-futurisms, and gestures of solidarity and community to Black conversations and exchange everywhere from Harlem's 125th St., Peckham London's grocery stores, to East African beaches and US prisons.
70 See Marcus Garvey, *Philosophy and Opinions of Marcus Garvey*, ed. Amy Jacques Garvey (New York: Universal Publishing, 1986).
71 Dead Prez, *Let's Get Free* (Loud Records, 2000).
72 Sister Souljah. *360 Degrees of Power* (Epic Records, 1992).
73 As it is for Black separatist movements to be mocked and derided as unfeasible even in a colony organized around nationalism based on settler separation from British colonists.

74 Toussaint Louverture, "Toussaint Louverture to Jean-Jacques Dessalines, February 8, 1802," letter, Accessed April 4, 2024, https://schlegiathanpost.files.wordpress.com/2013/07/primary-source-toussiant-louverture-to-jean-jacques-dessalines-february-8-1802-letter.pdf.
75 Emily Wagster Pettus, "Mississippi Police Officer Indicted in Activist's Death," *AP News*, published 2:19 PM PDT, April 21, 2023, Accessed April 2, 2024, https://apnews.com/article/jackson-mississippi-police-naacp-591246abb8f620f039ec33cf9f6e5e74#.
76 See Grace Nichols, *I is a Long-Memoried Woman* (London: Karnak House, 1983), 17–19.
77 Aptheker, *Revolts*, 201.
78 Aptheker, *Revolts*, 202.
79 The slaveholder author of the colony's anthem was unhappy that Black people (the British Colonial Marines) burned down the White House in 1812. He penned "No refuge could save the hireling and slave/From the terror of flight or the gloom of the grave" as a rallying cry for the colony against "the blacks." Glenn Johnston, "Racism or Rhetoric? Francis Scott Key and the Defence of Fort McHenry," *Stevenson University*, May 1, 2019, Accessed April 4, 2024, https://www.stevenson.edu/academics/undergraduate-programs/history/blog-news-events/racism-or-rhetoric-francis-scott-key-and-the-defence-of-fort-mchenry/.
80 Aptheker, *Revolts*, 191.
81 Aptheker, *Revolts*, 231.
82 Bryan Wagner, *Disturbing the Peace: Black Culture and the Police Power after Slavery* (Cambridge, MA: Harvard University Press, 2009), 70.
83 See Michel Foucault, *Discipline and Punish: The Birth of the Prison*, trans. Alan Sheridan (New York: Vintage Books, 1995), 3–31.
84 As South Carolina slaveholders declared in 1816, "Every measure that may lessen the dependence of a Slave on his master ought to be opposed, as tending toward dangerous consequences," Franklin and Schweninger, *Runaway*, 90.
85 Foucault opens *Discipline and Punish* with the scene of execution by torture of the regicide to begin his explanation of "the disappearance of torture as a public spectacle." Foucault, *Discipline*, 3–7. In the settler-colony, it is the Black person killing the master/police officer or white woman that is, functionally, considered the most heinous crime. The heretical act results in spectacles of grief for "fallen officers" killed in the "line of duty." These public funerals mirror the rituals of an English king's death. The punitive public spectacle of Black torture did not disappear in the eighteenth century either. Lynching bees multiplied the slave plantation's scene at the whipping tree.
86 Not only did the law excuse the master's killing of enslaved people if they were killed during the violence of "correction," but another law stated, "if any negro, mulatto, or Indian, bond or free, shall at any time,

lift his or her hand, in opposition against any christian, not being negro, mulatto, or Indian, he or she so offending shall, for every such offence, proved by the oath of the party, receive on his or her bare back, thirty lashes, well laid on." Black and Indigenous resistance to whiteness (even when conceived as "Christian") and authority must be harshly punished. "An Act Concerning Servants and Slaves, 1705," *Encyclopedia Virginia*, Accessed April 3, 2024, https://encyclopediavirginia.org/primary-documents/an-act-concerning-servants-and-slaves-1705/.
87 Ashley Williams, "Virginia Cops Arrest Employee for Stealing a Package That Resurfaced," *Atlanta Black Star*, February 21, 2024, Accessed April 2, 2024, https://atlantablackstar.com/2024/02/21/virginia-cops-arrest-employee-for-stealing-a-package-that-resurfaced/.
88 Fanon, *Wretched*, 2.
89 Rudyard Kipling, "'The White Man's Burden: The United States & The Philippine Islands, 1899," in *Rudyard Kipling's Verse: Definitive Edition* (Garden City, New York: Doubleday, 1929), Accessed April 2, 2024, https://historymatters.gmu.edu/d/5478/.
90 See note 11 in Colonial, "Meeting."
91 Samuel Sewall, *The Selling of Joseph: A Memorial* (1700), Electronic Texts in American Studies, Paper 26, 3.
92 Sewall, *Selling*, 2.
93 During the settler's war with the British in 1813, US officials worried about the enslaved African as the "internal foe." Aptheker, *Revolts*, 25.
94 Sewall, *Selling*, 2.
95 Lawrence W. Towner, "The Sewall-Saffin Dialogue on Slavery," *The William and Mary Quarterly: A Magazine of Early American History* 21 (1964): 40–52.
96 Sewall, *Selling*, 2. After Nat Turner's Revolt, free African Americans were banned from coming to Maryland. There were propaganda campaigns attempting to lure African Americans to Liberia as plans were devised to rid the state of free Black people. Aptheker, *Revolts*, 314.
97 Aptheker, *Revolts*, 314.
98 Aptheker, *Revolts*, 314.
99 John Saffin, "A Brief and Candid Answer to a late Printed Sheet, Entitled, The Selling of Joseph," in *A True and Particular Narrative. . . of the Author's Dealing with and Prosecution of his Negro Man Servant* (1701), Accessed April 4, 2024, from Oxford University Press website, https://global.oup.com/us/companion.websites/fdscontent/uscompanion/us/static/companion.websites/9780199338863/whittington_updata/ch_2_saffin_a_brief_and_candid_answer.pdf.
100 Saffin, "A Brief."
101 Towner, "Dialogue," 52.
102 Towner, "Dialogue," 5.
103 Fanon, *Wretched*, 6.

104 Colonial, "Meeting."
105 Fanon writes "... the colonist speaks of the colonized in zoological terms." Fanon, *Wretched*, 7.
106 Franklin and Schweninger, *Runaway*, 156–7.
107 Giorgio Agamben speaks of the werewolf as a metaphor of the being banned and thrown out of the city and yet human enough to be subject to law. Giorgio Agamben, *Homo Sacer. Sovereign Power and Bare Life* (Stanford: Stanford University Press, 1998), 104–11.
108 See Robert J. Devaux, *They Called Us Brigands: The Saga of St. Lucia's Freedom Fighters* (Castries: Optimum Printers, 1997).
109 Mary Guyatt, "The Wedgwood Slave Medallion: Values in Eighteenth-century Design," *Journal of Design History* 13, no. 2 (2000): 100.
110 Gordon Turnbull, *An Apology for Negro Slavery: or the West-India Planters Vindicated from the Charge of Inhumanity* (Printed by J. Stevenson for J. Strachan, R. Faulder, and W. Richardson, 1786), 33, http://reader.library.cornell.edu/docviewer/digital?id=may893207#page/10/mode/1up.
111 The "uppity" African American was especially hated as like the maroon and the disrespectful Black youth the character displayed a disinterest in remaining in the allotted "place." As George Fredrickson noted, in the antebellum world "the 'good negro' was always in his place and the 'bad nigger' outside it." Cited in Hartman, *Scenes*, 30.
112 Since the 1850s, the minstrel show addressed both working-class white audiences who enjoyed comforting representations of negro buffoonery and the happy and loyal slave as well as middle-class audiences who added to this the pleasure of the sentimental songs of the piteous enslaved. Brian Roberts, *Blackface Nation: Race, Reform, and Identity in American Popular Music, 1812-1925* (Chicago: University of Chicago Press, 2017), 182–3. This most visceral expression of anti-Black racism would also become the first colony-birthed form of mass entertainment. See Matthew D. Morrison, *Black Sound: Black People, Black Music, and the Racial Imagination* (Durham: Duke University Press, 2024).
113 Marshall, "Bleaching," 14.
114 Mark Twain, *The Adventures of Huckleberry Finn* (New York: Webster & Company, 1885), https://www.gutenberg.org/ebooks/76.
115 Emily Clark, "George Griffin: Devoted Friend to Samuel Clemens," *Connecticut History*, April 4, 2024, https://connecticuthistory.org/george-griffin-devoted-friend-to-samuel-clemens/.
116 Twain, *Huckleberry*.
117 Mark Twain, *The Adventures of Tom Sawyer* (New York: American Publishing Company, 1884).
118 Twain, *Tom*.
119 Twain, *Tom*.
120 Twain, *Huckleberry*.

121 See, James Elbert Cutler, *Lynch-Law: An Investigation into the History of Lynching in the United States* (London: Longmans, Green, and Co., 1905), 144. It is interesting that the militants thought the sheet was what was scary to the Black people. Most slave narratives, as Vincent Woodward notes, refer to masters cannibalizing Black people. Vincent Woodard, *The Delectable Negro: Human Consumption and Homoeroticism within US Slave Culture* (New York: New York University Press, 2014), 13.
122 Twain, *Huckleberry*.
123 Twain, *Huckleberry*.
124 See Stowe, *Uncle*, 351.
125 See Toni Morrison, *Playing in the Dark: Whiteness and the Literary Imagination* (New York: Vintage Books, 1993).
126 Aptheker, *Revolts*, 52.
127 See Carol Anderson, *The Second: Race and Guns in a Fatally Unequal America* (New York: Bloomsbury Publishing, 2021).
128 Eve Tuck and K. Wayne Yang, "Decolonization Is Not a Metaphor," *Decolonization: Indigeneity, Education & Society* 1, no. 1 (2012): 1–40.
129 Guy Adams, "Caught on Tape: Mel Gibson Race Rant to Girlfriend," *The Independent*, July 3, 2010.
130 Roberts, *Blackface*, 157–8.
131 Brian Howey, Nate Rosenfield, and Jerry Mitchell, "Six Officers Known as the 'Goon Squad' Plead Guilty to Torturing Two Black Men, Using a Sex Toy on Them and Shooting One of Them," *Mississippi Today*, August 3, 2023, https://mississippitoday.org/2023/08/03/six-rankin-officers-plead-guilty-to-torturing-two-black-men/.
132 Stowe, *Uncle*, 590.

Chapter 3

1 A law may no longer be on the books requiring a Black person to have to show their slave pass or, as in Mississippi 1866, not be found assembling together unlawfully with other freedmen, but it remains customary in the colony for the Black person to be prepared to give a defense of their being in public space if it is demanded by any white person. See Facing History & Ourselves, "Excerpt from Mississippi Black Codes (1865)," *Facing History & Ourselves*, March 14, 2016, Accessed December 17, 2024, https://www.facinghistory.org/resource-library/excerpt-mississippi-black-codes-1865.
2 Virginia, 1639 Act X: "All persons except Negroes to be provided with arms and ammunitions or be fined at the pleasure of the Governor and Council." Hening, *The Statutes at Large, Vol. 1*, 226.
3 Reform is a feature of every colony as every colony must adapt to conditions on the ground. This is necessary for the maintenance of settler

rule, especially in the context of an unsubdued colonized population. Reform, therefore, is a police instrument.
4 I am grateful to Elizabeth Gritter for this reference.
5 For a discussion on the limitations of "human rights" in a US hegemonic global order, see Joseph A. Massad, *Desiring Arabs* (Chicago: University of Chicago Press, 2007). Human rights under imperialism mirror Civil Rights in colonialism and in fact should be read as US apartheid law extended globally. A condition where Palestinian lives matter as much as Emmett Till's, and settler lynch mob of Israeli society expects as much reprimand as Roy Bryant and J. W. Milam did. Where all US colonial administrators presume preemptive immunity on the world stage, both neocolonial tyrants and the colonized world's human rights leaders are chased and murdered according to the requirements of capitalist rule and corporate interests.
6 New York Amsterdam News, "Dr. Martin Luther King Jr.: Celebrating the 90th Bornday of a King," *New York Amsterdam News*, January 17, 2019, Accessed January 10, 2025, https://amsterdamnews.com/news/2019/01/17/dr-martin-luther-king-jr-celebrating-90th-bornday/.
7 See Introduction.
8 Hartman, *Scenes*, 140.
9 See Marshall, *Bleaching*, 117–67.
10 See Marshall, *Bleaching*, 285.
11 Marshall, *Bleaching*, 284.
12 David Walker, *Walker's Appeal, in Four Articles; Together with a Preamble, to the Coloured Citizens of the World, but in Particular, and Very Expressly, to Those of the United States of America* (University Park: Pennsylvania State University, 2001), 42.
13 Walker, *Appeal*, xxxix–xli.
14 Walker, *Appeal*, 107–8.
15 See Fanon, *Wretched*, 8–9.
16 Roane, *Agoras*, 193.
17 Roane, *Agoras*, 24.
18 Roane, *Agoras*, 22.
19 In colonialism, apartheid and the "bifurcated state" are the rule and not a South African exception. See Mamdani, *Citizen*, 27–32.
20 "I Have a Dream," Speech in Its Entirety. NPR, Accessed April 4, 2024, https://www.npr.org/2010/01/18/122701268/i-have-a-dream-speech-in-its-entirety.
21 The hold that Dr. King and other charismatic Black male leaders have on dominant, published history is also due to what Erica Edwards points out is the fiction that Black leadership is "seductively troped as the motor of black history in a way that always hides and represses the heterogeneity of the movements toward black self-determination." A fiction that is disciplining so that radical work that seeks legitimacy must shape itself

in the mold of Black liberal leadership. Divergent aims of the radical Black women's work are pressured to fall in line with the narrative of the exceptional, seer Black male leader. Edwards convincingly stages the "inaugural scene" of twentieth-century Black politics, where middle class black leadership was crowd race representative and a bulwark against white supremacist ideology, to the 1893 Columbian Exposition in Chicago. "The World's Fair presented an ethnophilic panoply of colonial others: along the mile-long strip of the Midway Plaisance were a string of anthropological exhibits that presented folk representation of European villages followed by Chinese, Turkish, Arabic, Persian, Algerian, and Egyptian Villages. 'At the very end of the midway—and scale of civilization . . . was a Dahomyan village where sixty-nine Africans 'blacker than buried midnight and as degraded as animals capered nobly to the lascivious pleasing of an unseen tom-tom pounding within.'" Respectable, charismatic black leadership stepped forward to distance itself from the savage minstrel show of the human zoo and draw Black Americanness to the state and the civil, severing it from white white-supremacist-contrived Africanity. Erica R. Edwards, *Charisma and the Fictions of Black Leadership* (Minneapolis: University of Minnesota Press, 2012), 8–11.
22 Sundiata Keita Cha-Jua and Clarence Lang, "The Long Movement as Vampire: Temporal and Spatial Fallacies in Recent Black Freedom Studies," *Journal of African American History* 92, no. 2 (Spring 2007): 266.
23 See Marshall, *Bleaching*, 140–6.
24 Roberts, *Blackface*, 173.
25 Faith Salie, "Weaponizing the American Flag: Photographer Stanley Forman," *CBS News*, June 18, 2023. https://www.cbsnews.com/news/weaponizing-the-american-flag-photographer-stanley-forman/.
26 Another relatively muzzled contemporary of King and previous believer in what became known as Civil Rights, Robert F. Williams tellingly begins his *Negroes With Guns* with "Why do I speak to you from exile?" Williams looked even to Europe, abandoned by the NAACP who did not want to take up the sex case of two Black boys arrested for the capital crime of rape, being falsely accused of kissing a white girl. "The NAACP national office still wasn't doing anything about the case, but an English reporter who was a friend of Lynn's visited the reformatory and sneaked out a photograph of the boys, which appeared along with a story on the front page of the Dec. 15, 1958, London News Chronicle. Then all of Europe got wind of the case and there were protest demonstrations in London, Rotterdam, Rome, and Paris. Only then did many American newspapers begin to express 'concern' about the "Kissing Case." Williams, *Guns*, 59–60.
27 Ernest J. Cullen of East London, Cape Colony, sent a telegram to a US sheriff requesting photo postcard of a Black man burned at the stake in

Greenville, Texas. The telegram read, "I have just read in a New York paper of a lynching affair that has taken place in your county quite recently, a negro having been burned at the state for outraging a young white girl. The account also state that the affair was photographed whilst in full swing, and that picture post cards reproduced therefrom were all the go as souvenirs. Now Mr. Sheriff, I would esteem it a great favor if you would kindly obtain for me two of these postcards or photos and send them to me, as I should ver much like an idea of how these things are managed over the pond . . . ." The editors clarified that the writer made a mistake and the lynching did not happen in Fort Worth but Greenville. "African Official Sends For Picture Of Texas Lynching!" Fort Worth Star (Texas, USA), September 8, 1908.
28 Williams, *Guns*, 70.
29 Patrick Healy and Jeff Zeleny, "Clinton and Obama Spar Over Remark About Dr. King," *The New York Times*, 2008.
30 The nationalist political parties never insist on the need for confrontation precisely because their aim is not the radical overthrow of the system. Pacifist and law-abiding, partisans, in fact, of order, the new order, these political groups bluntly ask of the colonialist bourgeoisie what to them is essential: "Give us more power." On the specific issue of violence, the elite are ambiguous. Fanon, *Wretched*, 22.
31 Williams, *Guns*, 75–82.
32 Frederick Douglass, "Fifth of July Speech," delivered in Rochester, New York, July 5, 1852, Accessed April 4, 2024, https://housedivided.dickinson.edu/sites/teagle/texts/frederick-douglass-fifth-of-july-speech-1852/.
33 Roberts, *Blackface*, 20.
34 Kamau Brathwaite, *Roots* (Ann Arbor: University of Michigan Press, 1994), 260. Ngugi wa Thiong'o recalls the year when the colonial government took over the schools in 1952 during "The Emergency" in Kenya. Students were given corporal punishment for speaking Gikuyu near the school. "Three to five. Strokes of the cane on bare buttocks—or was made to carry a metal plate around the neck with inscriptions such as I AM STUPID or I AM A DONKEY," or fined. Stories of similar, if less corporal, punishments are heard in East Africa or the present. Ngugi wa Thiong'o, *Decolonizing the Mind* (Suffolk: James Currey, 2005), 11.
35 Indeed, if any enslaved did have the audacity to ask a master, plaintively, were they not a man and a brother in pleading against their bestialization, the expectation would be a response in violence.
36 Organization of American Historians, *Virginia Race Laws*, Accessed January 12, 2025, https://oah.org/site/assets/files/12011/virginia_race_laws_1.pdf.
37 Stowe allows Uncle Tom to die like Jesus, with two enslaved people charged with whipping him to death mocking him but eventually asking

for him to teach them more about Christ, like the two crucified next to Jesus in the biblical story. He dies ecstatic, saying, "heaven has come. I've got the victory" and that he hoped the master would repent and that he should not be hated for what he did because all he did was to open the gate of the kingdom for me." Echoing, with his broad Negro chest, Christ's "Into Your hands I commend my spirit" and "forgive them father for they know not what they do." Stowe, *Uncle*, 579–91.

38 Fanon, *Wretched*, 23.
39 Sister Souljah, "That One Time when Sister Souljah Schooled Cornel West," *Citizen Stewart*, YouTube, video, Accessed April 2, 2023, https://www.youtube.com/watch?v=JokCT0CAkE8.
40 Barack Obama, "A More Perfect Union," *NPR*, March 18, 2008, Accessed April 4, 2024, https://www.npr.org/templates/story/story.php?storyId=88478467.
41 Shakur, *An Autobiography*. (London: Zed Books, 1987), 13.
42 Marshall, *Bleaching*, 155–66.
43 See Ward Churchill, *A Little Matter of Genocide: Holocaust and Denial in the Americas, 1492 to the Present* (San Francisco: City Lights Books, 1997).
44 See Yannick Giovanni Marshall, "America, the Big Lie," *Al Jazeera*, February 8, 2021, Accessed April 2, 2024 https://www.aljazeera.com/opinions/2020/6/7/the-racists-peace https://www.aljazeera.com/opinions/2021/2/8/america-the-big-lie.
45 A history of colonialism from below, or from afar, from the viewpoint of marronage instead of romanticizing the slaveholding president might include the story of a runaway woman, Ona Judge, escaping George Washington. See New England Historical Society, "Ona Judge Staines: The Slave Who Got Away From George Washington," Accessed April 3, 2024, https://www.newenglandhistoricalsociety.com/ona-judge-staines-slave-got-away-george-washington/.
46 Woodard, *Delectable*, 60.
47 Caroline Elkins writes about the concentration camps to hold Indigenous African rebels during the uprising or "Kenya Emergency." Caroline Elkins, *Imperial Reckoning: The Untold Story of Britain's Gulag in Kenya* (New York: Henry Holt and Company, 2005), 141–211.
48 See Tuck and Yang, *Decolonization*.
49 See Horne, *Counter-revolution*, chap. 10.
50 National Museum of American History, *Star-Spangled Banner Lyrics*, Accessed January 12, 2025, https://amhistory.si.edu/starspangledbanner/pdf/ssb_lyrics.pdf.
51 The shooting location chosen for Jason Aldean's music video "Try That in a Small Town" was the site of the lynching of Henry Choate at Tennessee's Maury County Courthouse a century earlier. In the original music video, now removed news footage of 2020's Black Lives Matter protestors was projected onto the courthouse wall. See Adrian Horton, "Jason Aldean

'Try That in a Small Town' Video Edited After BLM Criticism," *The Guardian*, July 26, 2023, https://www.theguardian.com/music/2023/jul/26/jason-aldean-try-that-in-a-small-town-video-edited-blm.
52   Aptheker, *Revolts*, 167.
53   See Chap. 1.
54   Walker, *Appeal*, 23.
55   Lorenzo Kom'boa Ervin, *Anarchism and the Black Revolution* (originally published 1979), Accessed January 12, 2025, https://theanarchistlibrary.org/library/lorenzo-kom-boa-ervin-anarchism-and-the-black-revolution#toc15.
56   Hoover set out his reasoning for subverting militant Black nationalist groups and five goals to contest Black radicalism. "For maximum effectiveness of the Counterintelligence Program, and to prevent wasted effort, long-range goals are being set. 1. Prevent the COALITION of militant black nationalist groups. In unity there is strength . . . An effective coalition of black nationalist groups might be the first step toward a real Mau Mau [Black revolutionary army] in America, the beginning of a true black revolution.

2. Prevent the RISE OF A MESSIAH who could unify, and electrify, the militant black nationalist movement. Malcolm X might have been such a messiah he is the martyr of the movement today . . . King could be a very real contender for this position should he abandon his supposed obedience to a white, liberal doctrines (nonviolence) and embrace black nationalism. Carmichael [Kwame Ture] has the necessary charisma to be a real threat in this way.

   3. Prevent VIOLENCE . . . it should also be a goal of the Counterintelligence Program to pinpoint potential troublemakers and neutralize them before they exercise their potential for violence.

   4. Prevent militant black nationalist groups and leaders from gaining RESPECTABILITY, by discrediting them to three separate segments of the community. The goal of discrediting black nationalists must be handled tactically in three ways. You must discredit those groups and individuals to, first, the responsible Negro community. Second, they must be discredited to the white community, both the responsible community and to liberals who have vestiges of sympathy for militant black nationalist [*sic*] simply because they are Negroes. Third, these groups must be discredited in the eyes of Negro radicals, the followers of the movement . . .

   5. A final goal should be to prevent the long-range GROWTH of militant black organizations, especially among youth. Specific tactics to prevent these groups from converting young people must be developed. J. Edgar Hoover, "The FBI Sets Goals for COINTELPRO," *SHEC: Resources for Teachers*, Accessed April 6, 2024, https://shec.ashp.cuny.edu/items/show/814.

Chapter 4

1. See KRS-One, "Sound of da Police." *YouTube*, uploaded by KRSOneVEVO, June 5, 2015, https://m.youtube.com/watch?v=9ZrAYxWPN6c&pp=ygU aa3JzIG9uZSBzb3VuZCBvZiBkYSBwb2xpY2U=.
2. Often literally. Angola Prison (Louisiana State Penitentiary), for example, was a former slave plantation named Angola after the enslaved people's origins.
3. See Southern Poverty Law Center, "Council of Conservative Citizens," Accessed April 6, 2024, https://www.splcenter.org/fighting-hate/extremist-files/group/council-conservative-citizens.
4. See Franklin and Schweninger, *Runaway*, 79–83.
5. Franklin and Schweninger, *Runaway*, 135.
6. Landless peasants who have been pushed out of the countryside into the town become the lumpenproletariat. "It is among these masses, in the people of the shanty towns and in the lumpenproletariat that the insurrection will find its urban spearhead. The lumpenproletariat, this cohort of starving men, divorced from tribe and clan, constitutes one of the most spontaneously and radically revolutionary forces of a colonized people." Fanon, *Wretched*, 66, 81.
7. Fanon writes that in the colonized countries "the embryonic urban proletariat is relatively privileged. In the capitalist countries, the proletariat has nothing to lose and possibly everything to gain. In the colonized countries, the proletariat has everything to lose." Fanon, *Wretched*, 64. I would argue that the "US" settler-colony operates in between a colonized country and a capitalist country if we are following Fanon's schema, especially with regard to race. Black lumpen space is often seen as an "internal colony" (see Robert Blauner, "Internal Colonialism and Ghetto Revolt," *Social Problems* 16, no. 4 (1969): 393–408). The Black working class has nothing to lose due to exploitation and, for many, lives of base survival each day getting more dire. At the same time, unlike the peasants of Algeria who distrust the town-dweller, large elements of the working class, often with a view to upward social mobility, adopt white supremacist deriding and policing of Black lumpen cultures. Most infamously, telling lumpen youth not to "sag" their pants. See also Saidiya Hartman who argues that post-Emancipation obligations and morality around work, eschewing laziness, especially those espoused by Black people, made it possible to carry the whip into the age of abolition. The whip, in its disciplining and coercive power, was internalized. Hartman, *Scenes*, 125–51.
8. See Karl Marx, *Capital volume 1* (London: Penguin Books, 1990), 771–2.
9. Fanon, *Wretched*, 4.
10. J. T. Roane describes the 1964 North Philadelphia Black uprising and its aftermath as such a space of reversing the trap of the slum and

transforming it into a fort set against colonial order. Community members threw bricks and bottles at police officers who tried to arrest Odessa Bradford. "Residents claimed alleys, stoops, corners, rooftops, and other spaces as extensions of their apartments and as the primary sites of their social existence, in need of defense against the 'mushroom' of invading police." Their intimate knowledge of the space of the slum transformed it into spaces of fugitivity and refuge—a territory set against capital, property, and the police. Roane, *Agoras*, 181–7.

11 The "gig economy," "side hustles," cut hours, and part-time work have become the language that allows the unemployed, firmly cast away into the industrial reserve army to retain a working-class identity. But with the increase of capital comes the increase of the lumpenproletariat—the colony's gravediggers.

12 People's support and protection of the Mungiki in Kenya, Dudus in Jamaica, the FARC in Colombia, etc. are multifaceted but share an opposition to the dominant police order and settler-derived law.

13 That one is an American appears as a natural fact, or an obviousness. And all obviousnesses are a product of ideology. "It is indeed a peculiarity of ideology that it imposes (without appearing to do so, since these are 'obviousnesses') obviousnesses as obviousnesses, which we cannot fail to recognize and before which we have the inevitable and natural reaction of crying out (aloud or in the 'still, small voice of conscience'): 'That's obvious! That's right! That's true!'" Althusser, "Ideological," 104. This is a consequence of a colonist, nationalist ideology becoming hegemonic so that individuals, after being exposed to nationalist ideology for prolonged periods of time, begin, as if by osmosis, to recognize themselves through the nation, as national subjects. They become individuated by nationalist ideology or better, nationalized. See Balibar, *Race*, 93–100.

14 Lumpen cultures of spoken word poetry, Hip-Hop, and graffiti have ensured that this crafty rebranding does not go unnoticed.

15 Horizontal violence is a part of life in the native quarter. "At the individual level we witness a genuine negation of common sense. Whereas the colonist or police officer can beat the colonized subject day in and day out, insult him and shove him to his knees, it is not uncommon to see the colonized subject draw his knife at the slightest hostile or aggressive look from another colonized subject." Fanon, *Wretched*, 17.

16 Often including the Black working class. A significant element of Black liberal anti-racism is based on anger at the prospect of being confused with the Black lumpenproletariat.

17 Linda Diebel, "'Ghetto Dude' email sent by Mistake: Province," *Toronto Star*, July 21, 2007, Accessed April 4, 2024, https://www.thestar.com/news/ghetto-dude-email-sent-by-mistake-province/article_55f52158-5f7b-51e2-9429-3380f93bdfb6.html.

18 Southern plantations are a favorite wedding destination. In 2007, when Vincent Woodard visited Somerset Place in North Carolina, there was a gift shop not far from where a caught runaway was put into stocks and had to have her legs amputated. The plantation's tour guide said the enslaved were well-fed and each month adults received three pounds of dried meat and a ration of corn. Woodard, *Delectable*, 1–2.
19 A term popular in comment sections of white supremacist, that is, dominant social media. Video spectacles of arrests, perceived disorderliness, and "crime" involving Black subjects are circulated, and the Black people involved are described as usual suspects in the comments. A collective effort to identify Blackness with inherent criminality. The aim is to make the logic of the lynch mob hegemonic and to aid with the rationalization of all present and future violence against all Black people.
20 To stop runaways and control the slave population, the South used patrols. "They were organized in military fashion, with captains, sergeants, and patrollers [privates]; and they had legal authority to search virtually anywhere for fugitives." Franklin and Schweninger, *Runaway*, 152.
21 In St. Philip's Parish in Charles Town, African enslaved unrest led to the establishment of slave patrols in 1734. Aptheker, *Revolts*, 185. After Nat Turner's revolt, slaveholders fought for a reorganized and restructured patrol system, well compensated and organized by justices instead of militia captains. Patrollers should be employed by slave owners for the purpose of patrolling the enslaved population and receive fifty cents for every runaway they corrected and brought back to the owner. Franklin and Schweninger, *Runaway*, 156. The danger of the runaway and radical Black freedom, then, necessitated the further development of the modern police.
22 NBC News, "Bodycam Video Shows Ohio Officer 'Sicced' Police Dog on Black Man Defending Himself from Dog Attack," Accessed April 4, 2024, https://www.nbcnews.com/news/us-news/body-cam-video-shows-ohio-officer-sicced-police-dog-black-man-defendin-rcna97469.
23 Runaway slave catchers "were often illiterate, non-slaveholding whites who could earn what was for them, a sizable amount for bringing back a runaway." Some charged an extra ten dollars for administering punishment. Franklin and Schweninger, *Runaway*, 156. The history of the white working class' torture of the African colonized, in all settler-colonies has always made questionable talk of class solidarity. It has also always been easier for white Marxists (being Marxists of any race that minimizes racial violence and structural effects) to call for an overlooking of this torture and a denial of the centrality of white supremacy through appeals to "false consciousness." This has also led white Marxists to an embrace of even fascistic white workers in settler-colonies and be perennially disappointed that J.D. Vance and QAnon have not come around, and that

national socialism or "White Workers of the World Unite" Rand Rebellion folks cannot seem to see the light.
24 Aptheker, *Revolts*, 166.
25 The term helps legitimize the law.
26 In longstanding colonial tradition, if any person gives a hue and cry beforehand, they are not to be questioned if they kill a negro, Indian, mulatto, or slave for life runaway. This is laid out in the 1753 "An act for the apprehension and suppression of runawayes, negroes and slaves.": "FORASMUCH as it hath beene manifested to this grand assembly that many negroes have lately beene, and now are out in rebellion in sundry parts of this country, and that noe meanes have yet beene found for the apprehension and suppression of them from whome many mischeifes of very dangerous consequence may arise to the country if either other negroes, Indians or servants should happen to fly forth and joyne with them; for the prevention of which, Be it enacted by the governour, councell and burgesses of this grand assembly, and by the authority thereof, that if any negroe, molatto, Indian slave, or servant for life, runaway and shalbe persued by warrant or hue and crye, it shall and may be lawfull for any person who shall endeavour to take them, upon the resistance of such negroe, mollatto, Indian slave, or servant for life, to kill or wound him or them soe resisting; Provided always, and it is the true intent and meaning hereof, that such negroe, molatto, Indian slave, or servant for life, be named and described in the hue and crye which is alsoe to be signed by the master or owner of the said runaway. And if it happen that such negroe, molatto, Indian slave, or servant for life doe dye of any wound in such their resistance received the master or owner of such shall receive satisfaction from the publique for his negroe, molatto, Indian slave, or servant for life, soe killed or dyeing of such wounds; and the person who shall kill or wound by virtue of any such hugh and crye any such soe resisting in manner as aforesaid shall not be questioned for the same, he forthwith giveing notice thereof and returning the hue and crye or warrant to the master or owner of him or them soe killed or wounded or to the next justice of peace." Hening, *The Statutes at Large, Vol 2*, 1809.
27 Michaels, "Minneapolis Police Union President Allegedly Wore a 'White Power Patch' and Made Racist Remarks."
28 Mark Fuhrman, "CNN Special Reports," July 21, 2017, Accessed April 6, 2024, http://www.cnn.com/TRANSCRIPTS/1707/21/csr.01.html.
29 Michael Dunn, "Letter K," *Florida Justice*, Accessed April 6, 2024, https://floridajustice.com/wp-content/uploads/2021/11/LetterK.pdf.
30 Sabaah Folayan and Damon Davis, *Whose Streets?* (2017; directed by Sabaah Folayan and Damon Davis).
31 Lucy Tomkins, "Who Was Elijah McClain?" *The New York Times*, Accessed April 6, 2024, https://www.nytimes.com/article/who-was-elijah-mcclain.html.

32 Associated Press, "'Hoodlums' 911 Caller Indicted in Black Man's Fatal Shooting," *CBS News*, August 23, 2016, Accessed April 6, 2024, https://www.cbsnews.com/news/hoodlums-911-caller-indicted-in-black-mans-fatal-shooting/.
33 Victoria Moorwood, "Cops Shoot and Kill Black Man Standing in His Garage," *Revolt*, December 24, 2020, Accessed April 2, 2024, https://www.revolt.tv/article/2020-12-24/63146/cops-shoot-and-kill-black-man-standing-in-his-garage.
34 An attempt was made to defend the killing of Laquan McDonald with the claim that once an unarmed suspect is within 21 feet, they are a "significant threat to a police officer." See Radley Balko, "The 21-Foot Rule: A History," *Mother Jones*, December 14, 2015, Accessed April 5, 2024, https://www.motherjones.com/politics/2015/12/police-shootings-laquan-mcdonald-mario-woods-knives-21-foot-rule/.
35 Joe Biden, quoted in Nikki Carvajal, "Biden Reacts to Rittenhouse Verdict: 'The Jury System Works, and We Have to Abide By It'," *CNN*, November 19, 2021, https://www.cnn.com/2021/11/19/politics/joe-biden-kyle-rittenhouse-verdict/index.html.
36 See Chap. 1.
37 Joe Walsh, a former presidential hopeful, tweeted after Micah Johnson shot police in Dallas, "This is now war. Watch out Obama. Watch out black lives matter punks. Real America is coming after you." See Tara John, "Former Rep. Joe Walsh Blames Obama, Black Lives Matter for Dallas Shootings," *Time*, July 8, 2016, https://time.com/4397937/joe-walsh-war-black-lives-matter-dallas-shooting-police/.
38 Chris Hayes (@ChrisLHayes), Tweet, November 19, 2021, https://twitter.com/chrislhayes/status/1461765958712893443.
39 Chris Hayes, "Sean Collins Claims Trump Has Learned His Lesson," Youtube video, February 6, 2020, https://www.youtube.com/watch?v=NjfVWg_g1ls.
40 Biko, *Write*, 22.
41 See also Erica Edwards' analysis of mainstream Black political organizations mimicking the black church, its gender hierarchies, and autonomy even as they retain the fiery sermons about justice. The church became the handler of the black masses, and its leaders could be selected from to produce interlocutors and race informants to white liberal power for centuries to the useful exclusion of radical and anti-colonial voices. For centuries, the press corps have been seduced by the "narrative convenience of black exceptionality." A drive, I argue, which is inseparable from the dehumanization of the insurrectionary Black masses as an angry, riotous, unintelligible motley crew. Edwards, *Charisma*, 5.
42 Marshall, "Liberal."
43 Associated Press, "Man Accused of Attacking Nancy Pelosi's Husband Was Caught Up in Conspiracies, Defense says," *NBC News*, November 10,

2023, Accessed April 7, 2024, https://www.nbcnews.com/news/us-news/man-accused-attacking-nancy-pelosis-husband-was-caught-conspiracies-de-rcna124569.

44 James Baldwin, "An Open Letter to My Sister, Miss Angela Davis," *The New York Review of Books*, January 7, 1971, Accessed April 2, 2024, https://www.nybooks.com/articles/1971/01/07/an-open-letter-to-my-sister-miss-angela-davis.

45 Rachel Maddow, "Rachel Maddow Show Transcript," *MSNBC*, May 28, 2020, Accessed April 6, 2024, https://www.msnbc.com/transcripts/rachel-maddow-show/2020-05-28-msna1362721.

46 Yannick Giovanni Marshall, "The Racists' Peace," *Al Jazeera*, June 7, 2020, Accessed April 2, 2024, https://https://www.aljazeera.com/opinions/2020/6/7/the-racists-peace.

47 https://hoodcommunist.org/.

48 Yannick Giovanni Marshall, "The Coming Battle for the Racist Vote in America," *Al Jazeera*, June 7, 2020, Accessed April 2, 2024, https://https://www.aljazeera.com/opinions/2020/6/7/the-racists-peace.

49 PBS NewsHour, "What the 1960s Can Teach Us About Modern-Day Protests," *PBS*, May 31, 2020, Accessed April 6, 2024, https://www.pbs.org/newshour/show/what-the-1960s-can-teach-us-about-modern-day-protests.

50 Donna M. Owens, "Jim Clyburn Changed Everything for Joe Biden's Campaign. He's been a Political Force for a Long Time," *The Washington Post*, April 1, 2020.

51 See previous chapter.

52 Sen. Cory Booker's "Equality Act" Address to Congress June 3, 2020.

53 NBC News, "America, I Love You. Do You See Me? | NBC News NOW," YouTube video, June 3, 2020, Accessed April 6, 2024, https://www.youtube.com/watch?v=c4fKt_y6d6w.

54 CTV News, "Pelosi Thanking Floyd for 'Sacrificing' Life Sparks Outrage," YouTube video, April 21, 2021, Accessed April 7, 2024, https://www.youtube.com/watch?v=WQXF7LUDp5A.

55 Yannick Giovanni Marshall, "'He Was No Angel': The Rallying Cry of the Lynching Bee," *Middle East Eye*, July 10, 2020, Accessed April 2, 2024, https://www.middleeasteye.net/opinion/black-lives-matter-no-angel-rallying-cry-lynching-bee.

56 Steve Wyche, "Colin Kaepernick Explains Why He Sat During National Anthem," *NFL.com*, August 27, 2016, Accessed April 7, 2024, https://www.nfl.com/news/colin-kaepernick-explains-why-he-sat-during-national-anthem-0ap3000000691077.

57 See Debord, *Society*, 24.

58 A term that sanitizes colonial policing, implying the possibility of a non-brutal police. As possible as a nonviolent slave patrol.

59 Marshall, "Liberal."

60 Althusser, *Ideological*, 92–4.
61 Shakur, *Autobiography*, 13.
62 Oshinsky, *Worse*, 1.
63 Liberal white supremacy has been dominant in colonial administration at least until the second election of Donald Trump. The MAGA movement and the ascendancy of American Nazism will attempt to crush and permanently replace it with the white supremacy of the veld, the slave plantation, and European fascism.
64 It remains to be seen if this will be effectuated by Donald Trump's second successful presidential bid.
65 Douglass, "Fifth."
66 Yannick Giovanni Marshall, "A Short Dictionary of Liberal Language on Policing," *Al Jazeera*, May 25, 2021, Accessed April 2, 2024, https://www.aljazeera.com/opinions/2020/6/1/black-liberal-your-time-is-up. And https://www.aljazeera.com/opinions/2021/5/25/a-short-dictionary-of-liberal-language-on-policing.
67 Yannick Giovanni Marshall, "'The Only Common Denominator of American Conservatism is Anti-Blackness," *Religion Dispatches*, September 23, 2020, Accessed April 2, 2024, https://religiondispatches.org/the-only-common-denominator-of-american-conservatism-is-anti-blackness/.
68 An observer of Charleston, South Carolina, a central city of the enslaving South, described a virtual police-state where there are "police machinery such as you never find in towns under free government: citadels, sentries, passports, grapeshotted cannon, and daily public whippings of the subjects for accidental infractions of police ceremonies. I happened myself to see more direct expressions of tyranny in a single day and night in Charleston, than at Naples in a week; and I found that more than half the inhabitants of this town were subject to arrest, imprisonment, and barbarous punishment if found in the streets without a passport after the evening 'gunfire'. Similar precautions and similar customs may be discovered in every large town in the South . . . There is nearly everywhere, [in the South] always prepared to act, if not always in service, an armed force, with a military organization, which is invested with more arbitrary and cruel power than any police in Europe." F. L. Olmsted, *A Journey in the Back Country*, quoted in Aptheker, *Revolts*, 69.
69 See previous chapters.
70 As if Black people are spiritually condemned to always cowering in hovels with their children and waiting for white enlightenment to recognize their humanity. The settler-colony is a cosmological order in which Black people are always in a defensive posture and the unprovoked strike is always the privilege of white racists.

Conclusion

1 Shakur, *Autobiography*, 1.
2 Frantz Fanon, *The Wretched of the Earth* (New York: Grove, 1963), 311.
3 Isaac D. Williams, *Sunshine and Shadow of Slave Life: Reminiscences As Told by Isaac D. Williams to "Tege"*. Electronic Edition, ed. William Ferguson Goldie (Tege), 2003. Documenting the American South. University of North Carolina at Chapel Hill Library, Accessed April 6, 2024. https://docsouth.unc.edu/neh/iwilliams/iwilliams.html.
4 Claude McKay, "If We Must Die," *Poetry Foundation*, Accessed April 6, 2024, https://www.poetryfoundation.org/poems/44694/if-we-must-die.
5 Hall, *Wake*, 19.
6 Fanon, *Wretched*, 6.
7 Pooh Shiesty, "Back in Blood," Recorded 2020, 1017 Records.

SELECTED BIBLIOGRAPHY

Agamben, Giorgio. *Homo Sacer: Sovereign Power and Bare Life.* Translated by Daniel Heller-Roazen. Stanford: Stanford University Press, 1995.

Alexander, Michelle. *The New Jim Crow: Mass Incarceration in the Age of Colorblindness.* New York: The New Press, 2012.

Althusser, Louis. "Ideology and Ideological State Apparatuses (Notes Towards an Investigation)." In *The Anthropology of the State: A Reader,* edited by Aradhana Sharma and Akhil Gupta, 86–112. Malden: Blackwell Publishing, 2006.

Anderson, Carol. *The Second: Race and Guns in a Fatally Unequal America.* New York: Bloomsbury Publishing, 2021.

Aptheker, Herbert. *American Negro Slave Revolts.* Columbia: Columbia University Press, 1943.

Balibar, Etienne and Immanuel Wallerstein. *Race, Nation, Class: Ambiguous Identities.* London: Verso, 1991.

Bell, D. Procope "'Pick-Me' Black Women: Tactical Patriarchal Femininity in the Black Manosphere." *Feminist Media Studies* (2023): 1–19. https://doi.org/10.1080/14680777.2023.2262163.

Benjamin, Walter. "Critique of Violence." In *Selected Writings Volume 1: 1913-1926,* edited by Michael W. Jennings, 236–52. Cambridge, MA: Harvard University Press, 1996.

Biko, Steve. *I Write What I Like: Selected Writings.* Chicago: University of Chicago Press, 2002.

Blauner, Robert. "Internal Colonialism and Ghetto Revolt." *Social Problems* 16, no. 4 (1969): 393–408.

Bourdieu, Pierre. *On the state: Lectures at the Collège de France, 1989-1992.* Cambridge: Polity Press, 2018.

Brathwaite, Kamau. *Roots.* Ann Arbor: University of Michigan Press, 1994.

Césaire, Aimé. *Discourse on Colonialism.* New York: New York University Press, 2000.

Cha-Jua, Sundiata Keita, and Clarence Lang. "The Long Movement as Vampire: Temporal and Spatial Fallacies in Recent Black Freedom Studies." *Journal of African American History* 92, no. 2 (Spring 2007): 265–88.

Churchill, Ward. *A Little Matter of Genocide: Holocaust and Denial in the Americas, 1492 to the Present.* San Francisco: City Lights Books, 1997.

Colonial Society of Massachusetts. "Volume 1: Transactions 1892-1894: March Meeting, 1893." Accessed April 2, 2024. https://www.colonialsociety.org/node/51.

Cooper, Afua. *The Hanging of Angelique: The Untold Story of Canadian Slavery and the Burning of Old Montreal.* New York: HarperCollins Publishers, 2006.

Cutler, James Elbert. *Lynch-law: An Investigation into the History of Lynching in the United States*. London: Longmans, Green, and Co., 1905.

Dead Prez. *Let's Get Free*. Loud Records, 2000.

Debord, Guy. *The Society of the Spectacle*. Translated by Donald Nicholson-Smith. New York: Zone Books, 2006.

Devaux, Robert J. *They Called Us Brigands: The Saga of St. Lucia's Freedom Fighters*. Castries: Optimum Printers, 1997.

Diouf, Sylviane A. *Slavery's Exiles: The Story of the American Maroons*. New York: New York University Press, 2014. Accessed April 4, 2024. https://books.google.com/books?id=2OwTCgAAQBAJ&printsec=copyright#v=onepage&q&f=false.

Douglass, Frederick. *Narrative of the Life of Frederick Douglass, an American Slave. Written by Himself: Electronic Edition. 1818-1895*. Accessed April 2, 2024. https://docsouth.unc.edu/neh/douglass/douglass.html.

Douglass, Frederick. "Fifth of July Speech." Delivered in Rochester, New York, July 5, 1852. Accessed April 4, 2024. https://housedivided.dickinson.edu/sites/teagle/texts/frederick-douglass-fifth-of-july-speech-1852/.

Edwards, Erica R. *Charisma and the Fictions of Black Leadership*. Minneapolis: University of Minnesota Press, 2012.

Elkins, Caroline. *Imperial Reckoning: The Untold Story of Britain's Gulag in Kenya*. New York: Henry Holt and Company, 2005.

Equal Justice Initiative. Accessed April 3, 2024. https://eji.org/news/louisiana-judge-pressed-to-resign-after-racist-remarks/.

Ervin, Lorenzo Kom'boa. *Anarchism and the Black Revolution*. Originally published 1979. Accessed January 12, 2025. https://theanarchistlibrary.org/library/lorenzo-kom-boa-ervin-anarchism-and-the-black-revolution#toc15.

Facing History & Ourselves. "Excerpt from Mississippi Black Codes (1865)." *Facing History & Ourselves*, March 14, 2016. https://www.facinghistory.org/resource-library/excerpt-mississippi-black-codes-1865.

Fanon, Frantz. *Black Skin, White Masks*. New York: Grove Press, 2007.

Fanon, Frantz. *The Wretched of the Earth*. New York: Grove Press, 1963.

Fanon, Frantz. *The Wretched of the Earth*. New York: Grove Press, 2004.

Fleming, Walter. *Documents Relating to Reconstruction*. Morgantown: Morgantown, 1905.

Folayan, Sabaah, and Damon Davis, dirs. *Whose Streets?* New York: Magnolia Pictures, 2017. Documentary film.

Foucault, Michel. *Discipline and Punish: The Birth of the Prison*. Translated by Alan Sheridan. New York: Vintage Books, 1995.

Foucault, Michel. *Security, Territory, Population: Lectures at the Collège de France, 1977–78*. Edited by Michel Senellart and Translated by Graham Burchell. New York: Palgrave Macmillan, 2007.

Foy, C. R. "Eighteenth Century 'Prize Negroes': From Britain to America," *Slavery and Abolition* 31, no. 3 (2010): 379–93. Accessed April 2, 2024, doi: 10.1080/0144039X.2010.504532.

Franklin, John Hope and Loren Schweninger. *Runaway slaves: Rebels on the plantation*. Oxford: Oxford University Press, 2000.

Garvey, Marcus. *Philosophy and Opinions of Marcus Garvey*. Edited by Amy Jacques Garvey. New York: Universal Publishing House, 1986.

Guyatt, Mary. "The Wedgwood Slave Medallion: Values in Eighteenth-century Design." *Journal of Design History* 13, no. 2 (2000). doi:10.1093/jdh/13.2.93.

Haley, Sarah. *No Mercy Here: Gender, Punishment, and the Making of Jim Crow Modernity*. Chapel Hill: University of North Carolina Press, 2016.

Hall, Rebecca. *Wake: The Hidden History of Women-Led Slave Revolts*. New York: Simon & Schuster, 2021.

Harris, Lashawn. *Sex Workers, Psychics, and Numbers Runners: Black Women in New York City's Underground Economy*. Urbana: University of Illinois Press, 2016.

Hartman, Saidiya. *Scenes of Subjection: Terror, Slavery, and Self-Making in Nineteenth-Century America*. New York and Oxford: Oxford University Press, 1997.

Hartman, Saidiya. *Wayward Lives, Beautiful Experiments: Intimate Histories of Social Upheaval*. New York: W.W. Norton & Company, 2019.

Hening, William Waller, ed. *The Statutes at Large; Being a Collection of All the Laws of Virginia, from the First Session of the Legislature, in the Year 1619*, Vol 1. Richmond: Printed by and for Samuel Pleasants, junior, printer to the commonwealth, 1809. Accessed April 4, 2024. https://archive.org/details/statutesatlargeb02virg/page/270/mode/2up?q=negroes.

Hening, William Waller, ed. *The Statutes at Large; Being a Collection of All the Laws of Virginia, from the First Session of the Legislature, in the Year 1619*, Vol 2. Richmond: Printed by and for Samuel Pleasants, junior, printer to the commonwealth, 1809. Accessed April 4, 2024. https://archive.org/details/statutesatlargeb02virg/page/270/mode/2up?q=negroes.

Hoover, J. Edgar. "The FBI Sets Goals for COINTELPRO." *SHEC: Resources for Teachers*. Accessed April 6, 2024. https://shec.ashp.cuny.edu/items/show/814.

Horne, Gerald. *The Counter-Revolution of 1776: Slave Resistance and the Origins of the United States of America*. New York: New York University Press, 2014. Google Books. Accessed April 2, 2024. https://books.google.com/books?id=jC45AgAAQBAJ.

Horsmanden, Daniel. *A Journal of the Proceedings in the Detection of the Conspiracy Formed by Some White People, in Conjunction with Negro and Other Slaves, for Burning the City of New-York in America, and Murdering the Inhabitants*. New York: James Parker, 1744. Accessed April 2, 2024. https://quod.lib.umich.edu/cgi/t/text/text-idx?c=evans;cc=evans;rgn=main;view=text;idno=N04378.0001.001.

Hull, Gloria T., Patricia Bell Scott, and Barbara Smith. *All the Women Are White, All the Blacks Are Men, But Some of Us Are Brave: Black Women's Studies*. The Feminist Press at CUNY, 1982.
James, C.L.R. *The Black Jacobins: Toussaint L'Ouverture and the San Domingo Revolution*. New York: Vintage Books, 1963.
Kanogo, Tabitha, *Squatters and the Roots of Mau Mau, 1905-63*. London: James Currey, 1987.
Kipling, Rudyard. *Rudyard Kipling's Verse: Definitive Edition*. Garden City, NY: Doubleday, 1929.
KRS-One. "Sound of da Police." YouTube, uploaded by KRSOneVEVO, June 15, 2015. https://m.youtube.com/watch?v=9ZrAYxWPN6c&pp=ygUaa3JzIG9uZSBzb3VuZCBvZiBkYSBwb2xpY2U=.
Kubrick, Stanley, dir. *Full Metal Jacket*. Los Angeles: Warner Bros., 1987. Film.
Lorde, Audre. *Sister Outsider: Essays and Speeches*. Berkeley: Crossing Press, 2007.
Mamdani, Mahmood. *Citizen and Subject: Contemporary Africa and the Legacy of Late Colonialism*. Princeton: Princeton University Press, 1996.
Marshall, Yannick Giovanni. "Black Liberal, Your Time is up." *Al Jazeera,* June 1, 2020. https://www.aljazeera.com/opinions/2020/6/1/black-liberal-your-time-is-up.
Marshall, Yannick Giovanni. "The Bleaching Carceral: Police, Native and Location in Nairobi, 1844-1906." PhD diss., Columbia University, 2017. Accessed April 3, 2024. https://academiccommons.columbia.edu/doi/10.7916/D8W09JGD.
Marshall, Yannick Giovanni. "'He Was No Angel': The Rallying Cry of the Lynching Bee." *Middle East Eye,* July 10, 2020. https://www.middleeasteye.net/opinion/black-lives-matter-no-angel-rallying-cry-lynching-bee.
Marshall, Yannick Giovanni. "The Only Common Denominator of American Conservatism is Anti-Blackness." *Religion Dispatches,* September 23, 2020. https://religiondispatches.org/the-only-common-denominator-of-american-conservatism-is-anti-blackness/
Marshall, Yannick Giovanni. "A Short Dictionary of Liberal Language on Policing." *Al Jazeera,* May 25, 2021. a-short-dictionary-of-liberal-language-on-policing.
Massad, Joseph. *Colonial Effects: The Making of National Identity in Jordan*. New York: Columbia University Press, 2001.
Massad, Joseph. *Desiring Arabs*. Chicago: University of Chicago Press, 2007.
Marx, Karl. *Capital volume 1*. London: Penguin Books, 1990.
Michaels, Samantha. "Minneapolis Police Union President Allegedly Wore a 'White Power Patch' and Made Racist Remarks." May 30, 2020. Accessed April 6, 2024.
"Michigan State University, East Lansing, Michigan. 23 January 1963." *Columbia Center of Teaching and Learning*, Accessed April 2, 2024. https://ccnmtl.columbia.edu/projects/mmt/mxp/speeches/mxt17.html.

Mitchell, Timothy. "Society, Economy, and the State Effect." In *The Anthropology of the State: A Reader*, edited by Aradhana Sharma and Akhil Gupta, 169-86. Malden, MA: Wiley-Blackwell, 2009.

Morgan, Jennifer L. *Reckoning with Slavery: Gender, Kinship, and Capitalism in the Early Black Atlantic*. Durham: Duke University Press, 2021.

Morrison, Matthew D. *Blacksound: Making Race and Popular Music in the United States*. Durham: Duke University Press, 2024.

Morrison, Toni. *Playing in the Dark: Whiteness and the Literary Imagination*. New York: Vintage Books, 1993.

Moten, Fred and Robin D. G. Kelley. "Do Black Lives Matter." Vimeo video. Accessed April 5, 2024. https://vimeo.com/116111740.

NBC News. "America, I Love You. Do You See Me?" YouTube video, June 3, 2020. Accessed April 6, 2024. https://www.youtube.com/watch?v=c4fKt_y6d6w.

Ngugi wa Thiong'o. *Decolonizing the Mind*. Suffolk: James Currey, 2005.

Obama, Barack. "A More Perfect Union." *NPR*, March 18, 2008. Accessed April 4, 2024. https://www.npr.org/templates/story/story.php?storyId=88478467.

Oshinsky, David M. *Worse Than Slavery: Parchman Farm and the Ordeal of Jim Crow Justice*. New York: Free Press, 1996.

Paton, Diana. "Punishment, Crime, and the Bodies of Slaves in Eighteenth-Century Jamaica." *Journal of Social History* 34, no. 4 (2001): 923-54. http://www.jstor.org/stable/3789424.

Ritchie, Andrea J. "Dajerria Becton's Arrest at a Pool Party in Texas Went Viral: Where Is She Now?" *Teen Vogue*, Condé Nast, June 19, 2018. https://www.teenvogue.com/story/dajerria-becton-arrest-pool-party-viral.

Roane, J. T. *Dark Agoras: Insurgent Black Social Life and the Politics of Place*. New York: New York University Press, 2023.

Roberts, Brian. *Blackface Nation: Race, Reform, and Identity in American Popular Music, 1812-1925*. Chicago: University of Chicago Press, 2017.

Saffin, John. "A Brief and Candid Answer to a late Printed Sheet, Entitled, The Selling of Joseph." In *A True and Particular Narrative... of the Author's Dealing with and Prosecution of his Negro Man Servant, 1701*. Oxford University Press. Accessed April 4, 2024.. https://global.oup.com/us/companion.websites/fdscontent/uscompanion/us/static/companion.websites/9780199338863/whittington_updata/ch_2_saffin_a_brief_and_candid_answer.pdf.

Said, Edward W. *Orientalism*. Vintage, 1979.

Sewall, Samuel. *Diary of Sam Sewall 1674-1729 v. 1*. Boston: Massachusetts Historical Society, 1878. https://archive.org/details/samuel06sewa/page/41/mode/2up.

Sewall, Samuel. *The Selling of Joseph: A Memorial*. 1700. Electronic Texts in American Studies, Paper 26.

Shadle, Brett. *The Souls of White Folk: Settlers in Kenya 1900-1920s.* Manchester: Manchester University Press, 2015.

Shakur, Assata. *An Autobiography.* London: Zed Books, 1987.

Slave Voyages. "Intra-American Slave Trade." 2018. Accessed April 2, 2024. https://www.slavevoyages.org/american/about#methodology/0/classification/2/en/.

St. John, Maria. "'It Ain't Fittin': Cinematic and Fantasmatic Contours of Mammy in Gone with the Wind and Beyond." *Qui Parle* 11, no. 2 (1999): 127–36.

Stowe, Harriet Beecher. *Uncle Tom's Cabin.* London: Penguin Books, 1986.

Thomas, Taylor Simone, *Reclaiming Images of Black Women: An Investigation of Black Womanhood in Visual Communication.* Louisville, 2020. Accessed April 2, 2024. https://ir.library.louisville.edu/.

Towner, Lawrence W. "The Sewall-Saffin Dialogue on Slavery." *The William and Mary Quarterly: A Magazine of Early American History* 21 (1964): 40–52.

Tuck, Eve and K. Wayne Yang. "Decolonization Is Not a Metaphor." *Decolonization: Indigeneity, Education & Society* 1, no. 1 (2012): 1–40.

Turnbull, Gordon. *An Apology for Negro Slavery: or the West-India Planters Vindicated from the Charge of Inhumanity.* London: J. Stevenson for J. Strachan, R. Faulder, and W. Richardson, 1786. http://reader.library.cornell.edu/docviewer/digital?id=may893207#page/10/mode/1up.

Twain, Mark. *Adventures of Huckleberry Finn.* New York: Webster & Company, 1885. Accessed April 4, 2024. https://www.gutenberg.org/ebooks/76.

Twain, Mark. *The Adventures of Tom Sawyer.* New York: American Publishing Company, 1884.

United States Supreme Court. *Dred Scott v. Sandford,* 60 U.S. (19 How.) 393 (1857).

Wagner, Bryan. *Disturbing the Peace: Black Culture and the Police Power after Slavery.* Cambridge, MA: Harvard University Press, 2009.

Walker, David. *Walker's Appeal, in Four Articles; Together with a Preamble, to the Coloured Citizens of the World, but in Particular, and Very Expressly, to Those of the United States of America.* University Park: Pennsylvania State University, 2001.

Wells-Barnett, Ida B. *Southern Horrors: Lynch Law in All Its Phases.* 1892. Accessed April 3, 2024. https://ia800206.us.archive.org/6/items/southernhorrors14975gut/14975-h/14975-h.htm.

Williams Jr, Robert A. *The American Indian in Western Legal Thought: the Discourses of Conquest.* Oxford: Oxford University Press, 1992.

Williams, Robert Franklin. *Negroes with Guns.* Eastford: Marino Publishing, 2013.

Winston, Celeste. *How to Lose the Hounds.* Durham: Duke University Press, 2023.

Wolfe, Patrick. "Settler Colonialism and the Elimination of the Native." *Journal of Genocide Research* 8, no. 4 (2006): 387–409.

Woodard, Vincent. *The Delectable Negro: Human Consumption and Homoeroticism within US Slave Culture.* New York: New York University Press, 2014.

X, Malcolm. "The Race Problem." Speech, Michigan State University, East Lansing, MI, January 23, 1963. Columbia Center for Teaching and Learning. Accessed April 2, 2024. https://ccnmtl.columbia.edu/projects/mmt/mxp/speeches/mxt17.html.

INDEX

Abu-Jamal, Mumia 134
"Accidental Racist," (Paisley) 10
Act for Regulating of Free Negro (1711) 19
Adventures of Huckleberry Finn (Twain) 4, 76–9, 83
African American 17, 26, 62, 73, 84, 99
African anti-colonialism 45
African Internationalism 123–4
Africans 2, 44–7, 49–50, 74, 87, 112, 117, 146, 150
    charitable feelings toward 81
    depersonalization 21
    enslavement of 4, 30–1, 49–54, 64, 68–70
    as existential threat 44
    exploitation 45
    forcible deportation of 1
    free 61
    histories of devil-raising 44
    as human beings 68
    Indigenous 75
    practices of refusing colonialism 44
    rebellions of 21, 44
    revolt 52
Alexander, Archer 1
Alexander, Michelle 7
Alexander, Sadie Tanner 92
Allagood, F. M. 55
All In with Chris Hayes 130
Al Sharpton 134
American Colonization Society 141
Americanism 88, 93, 95, 98, 107, 112, 118–19, 145, 149, 164n.43
American justice 95

American liberal cable news channels 132
American nationalism 64–7
American Nazi movement 149
American Nazism 133
Americanness 125
American slave mill 21
"Am I not a Man and a Brother?" (Wedgwood) 2, 74, 95, 103, 157
Angelique, Marie-Joseph 54
Animal Liberation 113
"antebellum" period 66
anti-Black atrocity 34, 106, 140
anti-Black colonial culture 7
anti-Black derision 139
anti-Blackness 6, 32
anti-Black pogrom 25
anti-Black politics 32
anti-Black violence 31–2, 126
anti-Black xenophobe 48
anti-colonialisms 9, 86–7, 90, 105–6
anti-Crispus Attucks 90–1
anti-Indigenous atrocity 32
anti-slavery medallion 2, 4, 75, 81, 95, 130, 138, 141
Apartheid and Soweto raids 150
An Apology for Negro Slavery: Or the West-India Planters Vindicated from the Charge of Inhumanity 75
Appeal to the Colored Citizens of the World (Walker) 90–3
Arbery, Ahmaud 105, 138
Arendt, Hannah 36
atrocity 32, 34
audience as overseer 88–122
    King's dream 93–107

Obama, Barack   107–15
Walker, David   88–93
autonomy   3, 21

Baldwin, James   36
Balibar, Etienne   163n.41
Barbados   47
Beech, Lethie   55
Biden, Joe   129
Biko, Steve   132
Black anti-colonial insurrection   56
Black Codes   130
Black Codes of peaceful protest   5, 85, 88
Black crime   35
Black disposability   84
Black forgiveness   60
Black freedom   1–3, 5, 62–5, 112–13, 136–7
Black free people   70–1
black ghetto   55
Black Girl Magic   154
Black History Month   142
Black humanity   102–3
Black insolence   22, 40
Black international anti-slavery revolution   8
Black internationalism   99
Black liberal   9–10
Black liberal American nationalism   57–67
Black Liberation Army   65
Black liberation movements   97
Black liberatory politics   4
Black liberty   3–4, 15, 89, 121, 127
Black life   20–1, 31, 36, 84, 130–2
#Blacklivesmatter   139
Black Lives Matter   5, 74, 130, 136–9, 147, 188n.37
Black lumpen   125
Black lumpenproletariat   124–6, 137
Black masses   87
Black minstrelsy   139

Blackness   2, 4, 6, 8, 20, 32, 37–8, 46–7, 72, 82, 85, 90–1, 101, 112, 118, 121, 135, 141, 144, 146–7
Black obedience   85
Black people   52, 125
  anti-colonial life   13–42
  anti-colonial revolt   3, 135
  autonomy   55, 57, 85
  bodies   51–2, 134
  campaigns for justice   5, 85
  citizenship   84, 87, 89, 92, 107, 140–1
  freedom   1–5, 10, 14–18, 38–40, 45–8, 52–3, 57, 61–9, 71, 86–8, 93–100, 106, 110–14, 118–19, 121, 136–43, 156, 160n.14, 170n.10, 173n.49
  global sympathy for   138
  liberty   3–4, 15, 89, 121, 127
  revolt   4, 53, 92
  as shareholders in American dream   95–6
  suffering of   46, 98, 117, 134, 139–41
  torture   17, 27, 175
  violence against   129–32, 157
Black peril   35, 75
Black radicalism   4, 55, 92, 98–9, 110
Black riot   56–7
Black scholarship   9–10
Black separatism   58, 123–4
Black social media   90
Black Studies   6–7, 9–10
Black subservience   40, 147
Black supplication   3–5, 139
  animation of   130
  dictum against   110
Black Twitter   127–8
Black uprisings   5, 46, 54, 81, 116, 129, 130, 135, 139
Black vengeance   69
Black war   55

Black women 2, 48
Black writing 90
Bland, Sandra 36
Bloomberg, Michael 133
Booker, Cory 5, 136, 137
brotherhood 89
Brown, John 1
Brown, Mike 127, 138
Brown v. Board 37, 123, 142
Buttigieg, Pete 133
Byrd, James, Jr. 105

capitalism 75, 87, 123, 140, 155
Carceral violence 39
Castro, Ariel 35
Catawba 44
ChaJua, Sundiata Keita 96–7
chattel-making 20–1
Chattel slavery 39, 50, 66, 69, 119, 125, 146
Cheney, Dick 133
Cheney, Liz 133
childbirth 51–2
Christian humanity 70
Christian whiteness 104–5
Civil Rights 4, 85–122, 135–6, 142
    audience as overseer 88–122
    as colonial law 87
    concept 86–7
    discourse 5
    emancipation from 88
    era 87
    Fourteenth Amendment and 89
    ideology 5
    imagination of 86–7
    killing of 115–22
    King's dream 93–107
    laws 89
    leader 86
    millenarianism 102
    movement 24, 61, 64, 95–7, 115–16, 122, 139–40, 146–50
    muzzle of 85–122

Obama, Barack and 107–15
    resistance 86
    state 88
    struggle 6
    Walker, David and 88–93
Civil Rights Act (1866) 87
civil slavery 89
Clarke, Timothy 17
CNN 132
collective nationalism 89
Colleton County 44
Collier, Roxie 55
Collins, Susan 130
colonial exploitation, totalitarian nature of 19–20
colonialism 13, 34, 85–6, 95, 105, 123, 142, 155
colonial justice 28–30
Colonial life 51
colonial morality 48, 60
colonial reform 86
Colonial Society of Massachusetts 3, 19, 69
colonial violence 31–2
colonist media 140
colonists' economy 21
Colvin, Claudette 87
Cone, James H. 132
confederates 52
conflicts 3–4
Conservative Citizens' Councils 123
Constitution 107
Cooper, Amy 26, 33
Cooper, Christian 26–7
corporal punishment 40
court system 28–30
Covey, Edward 41
Cullen, Ernest J 181n.27

decolonization 9
Delaney, Martin 8
democracy 10, 23, 53–4, 93–5, 107, 110–14, 117, 130, 142, 148, 157

Dep, G. 39
de Tocqueville, Alexis 7
diversity 9
Dixon, Thomas, Jr. 1
Dom Rex v. Adam (1702) 17
Douglass, Frederick 10, 41, 50, 64–5, 102
Dred Scott v. Sandford (1857) 96
Dunn, Michael 126–7
Dyke, Jason Van 126

Emancipation Memorial monument 1, 136, 142
Emancipation period 123–4
Emancipation Proclamation 1
emotional abuse 125
enslavement 21, 45–7, 113
  bodies 51–2
  children 51
  farms 20–2
equality 2, 22–3, 30, 84, 87, 89, 118, 122, 132
Ethiopians 70, 71
Ethnic Studies 6–7
exploitation 20–1

Fanon, Frantz 36, 91, 101, 124
farm 20–2
fascism 21, 36
field negroes 48–9, 57, 157
Finn, Huckleberry 2, 79–80
Finney, Joshua 33
First Maroon War 54
Fitzhugh, George 75
Floyd, George (killing of) 2, 26, 92, 97, 127, 133, 135–9, 142
forgiveness 60–1, 98, 101, 111, 131, 134, 143, 154
Fox News 130
Franklin, John Hope 44
free Black people 70–1, 75
freedmen class 89
freedom

Black 1–5, 10, 14–18, 38–40, 45–8, 52–3, 57, 61–9, 71, 86–8, 93–100, 106, 110–14, 118–19, 121, 137–43, 156, 160n.14, 170n.10, 173n.49
  colonial 100
  from colonialism 45
  dream of 100
Fugitive Slave Law 1
fugitivity 45
Fuhrman, Mark 126

Gandhi, M. 104
Garner, Eric 127
Garvey, Marcus 98
Gibson, Mel 83
global Black revolts 2
Gone with the Wind and *Birth of a Nation* 27
gradualism 106
Griffin, George 76
Griffin, John 17
Grin-washing colonial violence 60–1
Guyatt, Mary 74

Hackwood, William 73
Haiti 62–3, 149
Haitian Revolution 73
Haley, Sarah 50, 55
half-devil and half-child 67–70
Hall, Rebecca 8
Hamer, Fannie Lou 87, 98
Harris, Kamala 133
Hartman, Saidiya 10, 21
Hayes, Chris 5, 129–36
Henkel, John 39
Hill, Andre Maurice 127
Hitler, Adolf 156
Horsmanden, Daniel 4, 50
hostile savage; *see* Indigenous anti-colonialists
house negroes 21, 48–9, 57, 157
Hughson, John 53

human rights   179n.5
human trafficking   68
Humphrey, James   67
hypocrisy   23–4

Indigenous Africans   75
Indigenous anti-colonialism
    123–4
Indigenous anti-colonialists   88–9
individual running away   45
inequality   108
insolence   13, 16–18, 20–3, 26, 38,
    40–1
insolent revolt   3
institutionalized racism   133–4
internalization of colonialism
    38–9
intra-American slave trade   17
Israel   107

Jenkins, Michael   105
Jim Crow society   7, 88
Johnson, Andrew   87
Johnson, Boris   6
Johnson, Micah Xavier   66–7
Jones, Van   137

Kaepernick, Colin   2, 138–40
Kemble, Edward Winsor   76, 82–3
Kennedy, J. F.   100
Kenya   150
Kenya Colony   6, 24, 88–9, 142,
    157
King, Martin Luther, Jr.   3, 9–10,
    93–107
    African Rifles   141
    Black life into colonial
        humanity   96–107
    Black people, attempt to
        integrate   96
    dream   93–107
    as salesperson of colonial
        reform   101–2
    speech   95

volunteer settler auxiliary
    force   141
King, Rodney   93
Klobuchar, Amy   133
Ku Klux Klan   1, 24, 62–3, 88

Lang, Clarence   96–7
law in colonialism   22–3
liberal abolitionism   6
liberal media   5, 27, 120, 129, 132,
    145–6, 150
liberal moral   85
liberty   15, 112
liberty for all   89, 137
Lincoln, Abraham   1, 109
Lundy, Benjamin   91, 98
lynching   24–6
lynch mob   24
Lynch mob society   56

Maddow, Rachel   132–4
Malcolm X   27, 86, 96, 98, 157,
    165n.47, 171n.32, 174n.60
Mandela, Nelson   104
maroon community   44–6, 65–7
Maroon-revolt Ayiti   156
maroon settlements   124–5
marronage   3–4, 44, 45, 57, 62,
    65–6, 72, 103, 105–6, 123, 154
    politics   123–4
    practices of   123–4
Martin, Trayvon   129, 138
Marxist   156
Massachusetts Bay   17
masterlessness   21
master race   4
masters' society   51
McClain, Elijah   127
McCloskey, Mark   55–6
McCloskey, Patricia   55
McDonald, Laquan   126
McDowell, Calvin   24
media   127, 132
Merian, Maria Sibylla   51

Middle East   107
Mitchell, Timothy   163n.42
monied class   89
Morgan, Jennifer   51–2
Moselle property   44
Moss, Thomas   24
MSNBC   132–3
Murdaugh, Alex   44
Murdaugh, Buster   44
Murdaugh property   44

Narrative (Douglass)   51
national security   18
Nazism   6
negro fiend   2
Negromantick summons   22
negro slave   3, 13–42
   colonial exploitation, totalitarian nature of   19–20
   cost   18
   court system and   28–30
   exorbitant practices   14
   farm and   20–2
   freedom   14, 16–17
   insolence   16–17
   law and   22–3
   police and   23–8
   recalcitrance   16
   rudeness   3, 14
   state and   30–2
   white society and   32–6
negro wench   2
negro women   22
neo-Black codes   7
neo-colonialism   38
Neo-Nuremberg rallies   155
neutrality   28
new negro   87
new type Negro   48
Nigeria   149
Nigger Jim   2, 79, 82, 137
"Nigger Jim" (Twain)   2
nonviolence   101, 104
N-word   150

Obama, Barack   5
   Civil Rights movement and   109–15
   on colonialism   110–15
   on freedom   112–13
   non-post-racial drone strikes and wars   110
   perfect union   107–15
   on race/racism   111–15
   speech   109–15
obnoxious agitators   160n.14
obscured war   44–67
old type Negro   48

Paisley, Braid   10
Parker, Eddie   105
The Patriot (2000)   83
Pelosi, Nancy   137
period of punishment   66–7
physical violence   94, 101
Pieh, Sengbe   61
plantation   21, 32, 55, 66, 88, 113, 123
police   2, 7–9, 16, 20, 22–8, 163n.38
   dogs attacking   2, 27
   encounter   7
   impunity   7
   power   2, 27, 30, 35, 39–40, 45, 116, 135
   riot   5
   in settlers' pocket   23–8
   sport-killing   134
   uprisings against   3
   violence   23–8, 39–40, 72
possession   20–1
proclamation   1
prostrate slave   101
Punch, John   17, 46
punishment   39

Quilombo   10

race   2
race massacres   126

racial antipathy   22
racial discrimination   140
racial equality   89
racial injustice   108
racial slavery   53
racial totalitarianism   3
racism   85–6, 141, 155
radical autonomy   86, 123
radical Black autonomy   55
radical class   124
radical reform   137
reform   179n.3
reverse racism   108
revolt   45
   Africans   52
   Black   2, 4, 53, 92
   insolent   3
   slave   19, 40, 45, 52, 55, 57–67, 86
revolutionary class   124
Rice, Benjamin   13, 33
Rittenhouse, Kyle   5, 129–36
Roane, J. T.   92
Rock, Chris   40
Romme, John   52
rule of law   129–30
runaways   123–5
running away   45

Saro-Wiwa, Ken   134
Schweninger, Loren   44
Scott, Charlotte   1, 2
Scott, Dred   97, 141
Scott, Walter   126
self-ownership   21
self-possession   85
The Selling of Joseph: A Memorial (Sewall)   3, 19, 68, 71
settler-colonialism   24–6, 31–2, 36, 44, 47, 56, 66, 72, 79, 105, 122, 132, 139, 141, 143, 149, 155–6, 162n.33
settler-colonial sovereignty   65
settler-colonial truism   70

settler-colony   24–6, 124
settler expansion   44
sexual abuse   125
Shakur, Assata   65, 110
Sharpeville Massacres   150
Shelton, William Henry   83
Slager, Michael   126
Slave Courts   29–30
slave/slavery   67–70, 123–4; *see also* negro slave
   abolition of   19–20
   Chattel   39, 50, 66, 69, 119, 125, 146
   civil   89
   codes   7
   conditions   51
   conspiracy   46, 54
   intra-American slave trade   17
   masters   88
   medallion   74
   patrols   125–6
   prostrate   101
   racial   53
   revolts   19, 40, 45, 52, 55, 57–67, 86
   trade   67–70
   womb in   51–2
Smith, Maxine   86
social justice   134
social media   139
soul force   104
Spanish Negroes   49–57
Sreenivasan, Hari   134–5
state   30–2
Stewart, Will   24
Stockholm Syndrome   42
Stono Rebellion   73
Stowe, Harriet Beecher   61
supplicant Blackness, ossification of   85
Supplicant Negro   2, 4, 20, 43–84, 142–3
supplication   2, 123–51
   Hayes, Chris and   129–36

Rittenhouse, Kyle and 129–36
    and spectacle 123–9
swamps 44
Sawyer, Tom 77

Tacky's Maroon War, Jamaica 73
Tate, Andrew 48
Ten-Point Program of Black Panther
    Party 6
Till, Emmett 28
totalitarianism 21, 35–6
totalitarianism of colonial
    capitalism 123–4
Townsend, Penn 15–16, 23
transnational human rights 86
Treaty of Paris 1783 73
Trumbull, Lyman 87
Trump, Donald 129, 133
Trumpism 133, 141, 149
Ture, Kwame 86
Turnbull, Gordon 75
Turner, Nat 62, 97
Twain, Mark 2, 4, 75–9, 83

Uncle Tom's Cabin 83
understanding 111
United States 1
Urban Area Act 113
US anti-Black pogroms 4

Vance, J. D. 156
vigilantes 24
vile Negro 17, 41
violence 3–4, 20, 130
    against Black people 129–32, 157
    of liberal hope 5
    physical 101
    police 23–8, 72
    against property 135
    of state 39–40
    of white society 88
Virginia 17, 29, 46–7, 64, 95, 102, 145

Virginia, 1639 Act X 179n.2
vulnerability 2, 101, 105

waKikuyu 88
Walker, David 58, 88–93, 100
    anti-Crispus Attucks 90–1
    Appeal to the Colored Citizens of the World 90–3
    Blackness *vs.* Americans 90–1
    text and strictures 93
Walz, Tim 133
waMeru 88
Wasow, Omar 134–5
Webber, Henry 75
Wedgwood, Josiah 2, 4, 73–74, 79, 95
West, Cornel 105–6
Western Hemisphere 3–4, 43–4, 54–5, 164n.43
    Africans in chains 1
    Black communities in 63–4
    colonization in 54–7
    enslavement farms of 21
    enslavement of Africans in 30–1
    slaveholding 46
West Indian Negroes 17
White abolitionism 74–5
"White Man's Country" 88–9
white masters and society 87–8
white neighborhood 22
white pleasure 51
white power 2–3, 7, 19, 22, 24, 27–9, 31, 34, 36, 40–1, 61, 63–4, 66, 78–9, 81, 83–4, 99, 124, 126, 130–1, 151, 158
white racism 105–7, 146
white Redemption 88
white society 32–6
white spaces 33
white supremacists
    assault 37
    colonialism 34
    murder 140
    power 129

society 88
totalitarian colony 13–42
violence 4–5, 24–5
white supremacy 3, 6, 25, 33, 41, 70, 89, 96, 100–1, 112, 115, 117, 119, 129, 136, 140–51, 155, 168n.68
Williams, Robert 102
Wilson, Darren 127
wisdom 23

womb in slavery 51–2
Wright, Jeremiah, Jr. 109
Wright, Reverend 108–9

Yankee voting laws 35
Yates, Emma 55

Zimmerman, Angela 8
Zimmerman, George 127, 130

ABOUT THE AUTHOR

Yannick Giovanni Marshall is a faculty member at *California Institute of the Arts*, teaching Contemporary Black Thought in the *School of Critical Studies*. He completed his doctorate in African Studies at *Columbia University*, writing a dissertation which explores whiteness as police-state in early Nairobi, and has written several articles on colonial policing, especially in the United States. He also writes creatively. More of his work is available at yannickgiovannimarshall.net.